Women organising

Do women organise differently? Can organisation theory meet the challenges of new forms of organisation? *Women Organising* is the first of its kind to bring together organisation theory and the real experiences of women organising.

This is the first book to analyse and explain what is special about the way women organise. Helen Brown relates the real-life struggles of groups of women seeking to manage without becoming bureaucratised, to find a sense of direction without relying on leaders, to participate fully as organisers, and above all to create a truly collective form of organisation.

'The story of Greystone Women's Centre is both interesting in its own right *and* a symbol of the alternative forms of organisation women have tried to build. . . . The lessons from this story will be salutory for those working in organisation theory, for the critique of those theories which accompanies the story of Greystone Women's Centre is thorough and convincing.'

Sarah Delamont, *School of Social and Administrative Studies, University of Cardiff*

The book will be of interest to all who have asked themselves 'how otherwise?', to students and teachers of organisation theory and women's studies, to those in the voluntary sector and to anyone wishing to see fairer and more active participation in organisation a reality.

Helen Brown has been active in the women's movement for many years. She is now a Fellow in Organisational Development at the Office for Public Management.

Women organising

Helen Brown

London and New York

First published 1992
by Routledge
11 New Fetter Lane, London EC4P 4EE

Simultaneously published in the USA and Canada
by Routledge
a division of Routledge, Chapman and Hall, Inc.
29 West 35th Street, New York, NY 10001

© 1992 Helen Brown

Typeset from the author's wordprocessing disks by
NWL Editorial Services, Langport, Somerset

Printed and bound in Great Britain by
Billings & Sons Limited, Worcester
Reprinted by Intype London Ltd 1995

British Library Cataloguing in Publication Data
Brown, Helen, *1946–*
    Women organising
    1. Management. Role of women
    I. Title
    302.35082

Library of Congress Cataloging in Publication Data
Brown, Helen, 1946–
    Women organising/Helen Brown.
    p. cm.
    Includes bibliographical references and index.
    1. Feminism – Great Britain – Societies, etc. 2. Women in
    community organization – Great Britain. 3. Women in
    cooperative societies – Great Britain. 4. Organization.
    I. title.
    HQ1597.B793 1992   91–12107
    305.42'06'041 – dc20   CIP

ISBN 0–415–04851–6

Contents

Acknowledgements   vii
Introduction   1

1   Collectivity, anarchism and feminist practice   6

2   Approaches to the understanding of organisation   31

3   Negotiated order, organising and leadership   52

4   Introduction to the case material   73

5   Greystone Women's Centre I: A community project   84

6   Greystone Women's Centre II: Moving out   110

7   Greystone Women's Centre III: Moving on   127

8   Creating non-hierarchical organisation   147

9   Organisation theory and non-hierarchy   166

10   Implications for feminist organising practice   180

Bibliography   193
Name index   201
Subject index   204

Acknowledgements

Very many people, most of them women, have contributed to this book. I am particularly grateful to all the members of the women's groups and organisations who helped me to understand; an award from the Economic and Social Research Council provided the initial time and space; and a special combination of personal and intellectual encouragement from Peter Burridge, Dian Hosking, Joanna Liddle and Sue Stirling kept the show on the road. Thank you all.

Introduction

Hierarchy is only one of the forms in which joint social action may be organised and yet the language of organisation theory is pervaded by talk of 'leaders' and 'subordinates'. As it stands currently, organisation theory has little to say about collective and non-hierarchical forms of organisation. The contention of this book is that organising activity which takes place in 'alternative' settings such as the Women's Centres explored here falls just as appropriately within the scope of organisation theory as that which takes place within complex hierarchically structured work organisations. If this contention is accepted it is then likely that the insights derived from an examination of organising activity in 'alternative' settings will aid the development of a theory of organising which is not tied to the dominant structures and discourses of contemporary capitalism.

Many of our current theories of organisation are close to being theories of managerial work, neglecting both the contribution of 'non-managers' to organising activity (Rosser and Davies, 1987) and the extent of lateral, cooperative linkages within hierarchically organised work places (Skinner, 1988). This neglect is in part a result of a conceptual framework which narrows the domain of what is appropriately 'seen' by organisation theory and partly a limitation of language to express forms of organisational relationships which are not predicated on hierarchical structuring. These issues are relevant to our understanding of what goes on within complex work organisations – those to which most theoretical development is referenced – but they also have particular salience when applied to other sites of organising activity. Here I have in mind organisations such as cooperatives, social movement organisations and those in some parts of the voluntary sector, where the form of collective social action adopted seeks to reduce differentials between members and in so doing to reduce or eliminate hierarchy. Whilst some might argue that it is inappropriate to expect organisation theory to provide a suitable framework to 'explain' what takes place within these 'alternative' organisations, this potential difficulty is precisely the point. If the theories in use can only be properly applied to certain kinds of organisational settings what are the implications of this limitation? Many, admittedly small, organisations do not fit the standard model, and the issues they raise are discounted – if they are identified at all. The intention of this book is to begin to establish an interchange between organisation theory and organising activity which takes place outside complex work organisations, to both stress current theory by exposing it to instances of non-hierarchical organising and to develop an analysis of organising in these settings which goes beyond notions of 'spontaneous' or 'natural' cooperation.

Against this background of neglect of non-hierarchical forms by organisational theorists it is ironic that there has recently been an acknowledgement, prompted by an examination of the management practices of some leading companies, that there is practical value in promoting 'flatter' (i.e. less hierarchical) forms of organisation; these being forms which emphasise autonomy, flexibility and collaboration, all of which are seen as positive features of 'new management'. To take one example: a study by researchers at Ashridge Management College led them to the view that:

> Organisations in future will be ... 'flatter' and more fluid in structure, and more fast-moving. They will be increasingly decentralised and fragmented, yet integrated by overall strategy, corporate culture and information technology. The need to manage issues ... across the organisation will lead to the growing importance of 'horizontal' management [i.e. the management of lateral relationships] as opposed to 'vertical' management [i.e. the management of hierarchical relationships].
>
> (Ashridge, 1988: 37)

The integrative mechanisms listed here – strategy, corporate culture and information technology – could be replaced by others, including the values of women's movement organisations, to produce the same kinds of structural processes. And yet Gareth Morgan, in his important and influential book *Images of Organization*, suggests that:

> emphasising the importance of activeness over passiveness, autonomy over dependence, flexibility over rigidity, collaboration

over competition, openness over closedness and democratic inquiry over authoritarian belief ... may call for a 'personality change' [for organisations] that can only be achieved over a considerable period of time.

(Morgan, 1986: 109).

To the extent that women organising autonomously are working to enact the positive attributes of Morgan's dichotomies, there may well be lessons from their practices which are relevant to all instances of organisation.

This is not, however, a book about women managers. Nor, although the arguments should be pertinent, is it about shedding light on the 'invisible' contribution of women to work in conventional organisations. But it is no accident that some of the most thorough-going criticisms of conventional organisation (for example, Asplund, 1988, Ferguson, 1984, Skinner, 1988) and many examples of practice which attempt to create alternative forms of organising come from a feminist perspective and conviction. The prescriptions for organisational change which follow these criticisms have a common format, focusing on networks, teams and other 'flat' structures, rethinking what it means to be 'a manager', and what is entailed in 'a career'. The elements are in many ways similar to the findings of the Ashridge study and Morgan's preferred *modus operandi*, and in each case justification is made in terms of greater organisational efficiency. However, there are differences as well. Skinner (1988: 162), for example, is clear that much of the change proposed by the 'new management' is 'cosmetic', concerned with managing change rather than changing management. Arguments from a feminist perspective insist that until we look closely at how women contribute (or are prevented from contributing) to organisation we will stop short of the radical reframing and restructuring of organisational life which is necessary both on the grounds of effectiveness and of equity.

I accept and endorse these arguments, and in that sense this book is written from a feminist perspective but, perhaps paradoxically, I want to argue that this perspective is not necessary to its contentions. On the one hand my experiences of feminist forms of organising were the trigger in that I felt I needed to find a way of connecting those experiences to my prior knowledge of organisation theory – and that was difficult – while on the other hand the complementary difficulty of generalising many of the insights of organisation theory across all forms and arenas where organising takes place was a concern. I wanted to look at settings where organising took place but which were very different from complex hierarchically structured organisations and specifically I wanted to explore the process of constructing non-hierarchical organisation. Autonomous women's organisations form an appropriate antithesis to conventional organisations on a number of counts; most pertinently they are oppositional groups in that they know what they are 'not like' as well as what they are, they demonstrate a principled objection to hierarchical forms, and they exhibit an unusual degree of agreement at the level of values. However, most existing studies of the autonomous women's movement have been concerned with exploring the capacity of the movement to bring about political change or as a means to the development of a collective consciousness.[1] Few commentators have been concerned to unpick the nature of organising within the autonomous social movement beyond agreeing that it is, or should be, characterised by an absence of hierarchy and resistant to individualised leadership; consequently questions about what organisation theory can learn from an examination of feminist organising practice, as an example of non-hierarchy, have rarely been asked. The overview of organisational and anarchist literature will also show that very little interest has so far been taken in the processes by which non-hierarchical organisation is produced. Typically characterisations such as 'natural' or 'spontaneous' have removed any sense of problematic from the processes involved. For organisation theory the implication of this is that forms of task allocation and of collaboration and integration other than super- and subordination are underestimated. It will be argued that non-hierarchical organisation is a far from spontaneously occurring phenomenon; that if the overlay of traditional forms of hierarchical organisation and super- and subordination be stripped away, no naturally occurring form of cooperative organisation lies revealed. Rather, social orders based on collectivist-democratic and non-hierarchical forms of cooperation have to be constantly negotiated and struggled for, in order to create new forms of organisation which embody and enhance the value of collectivism. This book, then, is an attempt to look more closely at what is special about the way in which women organise in order to develop a theoretical understanding of the processes which characterise organising activity in situations where there is a commitment to egalitarian values and where the intention is to organise without hierarchy and without leaders. This will involve challenging some of the prevailing limitations which are current in organisation theory. In particular this will involve making distinctions between the concept of organisation, as a noun, and organising activity, and between leaders, in the sense of the status of individuals, and leadership behaviour, and highlighting the role played by the exercise of skill in achieving successful organisation. The approach adopted is that of negotiated order theory which, with its emphasis on the processual, dynamic and political, has the capacity to capture the complexity of the 'reality' of social organisation (Brown, 1990b). This perspective implies close attention to the identification of the values which inform organising activity and the (negotiated) relationship between values and social action. This in turn can only be done by getting close to the action; by examining the *how* of organising at a micro level and over time, and relating these processes to the context in which they occur.

The data which are used to illustrate the arguments are drawn primarily from published 'first hand' accounts of women organising and from two case studies of Women's Centres; Greystone and Whitefield. Data collection took place in each case over a period of two years during which I participated in the activities of the Centres. On a number of occasions I also carried out interviews with other participants. What follows would not have been possible without the many women, who, through their interest and encouragement and their willingness to take time to reflect on their experiences, have contributed a great deal. I am very grateful to them all. In the interests of respecting confidentiality as far as possible the names of all people, places and institutions described in the case material (other than those that are nationally known) have been changed. However, as Burgess (1984: 206) has pointed out, it is not possible to disguise individuals and locations completely without distorting the data. I also accept that other participants may well have different perspectives on the events which occurred during the field work period and I take responsibility for the partiality of the accounts presented here.

NOTE

1 Explorations of these themes can be found in Coote and Campbell, 1987, Dahlerup, 1986 and Mueller, 1983.

Chapter 1

Collectivity, anarchism and feminist practice

THE COLLECTIVE DREAM

The ideal of genuine collectivity in forms of social organisation is a powerful one and one with a long history. In modern times it has been seen to underlie the concepts of community, social anarchism and feminist organisation, each of which expresses a desire to relate to others in terms which respect the capacities of individuals, which seek to avoid placing one group of people above another, and to promote collective ownership of the aims of the endeavour. Charles Handy (1988: 134) has termed this construct 'the collective dream', capturing a sense of both the strong attraction of the ideal and the difficulty, even unreasonableness, of attempting to attain it in practice.

The idealised quality of collective social life is much in evidence in the work of anarchist writers who, from Kropotkin (1904) onwards, have drawn on a romantic vision of a pre-capitalist world in which the 'natural state' of birds, animals, children or 'primitives' is cited as evidence for the possibility of anarchist society; one which emphasises equality, cooperation and the devolution of power. The assumption, in relation to the modern world, is that a naturally cooperative social order is available to be uncovered if the layers of authority structures which conceal it can, by some means, be stripped away: 'Man is always, if given the opportunity, a good fellow . . ., left in his natural state, man is cooperative' (Horowitz, 1964: 596). The plea is for a return to an earlier state of grace, uncontaminated by the corrupting forces of modern society. In these terms a noticeable failure of anarchist thought is its inability, even unwillingness, to provide a connection between immediate political goals and the desired end-state of existence. This is most clearly seen in the absence of any reference to the need for explicitly shared values as a necessary precedent to the production of the desired social order; since these are assumed to be innate they remain unarticulated, as does the means by which social order is produced. As Taylor (1982: 28) has observed, 'Communitarian anarchist writers . . . have not recognised that there would be a social order problem *within* the small community' (emphasis in original). Instead social order is commonly held to arise 'spontaneously', such that, 'given a common need, a collection of people will, by trial and error, by improvisation and experiment, evolve order out of a situation' (Ward, 1982: 28). This failure to consider just *how* social order might be achieved within an anarchist society is more than just neglect or oversight on the part of theorists in this tradition. Rather there is a strong sense that it is inappropriate to inquire too closely, or to risk being prescriptive, since to do so would undermine the essential sovereignty of the individuals concerned. A theory of society which is based on complete faith in the capacities of individuals for self-regulation may be in danger of demolishing the whole edifice if it takes too clear-sighted a look at the actual processes by which non-hierarchical organisation is pursued. If that were done it might expose some of the difficulties, struggles and confusion which more accurately charac- terise attempts to create non-hierarchy, and risk challenging its basic assumptions about the fundamental nature of human actors.

Although social anarchism no longer has the immediate appeal which it enjoyed in the 1960s, the long tradition of mystification and over-respect for the privacy of collective processes in small organisations has left a legacy. Handy's (1988) presentation of collectivity as highly desirable but totally impracticable captures the ambivalence which many theorists seem to feel – in passing. And those who pause, as Handy does, appear confused about their reference points. Is consensus 'a travesty . . ., time consuming, irritating and fraught with politics' (Handy, 1988: 6) or is it a process which 'takes time and costs money, but is worth it' (Handy, 1988: 137)? As a consequence of the inhibition engendered by this ambivalence organisation theory is underdeveloped in its understanding of forms of coordination and control other than those which derive from large-scale organised systems predicated on super- and subordinate relationships. The arguments which will be developed here will seek to redress this balance by emphasising skilled behaviour rather than innate human qualities, and organising activity rather than the condition of being organised.

FEMINIST VALUES

Many of the themes of social anarchism have been taken up and developed by feminists during the 1970s and 1980s. There are strong similarities between feminist practices in organising and social anarchism in the sense of a struggle against hierarchy. For example, one external (that is, male) observer, Bouchier in *The Feminist Challenge*, has characterised the women's movement in this way:

> [The women's movement] has sustained a co-operative, entirely decentralised and leaderless structure which approximates closely to the highest ideals of social anarchism: namely that people can work together for common goals without the need for a coercive, bureaucratic hierarchy to drive them on. It is an ideal which has been and still is held by many social movements, but which has never been made to work for so long or so effectively.
>
> (Bouchier, 1983: 218)

However, differences are also evident. One distinctive feature of the women's movement is the clear statement of shared values. In contrast to anarchism there is a recognition that the social order which feminist effort seeks to implement is informed by an overarching ideology. This ideology provides a motivating rationale for the adoption of values for cooperation and equality, which were previously identified as attributes of 'natural' or 'spontaneous' order. The identification of shared and overarching values means that feminist writers are concerned to draw attention to the interconnection of the specificities and generalities of social life, a viewpoint which is encapsulated in the widely adopted slogan 'the personal is political'. The implication this has for organising within feminism is that as much emphasis is placed on ensuring that means or present-time processes are enacted in accordance with the informing ideology as is given to depicting goals or end-states which embody full expression of these values. Thus, in contrast to the anarchist attempt to re-enact a romanticised past, under feminism the desired future is created by acting it out in the present, such that means and ends approach congruence.

As I have already suggested, in order to study the processes of non-hierarchical organisation it is not necessary to confine one's attention to women organising, but it is the case that in this arena the most, the most motivated and the most worked-through attempts to enact non-hierarchy are to be found. I have taken the term 'non-hierarchy' to summarise the dimensions of equality implied in this form of social organisation in preference to other possible terms such as 'collectivism' or 'participatory-democracy' because it seems to me that the way in which social relationships are structured is the fundamental element which distinguishes between organising forms. Both collectivity and participation are looser terms; they *may* imply non-hierarchy but it is not necessary that they do so. The use of a negative term is, of course, both indicative of its status as a signifier and unwieldy. However, it does capture accurately the stance of the women's movement which is simultaneously oppositional – to conventional forms of organising – and avocational – of something else. This 'something else' is broadly characterised as non-hierarchical organisation; that is, a form of organisation which promotes minimum differentiation between participants, particularly in relation to status position. It is usually, although not invariably, coupled with a commitment to collectivism, whereby the authority of the whole is paramount. Participation is part of the means by which non-hierarchy can be made to work. The widespread agreement on such organisational processes and structures as an expression of a value system provides the general loose-knit uniformity of the movement identified by Coote and Campbell (1987). In their account of the development of the modern women's movement in Britain they describe the dissolution of the National Coordinating Committee in London in 1971, and comment:

> Most women were confident that the movement would hang together without a coordinating committee – and it has remained a loose federation of small groups, linked chiefly by a sense of involvement and a common cause. That it has survived nearly two decades was a measure of the strength of the *idea* that held it together. It was also due to the fact that the movement's lack of formal structure was a positive, not a negative feature.
>
> (Coote and Campbell, 1987: 27, emphasis in original)

FEMINIST ORGANISING

Organising within the women's movement is thus a conscious political act. This has meant that the processes of organising are themselves subject to critical appraisal and scrutiny, unlike those of the early anarchists, and this has resulted in the production of numerous reflective 'grass roots' accounts of feminist organising practice which form a valuable source of data. These show how practitioners have themselves addressed basic questions about the strategies and tactics which may be employed in the implementation of non-hierarchical organisation. How, for example, is the pursuit of equality affected by variation in individual capabilities and how may these variations be minimised? What demands does non-hierarchical organising make of participants? How do individuals and groups manage different levels of commitment? What are the effects of mixing paid and voluntary workers? What are the advantages, both individual and collective, of non-hierarchical organising? These questions and the ways in which they are considered by practitioners provide a basis for identifying some of the main issues involved in non-hierarchical organisation. First, a brief overview of the development of the women's movement in Britain sets the context for what follows and illustrates the central importance of a particular form of organising for the definition of the movement.

The dissolution of the National Coordinating Committee described by Coote and Campbell (1987) took place in response to the realisation that it had become a sectarian battle-ground between various groups on the left. The first two National Conferences organised in Britain had admitted men and had been seen by some participants as being as much concerned with class issues as with women's issues. However, a number of unpleasant incidents led to mounting opposition to the involvement of men and, by 1973, when the women's liberation workshop opened in London, a series of meetings decided that men should be excluded from it: 'What [the majority of feminists] wanted above all was *autonomy*' (Coote and Campbell, 1987: 27, emphasis in original). From now on the women's movement was strictly women only. The separation from the broad sweep of left politics which followed this decision meant more, however, than the exclusion of men as individuals. It also rejected forms of organising which were defined as 'male'. In particular, rejection of hierarchical forms of organising and of leaders was seen as vital in defining the *difference* of the women's movement. To take just one example of the way in which these precepts inform feminist organising activity, Segal (1979: 167) has described the setting up of the first local Women's Centre, in 1972, as an expression of the fact that, 'We were opposed to all forms of leaderism and struggled for equality in all our social relationships . . . The idea of having a Centre was in itself different from the way in which most of the left organised itself. Interestingly and importantly Segal is aware that the enactment of equality in social relationships is a process which involves 'struggle'. In contrast to the anarchists' depiction of a natural process, a sense of problematic is introduced. This concern with the *how* of non-hierarchical organising – how the relationship between egalitarian values and appropriate social action is negotiated by participants – is a central issue, and the efforts of feminist organisers over two decades have produced a corpus of practical knowledge about the kinds of strategies and tactics which may usefully be employed in the pursuit of non-hierarchical organisation. An example of the kinds of organisational devices which are frequently used is given in the following account by Tyneside Rape Crisis Centre Collective:

> The Rape Crisis Centre organises along feminist lines. We are non-hierarchical – that is, we don't have an executive committee or elect officers, as these functions are shared among members . . . The tasks arising out of business meetings [are] undertaken by a member or members volunteering to carry them out . . . We also try to pay as much attention to the form and process of our meetings as we do to the content, trying all the time to be aware of each others' feelings, ensuring that all women are involved in decision-making and the tasks of the group. Often, those more used to formal structures and hierarchical organisations will query whether feminist principles are compatible with getting things done – but we can say that we managed to set up a rape crisis service after only a few months of work.
>
> (Tyneside Rape Crisis Centre Collective, 1982: 176)

The self-consciousness of this, and the many other similar accounts, is partly consequent on the *meaning* given to this form of organisation as demonstration of feminist values, and partly the self-consciousness of innovation. Between 1977 and 1980 a newsletter *Anarchist Feminist* debated the question of organisation within the women's movement. Whilst insistent on the fundamental need to pursue a non-hierarchical form of organisation, the authors recognise that the problems of so doing are exacerbated by the absence of available models of this kind of organisation on which to draw (Vere, 1977). Thus, while in general terms there is agreement that non-hierarchy is probably best approached through the introduction of such tactics as the sharing of tasks, skills, information and resources, and that it encompasses a balance of attention to the internal processes of the group as well as to the accomplishment of tasks, there is no 'off the peg' model which can be adopted simply and without effort. How in practice groups organising within feminism have variously sought to implement these aims, why the effort is seen as so important, and the problems which have been encountered in attempting to enact non-hierarchical organisation are the subject of the remainder of this chapter.

THE POSITIVE SIDE OF NON-HIERARCHICAL ORGANISATION

The moral imperative to organise non-hierarchically is, as we have seen, a central tenet of the autonomous women's movement, but beyond that practitioners have been able to identify a number of organisational efficiencies which support the desirability of developing non-hierarchical forms of organisation. In general the importance of *control* over work and organisational processes is widely considered to be a central reason for engaging in collective activity (see, for example, Cadman *et al.*, 1981, Rothschild-Whitt, 1982). The congruence between the design of work processes and values is seen as conducive to a situation where work is purposeful to participants and, typically, is contrasted with an alienated appraisal of work under a bureaucratic system, as in this statement by the Onlywomen Press Collective.

> In commercial publishing the process is incredibly split up from place to place. Here we are trying to pull the whole thing into a more integrated activity altogether. It's out of a feeling that we need control over our lives.
>
> (Cadman *et al.*, 1981: 33)

In more specifically organisational terms a number of claims are made for the advantages of non-hierarchical participatory groups which reflect Morgan's (1986) cluster of desirable attributes. These typically include some or all of the following:

(i) fast, flexible and adaptive responses to a given situation are more likely;
(ii) more innovative and 'creative' results are produced;
(iii) an individual's commitment to decisions is increased;

(iv) more personal and organisational risks are taken;
(v)   individuals develop a sense of personal autonomy which is
      transferable to other settings.

(Brown, 1986: 80)

Each of these claimed advantages has some reflection in accounts of
organising activity in the women's movement. The first appears,
initially, at odds with the widespread observation that 'democracy
takes time', but Rothschild-Whitt (1982: 39) has noted that with
practice groups can learn to speed this process up, and this view is
endorsed by a women's group producing a newsletter:

> We never found difficulty ... in meeting deadlines and making
> quick decisions. When an unexpected situation arose, such as
> being asked for information by a newspaper in a hurry, we'd
> promise to call them back within a few hours. That day's workers
> would discuss it, reach a possible solution and then contact
> everyone they could in the time, for their opinions.
>
> (W.I.R.E.S., 1978: 19)

This is an example of what consensus decision-making can be like
when the mechanisms have been set up and participants are aware of
their role in the process.

Flexibility and adaptiveness are seen by Col (1981: 193) to be
characteristic of the way in which groups (in her terms networks) are
formed in response to the needs of members and 'self-destruct' when
they are no longer useful; 'this life-cycle encourages the long term
expectation that whatever the need, some network will emerge to
cover the issues'. Networks are therefore not maintained for their
own sake but only to the extent that they are useful.

Clear examples of innovation and creativity are shown by the
tactics of women at Greenham Common peace camp – tactics which
have appeared to surprise journalists and other observers:

> One day some of the women began weaving webs of wool on the
> perimeter fence to remind those inside of their presence; since
> then webs have been used to entangle machinery, to string supine
> protesters together, and to baffle police officers trained to make
> baton charges but not to unpick knitting.
>
> (Davenport, *Observer*, 12.12.1982)

Without being told what to do, women on all sides of the base
began doing the same things, making the same decorations,

singing the same improvised songs ... It was a powerful
advertisement for anarchy.

(Gott, *Guardian*, 15.12.1982)

From the point of view of women in the camp innovative responses
also made organisational sense in terms of flexibility and speed, as
this interview with one member shows:

'How do you organise yourselves here?' I asked, 'Who makes
decisions? How does it run?' 'Chaotically', Helen said, 'and I think
that's our greatest strength in a daft way, we never seem to know
what we're doing from day to day, which makes it hard for the
authorities to know either. The chaos comes from people coming
and going. No one sits down and makes rigid plans, which is
excellent or you'd be stuck if something happened fast.'

(Jones, 1983: 82)

We have already noted that decision-making in collective
organisations involves a consensus process. It is the nature of this
process which allows the claim that an individual's commitment to
decision-making is increased. One experienced group gave this
account of the procedure they adopt:

We take turns to facilitate. This means preparing an agenda, seeing
that we stick to the point in discussions, are working reasonably
efficiently, and that everyone gets a chance to contribute. It's an
easy job in our group, for everyone is aware of these things, so the
facilitator just has to be a bit more aware, to notice the time, to
sense we are reaching a decision. We reach decisions by consensus.
If we cannot reach a decision it is usually because we are all unsure,
rather than because different women hold irreconcilable views.
We usually approach decisions by general discussion, and then let
each woman say what she thinks to see if there is a general
agreement. If one woman disagrees with a generally held view,
then we try to see if any accommodation can be made to satisfy her
as well. We will postpone a decision to another meeting if the
discussion goes on a long time without getting anywhere.

(Kanter *et al.*, 1984: 25)

This group took care to ensure that all participants were actively
engaged in the process, and was able to recognise when it was
inappropriate to 'force' a consensus. A statement from another
group highlights the fact that the affective nature of the group is

strengthened in the process, and that it can be a particularly effective form of decision-making:

> Through consensus we are working not only to achieve better solutions, but also to promote the growth of community and trust. ... Consensus does not mean that everyone thinks the decision made is necessarily the best one possible, or even that all are sure it will work. What it does mean is that in coming to that decision, no one felt that her position on the matter was misunderstood or that it wasn't given a proper hearing. Hopefully, everyone will think it is the best decision; this often happens because when it works, collective intelligence does come up with better solutions than could individuals.
>
> (Jones, 1983: 136, 137)

This process is very likely to increase an individual's commitment to a decision; the overt and explicit synthesis of views involves the participant in an understanding of the problem – the reasons why a decision is taken – in a way which is not possible when decisions are simply received.

One area where successful organisational risks have been taken is that of feminist publishing, to the extent that this has been one of the few examples of growth in an otherwise static market. Two kinds of risk-taking are apparent; starting with insufficient capital and believing, with only flimsy evidence, that a market exists for the product. One group which took the plunge said:

> We talked and decided that we could basically do two things: we could either set ourselves a time limit and get money together and all that, or we could literally just plunge in. It's a belief that women *can* do it. We've been told for so long we can't, it means capital and so on.
>
> (Cadman et al., 1981: 38, emphasis in original)

Another group, who were initially associated with a mainstream publisher but who later became independent, were able to benefit from their independence:

> What we discovered when we were at Quartet was that they did not understand ... that what we do is special. It would be fair to say that many of the books that Quartet would not take on, because they thought they were not viable, became very successful. They did not see the audience.
>
> (Cadman et al., 1981: 30)

Finally, as a comment on personal risk-taking and the development of autonomy, there is the later experience of the group producing the newsletter. For them the experience of working in that group had subsequent applicability:

> Most of us now have jobs which before we would not have had the confidence to apply for. Three of us have written a book about women. We say what we think at work, where once we might have been frightened of the consequences. We know we have the support of not being alone in our opinions.
>
> (W.I.R.E.S., 1978: 19)

Interestingly some of the key attributes described by groups who are organising non-hierarchically, in particular the need for an appreciation of the group's dynamics and the process of constructing consensus, closely accord with the characteristics of the 'mature group' identified by Bennis and Shepard (1965). They describe a process of group maturation which leads successively to a stage which is characterised by:

(i) the acceptance of individual differences between participants;
(ii) conflict only over substantive issues relating to group tasks, rather than over emotional issues;
(iii) decisions made through a process of consensus *which encourages dissent*; and
(iv) participants who are aware of the group's processes and their own involvement in them.

Thus, in terms of the ways in which non-hierarchical groups manage their internal relationships and their decision-making processes, these mechanisms represent the ideal type. However, the fact that the examples of women organising have so far been taken from experienced groups signals that the achievement of 'mature group' status is the result of a developmental process involving learning equally for all participants. This is unlikely to be achieved without effort and commitment. In the next section we will examine some of the difficulties which typically arise in attempts to implement non-hierarchical organisation through minimising differentials, in order to illustrate the argument that the production and reproduction of non-hierarchical organisation are not 'natural', but are struggled for and negotiated through shared learning and the development of skills. At the same time we need to recognise that organising is a process which is not limited to the management of within-group relationships. It is also crucially concerned with managing relationships with external others who, in the case of non-hierarchical groups, are likely to hold different values.

PROBLEMS OF IMPLEMENTATION

Sharing skills

> Today there is a new Women's Centre in Islington, but there is little continuity between the old one and the new one . . . Those feminists who were active in Essex Road have not become involved with the new centre, most of them saying, 'Oh, no, not the same problems all over again'.
>
> (Segal, 1979: 180)

As has already been suggested the process of negotiating a social order with reference to the core values of the women's movement is not necessarily problem free. To put it at its simplest, the espousal of a value for equality does not, *in itself*, ensure that equality will prevail. Rather the enactment of a value for equality in social relationships is dependent on participants' ability to find a way of managing a priori differences between individuals. Attempts to minimise individual differences may be directed at almost any personal attributes, but it is particularly the area of skill and knowledge differentials which is seen as crucial. The tactics of skill sharing and task rotation are widely advocated as a counter to this. However, as the following first-hand accounts illustrate, difficulties may arise when attempts are made to put these tactics into practice. For example, it may not be recognised that some tasks are too demanding for some participants, as in Charlton's account of a Children's Community Centre:

> By the summer we were aware of a few problems. Some parents who worked in the Centre, especially but not exclusively those without teaching experience, felt [unable to] and were ill equipped to cope with the work. It had been naive of us to expect anything else.
>
> (Charlton, 1977: 36)

Or the problem may be recognised but the 'remedial' action taken by the other participants is inadequate, as in Finch's account of a women's health group:

Some members have been women who ... have a genuine desire to help others in a similar situation. But other women joined because they themselves needed help. Where this was the overriding factor the woman has left. Those women experienced tremendous difficulty with the advice giving function. Some were seen as unreliable and 'in need of help', though members offered what support they could.

(Finch, 1982: 138)

Thus, the recognition of differences in abilities also places demands on those who are in the advantageous position. They are required to act as *enablers*, and the demands made on them are in terms of the time and energy which is required to make effective reductions in ability differentials. The extent to which effort is expended in this direction is likely to depend on the extent to which the value for equality is held. One group's account of producing a newsletter gives a good indication of the kinds of processes involved. The time period covered is two and a half years:

Collective working was a positive experience ... but there were problems. At the beginning 'leadership' was supposedly non-existent. Everyone was expected to do everything *immediately*, answer letters, file, type, duplicate ... it was pretty chaotic and not everyone could cope. Sometimes we were expecting far too much of people. It's a question of working out when someone is ready to take something on, and then encouraging them to do it.

Sharing skills wasn't always smooth and easy. We had to learn to criticise each other's work constructively, not to moan behind backs or secretly correct errors when the person who'd made the mistake had left for the day. Old-timers had to face their responsibility to teach newcomers, something we all found hard at first as it seemed like giving orders. As time went on some women did necessarily specialise; we only had one woman doing the accounts at one time. Other specialisations weren't so necessary and change involved the specialist letting go her hold and communicating her skill and the others having confidence in their abilities and willingness to learn. *In the end* the necessity to do things made us all able to do them.

(W.I.R.E.S., 1978: 1, emphasis added)

What is striking here is the amount of learning activity which is not simply directed towards the learning of tasks. Those who are initially skilled (in the sense of task competence) are required to learn as much as those who are less skilled. There is acknowledgement of the need to pace the sharing process appropriately, to make criticism overt but to label it in such a way that it is not construed as personal attack and to give instructions without giving orders. This group also found that temporary specialisms – one woman doing the accounts at one time – were organisationally useful and acceptable within the general ethos of equality as long as they were defined as temporary. Other groups have reported dealing less successfully with this issue. For example, members of the Women's Liberation Bookbus (1980) said, 'We have always tried to share out tasks equally [but] for a long time one woman did most of the accounts. We all talked a lot about how guilty we felt that we didn't share that work with her, but we let her do most of it just the same.'

These examples suggest that implementation of a value for equality through the process of minimising skill and task differentials places demands on all participants. It is not sufficient to recognise that there is some moral imperative to do so; a process of internal education, which may be difficult and will certainly be time-consuming, is also necessary. This effort only makes sense if it is understood as part of a struggle against the division of labour. It depends too on the capacities of participants to execute the demands made on them. The women in Finch's account and in Charlton's appear to lack the resources – whether in time, commitment or skills – necessary to manage effective reductions in differentials between more and less competent participants. An alternative outcome in such situations is reducing the demands of the task in order to maintain maximum involvement, such that reducing differentials may result in a 'levelling down' rather than a 'levelling up', leaving an overall deficiency in skills.

Influencing others

Within collective organisations all members have the right to full and equal participation in the formulation of problems and the negotiation of solutions. Achieving equality of *influence* in these processes is far less straightforward. The question of variation in the relative salience of individual contributions to organising processes is seen by many commentators as the most prevalent and persistent problem area. For example, Rothschild-Whitt considers that

individual differences in influence constitute a more or less inevitable
limit to what may be achieved in the pursuit of equality:

> Inequalities of influence persist in the most egalitarian of
> organisations ... Such individual differences may constrain the
> organisation's ability to realise its egalitarian ideals. The task of
> any collectivist-democratic workplace ... is to eliminate all bases
> of individual power and authority save those that individuals carry
> in their person.
>
> (Rothschild-Whitt, 1982: 44, 45)

Rothschild-Whitt's approach removes the issue of influence based on
personal attributes such as verbal fluency or social skills to an arena
where negotiation is not possible, and she does not suggest that the
group may seek to employ tactics which aim to reduce such inequalities. By contrast Mansbridge makes a similar distinction between
types of inequalities but fails to come to the same conclusion:

> Each individual brings to the group different levels of expertise,
> personal attractiveness, verbal skill, self-confidence, access to
> information and interest in the task. Therefore each group must
> (a) reduce inequalities that can be reduced and (b) understand and
> find ways to deal with inequalities that cannot be reduced.
>
> (Mansbridge, 1973: 361)

Thus, it is her contention that it is possible to find ways of 'dealing
with' even irreducible inequalities (although her distinction does beg
the question of how 'irreducible' inequalities are identified). For
example, the importance attached by collective groups to achieving
consensus in decision-making through discussion places a high
premium on verbal skills. But as before, behaviours can be learnt by
the more competent which foster reductions in the *effects* of
differences in this area:

> The less verbally facile can be assured that the group ... is willing
> to put up with stumbling or help them with longwindedness, and
> most important actually listens to and understands what they are
> saying ... The more potentially influential can themselves curb
> their impulses to speak or to try to influence the group.
>
> (Mansbridge, 1973: 363, 367)

This attention to the form of group processes in the furtherance of equality echoes the similar remarks of the Rape Crisis Centre Collective. However, Mansbridge concludes that even the adoption of such minimising tactics may not be sufficient to result in a genuine equality of influence, but that they can be successfully used to produce an equality of *respect* which 'is more important to most people'.

No such possibility exists for Freeman (1984)[1] who is unswervingly critical of the 'tyranny of structurelessness' in the organisation of the women's movement. She argues that advocacy of 'leaderless groups' leads inevitably to a situation where a 'myth of structurelessness' conceals an informal structure within which élite members are able to wield unchallenged, and unchallengeable, power. In Freeman's view, while this 'myth' prevails there are no mechanisms which can prevent the emergence of élites and 'stars', and consequently no checks on the increase in differentials of influence. Her assertion is that:

Informal structures have no obligation to be responsible to the group at large ... There can be no attempts to put limits on the use of power [and] they cannot be directly influenced by the group.
(Freeman 1984: 9)

This is an extreme statement. It appears to arise from a view that women are 'naturally' power hungry, in contrast to the 'naturally' cooperative man proposed by the anarchists. Both versions of human nature are clearly untenable when presented as baldly as this, and yet one or the other underlies most depictions of what collective social organisation is like. It is therefore unfortunate, in relation to the aim of developing a better understanding of non-hierarchical organisation, that the arguments of Freeman's pamphlet have, for some writers, acquired the status of 'facts' and are re-presented uncritically (see, for example, Carroll, 1984). The solution Freeman proposes to the problem of élite domination is that rules and structures must become formalised, but her appeal to formal rationality is, as Rothschild-Whitt (1982: 26) notes, directly counter to the substantive rationality of collectivist-democratic organisations. Under substantive (or value) rationality only decisions which follow from the consensus of the group carry the weight of moral authority; authority resides in the collective as a whole. The fact that Freeman fails to identify a value for equality in the culture of the women's movement prevents her appreciating that the élitist behaviours she identifies may be unacceptable at the level of the group and *may be addressed at that level* (Brown, 1989). As with differentials in ability, differentials in influence based on personal attributes may be handled by a group to the extent that participants are willing to engage in a learning process. Levine suggests some of the possibilities:

> The small ... group learns, first to recognise stylistic differences, and then to appreciate and work with them; rather than trying to either ignore or annihilate differences in personal style, the small group learns to appreciate and use them ... We are not going to obliterate personal-style-as-power except by constant recognition of these differences and by learning to let differences of personal style exist together.
>
> (Levine, 1984: 22)

Managing commitment

It is clear that participation and involvement in a collective organisation rely heavily on two-way communication. The idealised process of 'talking through' an issue until a consensus emerges is generally predicated on face-to-face interaction, and therefore to be part of the process an individual's physical presence is required, and in some cases it is also sufficient for group membership. For example Col (1981: 190) observed, 'In the Albany Women's Forum whoever comes to the steering committee at any meeting is considered a member for that meeting'. The converse is also true; those who do not attend will have less influence on the proceedings and possibly they may have none. While this issue obviously has some bearing on the processes in 'closed' or work-place groups, it has much greater salience in 'open' groups such as the Albany Women's Forum and Women's Centres where the question of who is or is not a member is less clear cut. In closed groups absent individuals are known and, if required, their views may be canvassed (as in W.I.R.E.S.' account of their practice), whereas in open groups those with the time and inclination to attend meetings may acquire a false representativeness of the group as a whole, or lead to a distinction between 'organisers' and 'organised' which is in conflict with the aim of non-hierarchical organisation. Even when this problem is noted it can prove hard to resolve, as in Charlton's account of the Children's Community Centre. 'The meetings were quite well attended, but always by the

same people, basically those who worked on the rota. Try as we did
we could not involve the others' (Charlton, 1977: 34). Charlton
reports that most of the non-attenders were in full-time employment.
The meetings were held at a time when they were likely to be
available – Sunday afternoons – but their level of commitment (that
is, a willingness to allocate personal resources to a particular activity)
was inadequate to bring about their attendance. In other instances
the limits of commitment may be collectively recognised and
collectively managed so that a level of commitment appropriate to
the particular context is negotiated by its members, as in Riley's
account of a women's employment group.

> Women in the group . . . feel that there is a limit to the amount of
> time and energy they are prepared to devote to fundraising and we
> have, therefore, always put a time limit when decisions will be
> made in the light of the situation at the time. I think that may be a
> reflection of the fact that for all of us in the group our lives are a
> precarious balance of job, children, other responsibilities,
> commitments to other organisations, etc, and additional
> involvements have to be weighed very carefully.
>
> (Riley, 1982: 46)

It is worth noting that there appears to be relative parity in the
situations of the members of this group, and that there was already
some experience in 'balancing' commitments. In this case the
likelihood of arriving at a consensus of an acceptable level of
commitment to *this* group is increased.

However, in open groups, of which Women's Centres are
examples, this adaptation appears relatively rare. The 1981
conference on Women's Centres observed that collectives do not
always work well in practice since individuals are not bound to turn
up to meetings. In some Centres this problem is overcome by the
instigation of a coordinating group, but this in turn raises the
question of the 'representativeness' of such a group. Many Centres
expressed concern at their failure to involve 'local' or working-class
women and a number of ramifications of this problem area will be
illustrated in the longer account of Greystone Women's Centre.
Segal's account of the Essex Road Centre points to the general
problem of initiating and maintaining a 'membership' and the
commitment of that membership which was adequate to the task of
maintaining the infrastructure:

> Despite all the creativity and energy which originated from the Women's Centre it was always hard to keep it open for more than a few hours a week ... and many women were only active in the Centre for about a year and would then drift off. It was often hard to get the new women who came along involved in the Centre, and it was difficult to keep up good communication between the different groups who did meet there.
>
> (Segal, 1979: 176)

Involving newcomers, maintaining the involvement of the already active and coordinating the activities of groups using the Centre are areas which require constant organisational attention. A recognition of the limits of voluntarism leads some groups to seek funds with which to 'buy' a quantity of commitment in the form of one or more paid workers in order to ensure these tasks are carried out more reliably. At Essex Road this proposal was considered, but rejected because of its possible implications for the structuring of the Centre; if a hierarchy were to be introduced it would undermine basic values:

> Some of us wanted to obtain money for a paid worker at the Centre in order to keep it open to plan and co-ordinate activities. But others rejected such an idea out of hand, believing it would be 'selling out' to obtain money from the local council or the state ... Women also feared that a paid worker would create a hierarchical structure. There seemed a contradiction between our emphasis on self-help and collective activity and the idea of state funding.
>
> (Segal, 1979: 176)

Other groups do not see the problem in the same terms, or they accept that without paid workers they are unlikely to be able to implement their project. Tyneside Rape Crisis Centre is a case in point. However, after the decision had been taken the group found they had to deal with some unanticipated consequences of their actions.

> The presence of paid workers in the group created a whole new set of problems. The meetings subtly changed; sub-groups tended to fold up and energy seemed to evaporate ... This is a serious problem for any organisation employing paid workers. The group is no longer working collectively towards a common goal; a division developed between volunteers and paid workers – a

division with possible sources of resentment on both sides. This still is, to an extent, the case . . ., work tends to be left to the paid workers, which seems fair enough as they are being paid. The workers can often feel, however, that other women have little interest in the day-to-day running of the organisation, and that without this interest, the full responsibility for important decisions is being left to them – but how could the members give that much time? ... With the best will in the world, when a person's unemployed it's not easy for them to work with people who are paid for their time. Unless steps are taken to intervene in the process, the people who started the project in the first place, the collective, can feel left out as information and experience accumulates in the hands of the paid workers.

(Tyneside Rape Crisis Centre Collective, 1982: 177)

In this case the intervention strategy adopted was for each paid worker to choose a personal support worker from the members of the collective. The group reported that this system appeared to be working, 'but no doubt we will come up with other ways of tackling the problems we've had to deal with ever since we became employers of paid labour' (ibid., 1982: 178). In this case the concept of equality was treated differentially in relation to different aspects of the organisation: it *was* considered reasonable for paid workers to take on more of the work of implementation, it *was not* reasonable for decision-making to devolve to this group alone. But the consequences for the maintenance of the original organisational structure look like being considerable as volunteer members feel distanced from core processes and express this feeling by further reducing their involvement. In general terms participatory groups who cannot assume adequate or persistent commitment on the part of their members, as, for example, where members are not paid or where an open policy makes it unclear who members are, must devise some means of dealing with a possible shortfall in commitment. This may be done by attempting to find ways of increasing the commitment levels of volunteers, or by paying some members for their expenditure of time and effort. In the latter case, to the extent that the value for equality is seen to be threatened, innovations directed towards minimising differentiation between paid and unpaid members may be introduced, but these may also be accompanied by differentiation between the requirement for equality in relation to different organisational tasks.

Relating to other value systems

Rothschild-Whitt (1982: 44) has pointed out that collectivist-democratic organisations may face particular problems when they are operating in a capitalist-bureaucratic context. The extent of the problem will depend on how much and in what way a group organising along non-hierarchical principles interacts with a hierarchically organised environment. For example, if a group is receiving funding from a state body it may be required to justify its activities in terms of 'outsider' criteria of cost-effectiveness. At the 1981 conference on Women's Centres a number of groups reported that they were 'checked up' on frequently, and one group said that they were required to account for the minutes of their meetings. This kind of pressure from the environment can lead to a group working with two versions of 'reality'; one for internal use based on substantive rationality and another for external use based on formal rationality. Rothschild-Whitt (1982) has termed this phenomenon 'cultural disjunction' and observes that 'in part, the low wages, hard work and intense personal involvement that make collectivist organisations seem so costly may be due to costs imposed by the environment'. These costs may be in terms of the additional requirements of time and effort to produce an acceptable face to funding bodies, or other controllers of resources or, if such an approach is not adopted, on a limitation of the activities which are possible in an under-resourced situation. Newman (1980) has in fact proposed that the need to present an acceptable face to funders leads to a more or less inevitable development of hierarchy in previously egalitarian organisations. Although her argument is over-deterministic, it is indicative of the considerable difficulties of maintaining internal organisation which is non-hierarchical while interacting with a hierarchically structured environment. Such problems may be mitigated to the extent that a participatory group is able to locate in a network of similarly organised groups which also have control of resources, such as the Mondragon system in Spain or the women-owned banks in the United States, but such examples are rare. It is more usual, at least in Britain, for groups to exercise some choice as to whether they locate in a position which offers strong support for their collective principles or in one which affords good access to resources (or, of course, in a number of interim positions if these are available). In the women's movement some groups choose to operate in an entirely 'within movement' space. For others, and

Women's Centres are an example here, the decision to acquire premises and funding almost always makes inevitable some interaction with a hierarchically organised environment. The later case material will show that groups may acquire, or seek to acquire, different social locations at different times.

However, the process of achieving a location in a particular part of social space is one which is subject to negotiation. Typically negotiation takes place at two levels; that is, internally where the group decides where it wishes to be located, and externally where it seeks to achieve that location. Riley makes a general observation about one difficulty groups can face in achieving their desired social location and also adds a comment on the limits of voluntarism:

> The timescale of gaining support from a funding organisation and then that organisation incorporating the finance required into its budgets is getting longer and means that any community group that wants to get funds to employ its own workers or acquire premises is likely to have to sustain itself over years rather than months and may still not be successful. Such projects are likely to become unviable.
>
> (Riley, 1982: 46)

This group also considered that it spent insufficient time locating itself in a network from which it could have gained support to sustain its activities.

> We cut out [a] desirable phase – making relationships with other relevant projects (women's groups, trades councils, employees' organisations). This omission was not as serious in Milton Keynes as it might have been elsewhere. Such bodies are not exactly thick on the ground.
>
> (Riley, 1982: 44)

Particularly for a newly constituted group, but also as part of a continuing process, the question of where to locate in relation to other groups and organisations is likely to be a matter of some concern, in terms of the consequences these relationships will have for the identity of the group in question. After two months of operation Sheffield Women's Centre (1978) noted:

> There are still lots of questions like who is the Centre for? The community? Or is it a place where women in the movement can go to explore their ideas and feelings? We are starting to have open

monthly meetings soon and hope to resolve who we want to attract to the Centre.

The three extracts above give some indication of a further complication in the area of organisation-environment relations. If we set aside the extreme cases where a movement organisation locates wholly within a collectively organised environment or a bureaucratic organisation locates wholly within a bureaucratically organised environment, we are left with a number of 'mixed' cases where the organisation forms different relationships with different segments of the environment. Taking the instances above it is possible to outline four areas where women's movement organisations may form relationships with the environment:

(i)   with those whose values accord with those of the organisation and are potential participants – for example, women in the women's movement;

(ii)   with those whose values are not known and are potential participants – for example women in the community;

(iii) with those whose values may accord with those of the organisation but are not seen as potential participants – for example, trades councils, some funding bodies;

(iv)   with those whose values do not accord with those of the organisation and are not seen as potential participants – for example, some funding bodies, most local authorities.

In general forming relationships with the environment places demands on participants; 'it is asking, in effect, that people in collective organisations constantly shift gears, that they learn to act one way inside their organisation and another way outside' (Rothschild-Whitt, 1982: 41, 42). Or, as Newman (1980) suggests, internal values may become modified to fit better with those of influential others. In general the choices made about those relationships with others which are deemed to be necessary or desirable are themselves expressions of how those within the organisation see themselves – either in the present or as they wish to become. The relationships which are formed in this way are often identified primarily as channels of resources or information, but they also carry meaning about what the organisation is. In the commonest form of organisation/environment relationship, where a collectivity interacts with a bureaucracy, the meaning embodied in that relationship may be resisted, with an effort, as Rothschild-Whitt indicates, or it may lead to a change in the values and structuring of the collectivity so that it more closely resembles its external partners (Newman, 1980). These, however, are not the only adaptations possible and in the later case material the variable and negotiated quality of organisation/environment relationships is examined over time.

SUMMARY

This chapter has shown that the idea of genuine collectivity or non-hierarchical organisation is a powerful dream which has inspired many attempts to describe and enact a form of social organisation which is based on a value for equality. Beyond this there are claims that non-hierarchical organisation offers advantages in terms of flexibility, innovation, and personal commitment, all of which are generally regarded as desirable attributes of organisational arrangements. In recent times the nature of organising activity within the autonomous women's movement is clear expression of a strong motivation to devise practical means to achieve this dream. As such, case material of women organising collectively provides an appropriate context through which to explore the dimensions of non-hierarchical organisation and to develop a theoretical understanding of the processes which characterise organising activity in situations where there is a commitment to egalitarian values.

So far we have seen how women organising have identified and implemented strategies to reduce differentials between participants through skill sharing, task rotation and attention to within-group processes, how they have sought to attract and maintain resources, create a sense of direction and identity, and to manage relationships with others who do not necessarily share their values. Ideally these organisational processes lead to a situation of non-hierarchy, where there is equity between participants, where individualised leadership is absent, and where decisions are taken on the basis of consensus. In practice, as the examples have shown, this situation is unlikely to be achieved without commitment and effort on the part of participants, in contrast to the anarchists' depiction of spontaneous or natural processes. Typically these groups implement some form of ongoing reflexive monitoring which compares the current state of organisational processes with the ideal situation and initiates modifications. But are these groups of women 'really' organising?

The next chapter will review the main themes of the organisational literature and show that there is a strong, although rarely examined, assumption that organisation is an activity which takes place exclusively within hierarchically structured contexts. If, on the other hand, we conceive of social organisation as a cycle of tasks to be accomplished – working out what is going on and why, what to do about it and the translation of these understandings into action (Hosking, 1988) – no assumptions are necessary about who does what, or about the relationships between actors, and it would appear indisputable that these women *are* organising.

NOTE

1 This article first appeared in 1970 but references are to the 1984 reprint.

Chapter 2

Approaches to the understanding of organisation

The task of this chapter is to review the main themes of the organisational literature, looking in particular at the assumptions that are made about where organisation takes place, what it is, and what relationships are proposed between individuals, processes and contexts.

Key features of organising non-hierarchically which have emerged from the first-hand accounts in the previous chapter are the need to manage relationships between individuals and the group, and between the group and other actors; to create and maintain commitment; to enhance the competence of participants; and thereby to ensure the survival of the social order. It is argued that these activities are features of any setting in which organising takes place. What distinguishes organising within the women's movement is the clearly articulated and widely accepted system of values which informs the *way* in which fundamental organising activities are carried out. It is because the concern here is to move beyond descriptions of non-hierarchical organising as 'spontaneous' or 'natural', predicated as these are on particular assumptions about human nature, and to get closer to how non-hierarchy 'works', that the discussion is grounded in organisation theory. It is therefore accepted that some readers will perceive gaps, while others will prefer development in areas which are here underdeveloped, and it does mean that the case material is available to different readings in relation to different theoretical bases. Most obviously, perhaps, the literature on social movements, voluntary associations and self-help groups attends to aspects of social life which in terms of their defining characteristics – lack of monetary incentives, oppositional stance and skill and information sharing – clearly have some parallels with the organising efforts of the women's groups described in chapter one. On the other hand the main interest of much of this literature is in developing comprehensive classificatory schemes, and, with a few notable exceptions (for example, Rothschild-Whitt's (1982) work on collectivist-democratic organisations and Freeman's (1975, 1984) work on the women's movement in the USA), the concern of a great deal of the social movement literature in particular is to attempt an assessment of the political effectiveness of social movements rather than to understand their characteristic forms of organisation (Brown, 1989). This observation applies as much to studies of the women's movement (for example, Coote and Campbell, 1987, Dahlerup, 1986) as to other social movements. However, in other respects the wealth of anecdotal evidence describing experiences of organising in the women's movement which was reviewed in the previous chapter both broadens the empirical base of the study and is useful in drawing attention to areas which are seen as problematic – a source of questions if not an answer to them.

In this chapter it will first be established that within the organisational literature organising activity is generally assumed to take place in hierarchically structured contexts. In view of this we will then be concerned to identify and assess such evidence as exists at present about the nature of non-hierarchical organisation, to draw attention to the importance of identifying the values which inform the form of organising in different settings, and to highlight the negotiated nature of the interrelation between values and action.

Within the *human relations school and socio-technical systems* attention has been given to informal and autonomous groups within organisations, but it is also the case that there is little or no consideration of how social order within such groups is negotiated, since this is once again assumed to be the outcome of natural or spontaneous processes. Further, it is frequently the case that autonomous or non-hierarchically organised groups are embedded within a hierarchical context. This has the effect of removing managerial tasks such as task definition and boundary management from their remit; this omission has implications for the later arguments concerning organising skills. In this section the idea that there are organisational advantages in pursuing participation rather than bureaucratic control is introduced. This idea is developed in looking at the *human resources approach*. Specifically the moral or value component of this approach is noted, and also that some work in this area (for example, Likert and Likert, 1976) contains strong suggestions that there is an inevitable de-emphasising of hierarchy within organisations if interpersonal and organisational skills are valued and developed.

Turning next to approaches to the study of organisations *systems theory* is discussed and linked to the preceding sections by noting that, at the level of the organisation, the 'spontaneous cooperation' of the human relations approach now becomes 'equilibrium' or 'dynamic homeostasis' and is subject to the same criticism of unexplicated processes, in this case within the organisation. *Criticisms and alternative approaches* come primarily from interactionism and ethnomethodology, and are concerned to assert the active role of participants in creating organisation and to indicate the complexity of organisational realities. In particular, ways of transcending the static connotations of 'structure' are examined and of giving due space to the negotiated and reflexive quality of organisational life.

THE DOMINANCE OF HIERARCHICAL ASSUMPTIONS

It has become commonplace among radical theorists to criticise organisation theory for its managerial bias – that is, to treat the goals and values of the management of an organisation as if they were identical to those of all organisational members (see, for example, Burrell and Morgan, 1979). However, from the point of view of our present concerns, a more fundamental and generally unexamined bias is the assumption that organising takes place exclusively in hierarchical contexts. Among those who have recognised this bias Herbst (1976) suggests that it may be brought about by a failure of the imagination; it is very difficult to conceive of organisations which do not have a hierarchical structure and consequently where they do exist they often remain unrecognised. Gerlach and Hine (1970), in their classic study of social movement organisation, identify the fact that this failure of the imagination can apply to participants as much as to analysts:

> One of the most significant and least understood aspects of a movement is its organisation or 'infrastructure'. We have found that movement organisation can be characterised as a network – decentralised, segmentary and reticulate. Most people, even those participating in movements, are not able to imagine an organisation of this type. There is a marked tendency in our society

to identify an organisation as something which has clear-cut leadership and which is centrally directed and administered in a pyramidal, hierarchical pattern.

(Gerlach and Hine, 1970: 33)

There are implications in these observations for both theory and practice. Westerlund and Sjöstrand (1979) also identify hierarchy as 'one of the most deeply rooted notions of how organisations should be structured', and point out that a failure to challenge the universality of hierarchical organisational structures leads to a situation where means of carrying out the basic tasks of organisation such as task allocation, coordination and integration, other than through a system of super- and subordinate relationships, are not explored. It follows that the process of developing an analytical approach to non-hierarchical organisations through an examination of the literature is more likely to take the form of piecing together suggestive clues rather than seeking out fully developed formulations. For groups attempting to work in a non-hierarchical way there is a persistent question of 'imagining' what it is they are trying to create. We are all, in Western cultures at least, socialised into hierarchically organised societies. To work in other ways therefore means more than simply adopting a different model from a range of possible alternatives. It means actively creating a vision of what an alternative form of organisation looks like and working towards bringing this vision into being. From a theoretical perspective this may involve some modification to the current tenets of organisation theory.

HUMAN RELATIONS AND SOCIO-TECHNICAL SYSTEMS

One of the key activities of the women's groups reviewed in chapter one is managing the relationships between individuals and the group. Within organisation theory the small group has a particular, but limited, significance. The early work of Mayo (1933, 1949) and other exponents of the human relations approach drew attention to the existence of informal groups within work environments and to the fact that people fulfil social as well as economic needs in the process of working. While it is undoubtedly true that the identification of informal groups was a major contribution of this early work to organisation theory the work has also been widely criticised for its managerial bias; as an attempt by management to retain the benefits of authority structures while avoiding their costs by using the social needs of workers to involve them in an integrated community of purpose. From this perspective there is an assumption of consensus between the goals of management and workers which is not warranted. It is also true, as Kanter (1975: 48) points out, that 'informal organisation was studied more often among workers or between workers and supervisors, leaving the impression that only workers have informal ties – managers do not'. Thus engaging in cooperative behaviour is something 'other people' do; an activity which is marginal to the 'real' business of managing the enterprise. Thus this human attribute constitutes a tool for managers while management itself remains at a distance, charged with organising the cooperative behaviour of others but remaining separate from it.

This evidence of bias suggests why little interest has been taken in how cooperative behaviour occurs within work-based groups. A view which sees this as a 'natural' outcome of social interaction removes any sense of curiosity or problematic which might otherwise invite inquiry into the processes involved. Douglas (1983: 120) has in fact gone further in his criticism of the effects of managerial bias. He contends that the available knowledge of group dynamics has been largely rejected, precisely because of its narrow use, in the context of work-based groups, to increase productivity.

The importance of satisfying social and psychological needs in organisational settings, identified by Mayo, was taken up and developed by Trist and his colleagues at the Tavistock Institute during the 1950s. Under the banner 'socio-technical systems' they introduced organisational practices which had the twin intentions of improving the quality of working life and of creating forms of organisation which could operate efficiently in changing environments. One of the contributions of this strand of work to organisation theory was the recognition that it was not always adequate to treat the environment of an organisation as a relatively constant quality, and the continuum 'turbulent/placid' was devised to describe the nature of environments. This recognition meant that attention to the nature of the environment was now seen as an important component of management practices. An example of the application of socio-technical thinking is the work of Rice (1958) in an Indian textile mill. Here the problem of an overstretched supervisor was solved by an arrangement which maximised the responsibility of the work group for its own internal organisation, 'thus freeing the supervisor for his *primary* task of boundary management' (Pugh *et al.*, 1983: 86, emphasis added). A similar pattern is evident in the work of Trist and Bamforth (1951). Following mechanisation in the coal industry the primary work groups which had characterised the pre-mechanisation period were dispersed. This led to production problems in the form of frequent stoppages, increased stress for the deputy (supervisor), and to the management complaining that they no longer had the support of the men. Trist and Bamforth's proposal in this situation was to pursue some means of incorporating the advantages of the pre-mechanisation work groups (characterised as having 'responsible autonomy' with leadership and supervision internal to the group) into the requirements of the new technology. 'Only if this is done will the stress of the deputy's role be reduced and his task of maintaining the (work) cycle receive spontaneous support from the primary work group' (Trist and Bamforth, 1951: 38). By this means the workers at the coal face are allowed the advantages of self-regulation within the confines of their allotted task while at the same time freeing those at higher levels within the organisation from attention to internal matters. It is interesting to see the use of the term 'spontaneous' here to describe the behaviour of the primary work groups, similar to the 'natural cooperation' identified by Mayo.

Later work (for example, Hedberg *et al.*, 1977, Nystrom and Starbuck, 1977) identified a requirement for the efficient organisation to be flexible and adjustable in its internal design; that turbulence in the environment should be paralleled by internal turbulence. This meant that the characteristics which had been identified in the 'naturally cooperative' groups were taken up and adopted in a more self-conscious way. Thus the 'one-man-one-task' principle was abandoned in favour of task repertoires whereby an individual worker has the capacity to undertake a range of tasks, direct supervision through line management was replaced by the idea of group responsibility and the emphasis was placed on collaboration rather than competition between workers. Overall these innovations were intended to have the effect of increasing participation and decreasing the weight of hierarchy. They should also increase the involvement and commitment of organisation members and lead to an increased capacity for risk-taking and innovation in response to the demands of a changing environment.

The positive features of small groups within organisations described by these writers appear to be similar to many of those which are identified in women's organisations. However, the correspondence is not complete because one crucial dimension is missing. Herbst (1976: 38) notes that 'autonomous type groups have for the most part been implemented within the structure of existing hierarchical type organisation, specifically in bottom-up change strategies, and thus built at least temporarily into an at least partially inconsistent context'. Notwithstanding the number of qualifiers in this observation it is certainly true that job design projects which introduce autonomous, non-hierarchical groups typically do so in relation to a specific and contained task such as assembling cars. They can take place within a range of wider organisational contexts but these will, almost universally, maintain a basically hierarchical form (Child, 1984). However, the question of how participants in these groups manage, in Rothschild-Whitt's (1982) terminology, to 'change gears' between internal collectivity and external hierarchy is not considered. It is still the case that the focus of attention rests on the managerial tasks which circumscribe the activities of the autonomous work group. For example, in a retrospective look at the work in the Indian textile mill, Miller (1975) reinforces the point that management has a key function in the management of boundary conditions. However, it is clear that if non-hierarchical groups are not contained within a larger organisational structure, as is the case for autonomous women's organisations, then the 'managerial' tasks such as boundary management must form components of the total range of activities undertaken by the group. In Herbst's (1976) work for the Norwegian navy status differentials between officers and other ranks were considerably reduced and this example provides perhaps the closest comparison in terms of conventional organisations. However, his primary interest in discovering the maximum possible size of non-hierarchical organisations left the question of how exactly such novel organisations organise themselves off his research agenda: 'This type of organisation ... can adopt any temporary structure which is judged by the members to be appropriate at any one time' (Herbst, 1976: 32).

The literature which has been discussed so far is curiously uninterested in the organising processes of non-hierarchical or collective-democratic groups. It has also failed to engage with the possibility that these kinds of group can occur outside the context of the large conventional organisation. Any group which is engaged in attempting to implement a complete (i.e. non-bounded) form of non-hierarchical organisation must be concerned with devising ways of distributing 'managerial' as well as executive tasks within the group. There are only a few observations to suggest further lines of inquiry. For example, Miller (1975) suggests that autonomous working groups cannot function effectively unless they receive training and members have the 'necessary ability', while Kerr and Jermier (1983) have suggested that leadership may be redundant in certain situations, one of which is when 'subordinates' (their term) find the task intrinsically motivating and have all the skills and knowledge they need. ('Leadership' is used here in the traditional 'focused' sense (Gibb, 1954, 1969) to denote the influence of a minority, including a minority of one.) It appears likely from these observations and on the basis of the experiences of women organising reviewed in the previous chapter that non-hierarchical organisation depends on the skills, abilities and motivation of participants and on them devising a way of exercising these skills in a way which does not reproduce hierarchy. Thus, while leadership in the focused sense may be redundant, or more accurately *unacceptable* in non-hierarchical settings, it will be argued here that leadership must still be accomplished by some means if successful organisation is to be achieved. First, the next section looks at the role of motivation and commitment in organisation.

HUMAN RESOURCES

Concluding his discussion of the philosophy of anarchism Read (1954: 51) says, 'I have said little about the actual organisation of the anarchist community... The main thing is to establish the principles – the principle of equity, of individual freedom, of worker control. The community then aims at the establishment of these principles from the starting point of local needs and local conditions.' The clear assumption is that there is some connection to be made between the principles or values which inform organisation and the nature of the organisation which ensues. What may be termed the 'moral' component of the human relations approach – the attention to self-direction and self-actualisation – has been developed and given more widespread application in the human resources approach, notably in the work of McGregor, Likert and Argyris.

McGregor's (1960) classic formulation of 'pyramidal values' and 'cooperative values' as Theory X and Theory Y is composed in terms of alternative assumptions about the nature of human motivation. Briefly, pyramidal values describe the assumptions that people have an inherent dislike of work, prefer to be directed and must be directed to get them to make adequate effort. Cooperative values, on the other hand, assume that the expenditure of effort is normal, that people can exercise self-control and can gain personal rewards from working towards organisational objectives. We have already seen how Theory Y assumptions underlie anarchist beliefs about the potential for self-regulating communities. However, for the purposes of the present inquiry it is less important to engage with debates, the terms of which are clearly over-dichotomised, about the 'true' nature of human beings, than to focus on the form of relationships implied by these different formulations and to relate these to processes of organisational structuring, given the emphasis on the appropriateness of certain kinds of relationships under non-hierarchy. Argyris (1957, 1965), for example, draws attention to the constraining effects of pyramidal values on behaviour such that organisations are unable to utilise fully the capacities of individual members. Thus the emphasis on external direction and control via the process of direct supervision under simple hierarchies (the Theory X model) is replaced, as in Likert and Likert's (1976) System 4T (a Theory Y model), by group-based organisation and 'the principle of supportive relationships'. With these developments the types of relationship which are assumed to occur 'naturally' within autonomous work groups are now seen to have useful applicability at higher levels in the organisation. The intention underlying these innovations is to find a way of directing the positively identified aspects of human behaviour in ways which are congruent with the needs of the organisation; ideally both individual and organisational goals will be met simultaneously. 'It means that [the individual] will continuously be encouraged to develop and utilise voluntarily his capacities, his knowledge, his skill, his ingenuity in ways which contribute to the success of the enterprise' (McGregor, 1984: 332). However, McGregor also warns us that this intent in no way implies an abdication of managerial responsibility. The task of constructing *commitment* to the attainment of organisational objectives by individual workers remains within its domain.

Likert's work along similar lines introduces the question of how far developments in organisations which are 'employee centred' and structured around group-based participation processes may in fact be contained within a system which remains fundamentally hierarchical. His System 4 management (1961) (later developed as System 4T) meets the 'efficiency' criteria of high productivity, greater involvement of individuals and better labour–management relations when compared with other systems of management. It is characterised by participative group management – a series of groups throughout the organisation linked together by individuals who are members of more than one group. Likert has inquired more closely than some writers into the nature of relationships in this type of organisation and his observations, or perhaps prescriptions, are interesting. As a counter to the low level of interpersonal competence under pyramidal values identified by Argyris, he states (1984: 295) 'sensitivity to others and relatively high levels of skill in personal interaction and the functioning of groups are present [under System 4T]. These skills permit effective participation in decisions on common problems.' His description of the effectively functioning group as one which is 'pressing for solutions in the best interests of *all* members and refusing to accept solutions which unduly favour a particular member or segment of the group' (1984: 306, emphasis in original) echoes the similar descriptions of decision-making processes in the women's groups. However, while Likert reduces the importance of hierarchy within the system it is not removed, and all his prescriptions are presented in terms of 'leaders' and 'subordinates'. The validity of this position becomes questionable when posed in terms of the accumulation of skills by participants. For example, the observation that 'these people become experienced in effective group functioning. They know what leadership involves ... The members will *help* by performing leadership functions' (Likert, 1984: 308, emphasis added) may be taken as indication of some spread of 'leadership' between ordinary group members irrespective of the existence of a nominal group leader. Similarly the observation that 'hierarchical status acts as a strong deterrent on the willingness of group members to speak up' (Likert and Likert, 1976: 33) leads Likert to acknowledge the usefulness of de-emphasising status differentials. The logic of this position is expressed in the possibility of a System 5 organisation which is described (Likert and Likert, 1976: 33) as 'an even more effective, complex and socially evolved management and social system ... It appears it will have the structure and interaction processes of System 4T but will lack the authority of hierarchy.'

Unfortunately this insight came near the end of Likert's working life and the possibilities it represents were not explored.

To summarise: the suggestion is that organisations which deal effectively with intraorganisational conflict and are appropriately poised to meet changing conditions in the environment must have a structure which facilitates constructive interaction, have members who are skilled in these processes and show high levels of trust and motivation. It appears that there is an incompatibility between this type of structure and one which is to any degree hierarchically structured. For there to be an adequate degree of harmony between organisational objectives and the needs and desires of individual members 'the organisation' (or its management) cannot be superior to the organisation as a cooperative of members. If this is the case it is necessary to look elsewhere for the sources of motivation which McGregor insists are the concern of management.

The application of psychological insights to the field of organisation theory (see, for example, Herzberg, 1976) leads to observations about the nature of interpersonal relationships. If psychological 'goods' such as self-actualisation and self-regulation are valuable in themselves (as well as contributing to organisational effectiveness) then a value component can be attached to the kinds of interaction processes which facilitate the enactment of these psychological 'goods'. These kinds of interaction processes have been summarised by Morgan (1986: 109) as those which emphasise activity, autonomy, flexibility, collaboration, openness and democratic inquiry. It therefore seems probable that non-hierarchical organisation is more likely to be accomplished in situations where value is attached to a particular mode of conduct which emphasises some or all of the attributes Morgan describes; where motivation, in some part at least, depends on seeing the *form* of organising activity as valuable in itself. In traditional organisations this may be difficult. It has been pointed out by a number of writers (for example, Mangham, 1979, Morgan, 1986) that there are problems in implementing the intentions of the human resources approach in that evidence for the existence of open and supportive forms of relationships is limited, both in the majority of organisations and in society at large. Those who attempt to work in this way may be faced with the need for a major change in their attitudes and values if they are to be successful, and equally are likely to be confronted with the difficulty that there are 'no scripts to follow' (Mangham, 1979: 141). However, in contrast to traditional organisations, women's organisations hold a real possibility as locations where the assumptions of Theory Y might be implemented. Not, however, because human actors are naturally cooperative, but because of the value placed on equality in social relationships. Certainly the widespread agreement about the core values which inform organising activity in the women's movement is part of the identity of the movement and a description of its difference from other societal groupings. The second concern – of innovation in the absence of 'scripts' – has already been identified as a potential stumbling-block.

SYSTEMS THEORY AND ITS CRITICS

So far we have been mainly concerned with processes and relationships within 'organisations' and between organisations and their environments. But what is 'organisation'? Or perhaps more reasonably, what are the different ways in which organisation has been conceptualised and how useful are they as paradigms for describing the phenomena we are seeking to explore? Until recently the study of organisations was dominated by a systems perspective. This approach, as the discussion above has indicated, focuses principally on interchanges between an organisation and its environment and on relationships between organisations. In response two interconnected criticisms have been offered – that within systems theory the organisation as such is over-constructed and assumes an unjustifiable reification, while the activities of participants as crucial to the construction of organisation are under-emphasised (see, for example, Elger, 1975, Giddens, 1984). Acceptance of these criticisms makes it imperative that attention is directed towards the dynamic aspects of organisation; to treat organisation as activity, and moreover activity which is historically and contextually located (Burowoy, 1979). By conceptualising organisation as activity it is possible to avoid being drawn into possibly unrewarding debates concerning the ontological status of organisation. As Burrell and Morgan (1979: 398) have commented, 'the notion that one can measure an organisation as an empirical facticity is as extreme as the notion that organisations do not exist'. By 'extreme' they are suggesting 'not helpful'. It is clear that approaches to organisation which counterpoise structure and process, the formal and the informal or constraint and choice as dichotomous options can produce logical alternatives whose value is more in redressing a perceived imbalance in theoretical development than, in themselves, contributing to a holistic analysis of organisational activity. Such an analysis is a more complex undertaking than it is perhaps comfortable to acknowledge.

So far the discussion has examined the pervasiveness of hierarchical assumptions in the organisational literature and the curiously unexamined nature of autonomous or semi-autonomous groups, which are seen as having a self-regulatory quality freeing higher-level organisational members for the tasks of managing 'boundary interchanges'. This approach can be traced back to Comte's description of 'natural' and 'spontaneous' social organisation which, via the human relations school, is expressed in cybernetic versions of systems theory. In these terms 'organisational structures are viewed as spontaneously and homeostatically maintained [by means of] shared values which are deeply internalised in the members' (Gouldner, 1959: 405). ('Homeostasis' refers to the ability of a system to maintain a state of equilibrium in the face of changing conditions.) In this context the assumption of shared values allows 'the organisation' to be treated as an entity – as a 'thing' which is capable of acting in its own right – while leaving unexamined the precise means by which homeostasis is achieved (see, for example, Katz and Kahn, 1978, Simon, 1957). Other versions of systems theory, deriving from Weber's rational-bureaucratic model, construct 'the organisation' as an instrument, as a rational means of achieving expressed group goals. In these versions formal rather than informal aspects of organisation are given prominence, but in either case we are presented with the implication that organisational structures, however produced, are amenable to observers' definitions. That is, they have the status of a social fact.

This view is only possible if, following Parsons (1960), it is considered reasonable to assume that society is characterised by generalised consensus values. If this is the case then differences between individuals or between groups are minimal when compared with the degree of agreement between them. This seems unlikely and yet, within some versions of organisational analysis, consensus assumptions have been adopted which permit treatment of 'the organisation' as a unity with explicit goals and clear operating procedures. In these terms the relationship between structure, function and normative order appears unproblematic since pertinent values designate the goal of the organisation and inform all aspects of organisational structure. Within this model organisations are characterised by equilibrium processes and role-determined behaviour on the part of participants and, as this aspect of organisation appears as relatively uninteresting, the attention of analysts is more often focused at the macro level, for example, at the responses of organisations to changes in technology or the environment (for example, Aldrich, 1979, Woodward, 1965).

Some criticisms of this model are obvious, particularly perhaps the questionable validity of assuming consensus values, and yet the discussion so far has been concerned to draw attention to the existence of agreement around the core values of the women's movement. A necessary distinction is between a specific system of values which identifies and defines a sub-group within wider society and the grosser assumption that such specific sub-systems are of minimal importance when compared with unanimity at a system level. Nevertheless, we need also to take note of the assumption that, where there is agreement around core values, other aspects of organisation fall easily into place. Does this mean that there is little more to be said? The evidence from chapter one suggests otherwise, rather it suggests that attempts to achieve non-hierarchy are troublesome and time-consuming. This anomaly arises because the processes by which values and actions are connected are insufficiently explicated in the Parsonian model.

The interactionist critique

One explanatory example may be found in the meaning attached to the term 'consensus'. Consensus is, as we have seen, the *outcome of a process* in which differences have been aired and conflicts resolved or accommodated. It is not the same as a state of 'complacent unanimity' (Likert and Likert, 1976: 153), although this meaning is perhaps closer to the interpretation placed on the notion of consensus by some systems theorists. Other critics of the entitative view of organisation (for example, Brown and Hosking, 1986) reflect this lack of concern with individuals and group processes: that the organisation 'is not merely greater than the sum of its parts, but so superior that it is effectively divorced from the influence of its parts' (Giorgiou, 1973: 77). Thus the corollary to the promotion of organisational goals and structures is the neglect of participants' involvement and actions. Writers in the interactionist tradition (for example, Bittner, 1974, Silverman, 1970) insist that an analytical approach to organisation must take account of the way actors actively and variously interpret, create and respond to organisational settings and that therefore there is a serious omission if the behaviour of people in organisations is considered to be no more than that which is prescribed by organisational rules. In Bittner's view this selective viewpoint comes about through over-identification with the efficiency principle 'which merely selects, identifies and orders those elements of a scene of action that are perceived as related to it . . . Instead, one is confronted with a rich and ambiguous body of background information' (Bittner, 1974: 72–3). This criticism is, in essence, the same as the managerialist bias discussed earlier. Acceptance of this criticism demands certain modifications to the dominant mode of research in organisations. The importance of the interactionist critique is in drawing attention to the existence of individual agendas within organisational settings (Perrow, 1978), and consequently to the fact that members participate in an active and variable manner (Strauss, 1978), a point which is obscured when role-determined behaviour is treated unproblematically.

The Marxist critique

This urge to attend to micro levels of analysis is balanced by arguments, frequently from a Marxist perspective, which propose that 'explanations of organisational phenomena cannot be sought within the boundaries of the organisation' (Benson, 1977: 11). In this view organisations are, in part at least, locations for the expression of class interests and reflect within them the inequalities of power which are the defining characteristics of capitalist society. Thus, in general terms, the plea from this quarter is for a sociology of organisations which 'takes as its topic to be investigated exactly that which is assumed and glossed over by contemporary organisational analysis: the relationship between internal organisational structures, processes and ideologies and the society in which they exist' (Salaman, 1978: 519). The importance of this perspective is that it identifies a relationship between micro and macro levels of analysis and also offers the possibility of incorporating context and history into organisational analysis. However, precisely how this is to be done is less clear, and Salaman has been criticised (Pettigrew, 1985) for failing to provide the necessary theoretical language to connect the two levels.

Before going on to consider how micro and macro levels of analysis may be connected a short digression is in order. Marxist approaches to organisational analysis are constructed in terms of different interest groups (classes) under capitalism, which are understood in relation to their differential access to resources and the maintenance of these differentials. To the extent to which the terms of the discussion are wholly located within the problematic of capitalist production and reproduction, the relevance to organisational settings, such as Women's Centres, which are not specifically of this type is less certain. The relationships between Marxism and feminism, between capitalism and patriarchy are complex, and have been debated in terms of both incorporation and separation (Sargent, 1981). Acknowledging that this may be a controversial interpretation given that the women's movement is often labelled as a middle-class phenomenon, the view is taken here that, while the constraints and structural processes of capitalist production cannot be claimed to be totally absent in women's organisations, they intrude less immediately and directly than is the case for the majority of settings where organisational behaviour is studied. The reason for raising this point is that class interests and values provide different bases for affiliation and it is important to differentiate between them (see, for example, Westerlund and Sjöstrand, 1979), although it is not uncommon to find references to 'values and interests', treated as an undifferentiated bundle in the literature. In this research the emphasis is on ideology and values as the *primary* base for affiliation, and in this respect Salaman's request for attention to the relationship between organisational processes and ideological contexts has been heeded. Clearly class differences between participants are a part of the dynamics of organisation, but it is argued that essentially it is differences in familiarity with the ideology of the women's movement and in the nature or extent of skills and knowledge[1] which require negotiation between participants in these examples of attempts to create non-hierarchical organisation.

The action critique and negotiated order

A number of writers (for example, Benson, 1977, Giddens, 1976, Perrow, 1978) have pointed to the convergence of Marxism and interactionism in their (action) critique of approaches which assume and depict a singular organisational reality. To quote Benson's description:

> The action critique forces us to attend to the processes through which particular organisational patterns have been generated and are sustained. Explanations based solely in the morphology of a produced, taken-for-granted reality are no longer acceptable. This forces attention to the history, to the sequence of events and contexts through which the present arrangements have been manufactured. It also directs attention to the ongoing day-to-day interactions through which a produced reality is sustained.
>
> (Benson, 1977: 8)

This alternative approach makes a number of demands on organisational analysis; that the inquiry must be wider than the narrow confines of conventionally understood organisational analysis, that a complete picture requires more than one level of analysis and that 'structure' must be reconceptualised in a way which incorporates its dynamic and dialectic aspects.

The first point reflects Salaman's plea to locate organisational analysis in its societal context. The dilemma this poses is that to take on all that is implied by this perspective may easily lead to a degree of complexity which approaches the 'unresearchable'. Some means of relating to and yet selecting from the 'rich and ambiguous body of background information' (Bittner, 1974: 73) which characterises a less narrowly framed approach to organisation are required. Successful ethnographic studies (in particular Beynon, 1975, Willis, 1977) succeed because they place participants' involvements and definitions centrally such that these provide a vehicle for interpreting a complex reality and illustration of the relationship between day-to-day interactions and larger social forces. Thus an important component of the case study material is that it provides a mechanism for presenting the voices of individual participants as they seek to describe and interpret their actions and those of others.

Attention to the voluntaristic aspects of organisations is also pertinent to considering the notion of 'structure' in ways which transcend the static connotations of the term. Writers who have addressed this issue have sought to incorporate a temporal dimension, either retrospective or prospective, or to find some way of indicating the processual and active dimensions of structure. Thus

Perrow (1978: 117) says 'that what we see as structure is only the trace of past movement', while Silverman (in Pugh *et al.*, 1983: 93) sees structures as 'immanent', 'continuously constructed and reconstructed out of the meanings that actors take from them and give to them'. Similarly Strauss (1978) discusses 'structural processes' and Giddens (1984), in the most fully developed version of this approach, presents a theory of structuration. In common the point is made that human behaviour cannot be fully understood simply by reference to a normative order or a set of rules and, crucially, attention must be given to the arena of negotiation between action and its symbolic referents – whether expressed in terms of goals, rules or values. Within this arena actors, both individually and collectively, bring to organisational encounters differences in interests, perceptions, values and resources in a process which is inherently political (Pettigrew, 1973) and negotiated; political because interpretations have to be made, choices determined and resources allocated in a continuous, iterative process, and negotiated because interpretations, choices and allocations are the outcome of influence and exchange both within and between groups. In these terms social order is shaped, in some part, by participants who act in a self-conscious and reflexive manner. This attention to the mediating social processes which interpose between reference points or end-states and their implementation in day-to-day organisational activities highlights the ambiguous and conditional nature of much that is involved in 'making' organisational actions (Elger, 1975). Thus Day and Day summarise negotiated order theory as:

> [emphasising] the fluid, continuously emerging qualities of the organisation, the changing web of interactions woven among its members, and [suggesting] that order is something at which the members of the organisation must continually work. Consequently conflict and change are just as much a part of organisational life as consensus and stability. Organisations are thus viewed as complex and highly fragile constructions of reality which are subject to numerous temporal, spatial and situational events occurring both internally and externally. [This] involves the historical development of the organisation ... as well as those relevant changes taking place within the broader social, political and economic spectrum of the organisation.
>
> (Day and Day, 1977: 134)

This summation brings together process, context and history as necessary components in organisational analysis and clearly has much to offer as an alternative to structural theory. However, as Giddens (1984: 26) has warned, it is important to avoid the excesses of phenomenology in regarding society as 'the plastic creation of human subjects'. The debate between Strauss (1978) and his critics (Benson, 1977, Day and Day, 1977) has drawn attention to some concerns about the phenomenological aspects of negotiated order theory. First, there is a failure of practice, if not of intent, to adequately locate negotiative processes in their contextual framework and thus to relate macro-level issues to what occurs within organisations. Second, negotiated order theorists may have fallen into the error of disregarding structural limits by focusing on the small-scale adjustments possible within the limits posed by structural arrangements. In response Strauss (1978: 249–59) has argued that these criticisms derive from a misreading of some aspects of negotiated order theory. Wider contextual frameworks and limitations are not neglected if importance is attached to seeking to discover 'just what *is* negotiable at any given time' (ibid.: 252). Thus the longitudinal component of the case material will bring into relief the shifting arena of negotiation over time.

Beyond this, the addition of a temporal dimension to organisational analysis provides a method for identifying different levels of order from the same stream of action. They argue:

> We would expect actors and transactional patterns to be determinate in the uncertain day-to-day experience of organisations; emergent regularities of size, technology and environment to become apparent in the medium term; and an order of meaning, value and belief to be sedimented in the long-term structuring of organisations in their contexts.
>
> (Ranson *et al.*, 1980: 14)

By this means they evoke the possibility of a more holistic approach to analysis which transcends the seemingly disparate viewpoints offered by phenomenology, traditional ahistorical approaches and broader sociohistorical perspectives. The particular usefulness of these insights is that one level of analysis is not logically prior to another, nor do they operate exclusively; an understanding of organisational phenomena must take into account individuals, processes and contexts and their interrelations over time.

IMPLICATIONS FOR THE UNDERSTANDING OF ORGANISATION

In this overview of the main themes of the organisational literature a partiality of attention has been noted which has left under-examined some aspects of organisational behaviour which are of particular relevance to the study of Women's Centres, taking these as an example of a type of organisation which seeks to operate in a non-hierarchical and collectivist mode. In particular it has been pointed out that 'organisation' is generally assumed to take place within an hierarchical context and that this assumption has limited examination of the process of 'spontaneous cooperation' in the settings where it is presumed to occur. It has been argued that it is inadequate to adopt an 'efficiency' rationale towards understanding non-hierarchical organisation and that it is also necessary to take into account the value or 'moral' component in such agreements to cooperate. The value dimension – defined as a basic attitude towards certain broad modes of conduct or certain end-states of existence (Rokeach, 1968, 1973) – is important in providing a motor to drive the process of constructing a particular social order. Gerson (1976: 797) has commented that 'participation in any ... situation is simultaneously constraining in that people must make contributions to it, and be bound by its limitations and yet enriching, in that participation provides resources and opportunities otherwise unavailable'. In drawing attention to the fact that social organisation offers participants rewards which are, crucially, a product of interaction, and that different forms of organisation provide different interaction products, it is apparent that the establishment of a social order with particular characteristics can be valuable in itself in terms of the rewards and opportunities which it can offer its participants. Further, it is worth reflecting Salaman's (1978) observation that the apparent logical base of many organisational rationalities is, in fact, founded on value premises. In these terms the 'efficiency' rationale appears as an example of managerial values and points to the need to acknowledge the value component in all examination of the process of social organisation, and to do so in a way which connects structure and process.

These observations also have implications for methodology. Hall (1987: 18) argues for 'methodologies which are sensitive to the problematic and processual nature of social life', and continues by saying, 'everyday behaviour, interactions and relationships cannot be understood except as contextualised, . . . social forces need to be analysed by attending to the processes and activity that give them life, form and content'. These prescriptions signal a requirement for observation *in situ*, for attention to actors' accounts of their values, motivations and understanding of organising processes, and for a longitudinal format. In short, for case study analysis.

NOTE

1 See also Haug's (1989) discussion of the increase in women's education.

Chapter 3

Negotiated order, organising and leadership

The concept of the meso domain has been introduced (Altheide, 1988, Hall, 1987, Maines, 1982) as a means of bridging the macro–micro gap. Hall identifies the meso domain as the area where situated activity, history and structure converge, and reiterates our earlier emphasis on the necessity of a processual analysis, linking pasts, presents and futures. The use of the plurals is important; there is always more than one reading of past events which can be made, 'always more than one possible course of action' (Altheide, 1988: 343), and more than one meaning which can be attached to present time actions. Within the meso domain societal and institutional forces mesh with human agency to produce structural processes which are always *emergent*, identifiable and comprehensible only through their enactment, but enacted in a way which is conditioned by previous structurings. Negotiated order thus refers to the (temporary and repetitive) process of defining a situation within the context of a social order, which included the identification and selection of those experiences and resources which contribute to a definition of the situation, and the effects of that definition on the specific situation as well as on its external context. The way in which these definitions are constructed and enacted will depend on the content of values and goals of the social order in question and on the preferred mode of conduct. This attention to the interactive and dialectic processes which are involved in 'making' social actions is in contrast to the reification of 'organisation' and the associated assumptions of the basic separability of actor, organisation and society discussed in chapter two. However, attention to these processes does demand that we devise a framework for codifying and communicating what is going on.

LINKING VALUES AND ACTION: (I) THE PROBLEM

First we need to understand something of the problems involved in linking values and actions; problems which are experienced routinely by participants, as well as posing questions for theorists. Taking the problem of social order and organisation within Women's Centres as an example of non-hierarchy invites comparison with other investigations of organisations which fall outside the mainstream of organisation theory. Examples include Abrams and McCulloch's (1976) work on communes, Thompson's (1973) on religious organisations and Gerlach and Hine's (1970) examination of social movements. In common these writers draw attention to the role played in organisational structuring and processual activities of values, ideology and symbolism. Gerlach and Hine (1970: 60) consider that, 'the ideology is perhaps the key to the infrastructure of the movement', while Thompson (1973: 301) observes that 'religious organisations are judged not only for their efficiency, but also for their symbolic appropriateness'.

However, if we argue or observe that people cooperate on the basis of shared values we must be clear what we do and do not understand to follow from this. The relationship between values and action may be unclear, ambiguous or disputed (Brown, 1990b). Organising activity in Women's Centres makes reference to the values of the autonomous women's movement, but as we shall show the relationship between values and action is one which is continually negotiated by participants; the terms of the negotiation and the arenas in which negotiation occurs vary over time and between situations. There is a general requirement that actions be legitimated by linking them to values, but the process by which this legitimacy of action is demonstrated is a political one. Thus, as we have already noted, while both action and its symbolic referents may be expressed in terms of agreement about a shared set of core values, particular attention must be paid to the arena of negotiation between the two. To do otherwise is to fall into the trap of determinism which arises from a Parsonian sense of shared values, such that social integration follows mechanically from an assumed consensus around generalised values. For this reason Martins (1974: 263) prefers to distinguish between 'valuations' and 'values'; 'values as schemata of valuations, actual values being susceptible to wide margins of indeterminacy, variation and fluctuation'. In these terms 'valuations' takes the place of the more frequently used 'values' to refer to a summative abstraction from multiple *evaluations*. 'Actual values' are the negotiated and variable evaluations made of particular items of social action, which make reference to but are not necessarily identical with generalised 'valuations'. The role of values as a source of meanings and in the creation of a shared sense of social order is accepted by many commentators, but in making this point Emery and Trist (1965: 28) also observe, 'values are not strategies or tactics; . . . they have the conceptual character of "power fields" and act as injunctions'. The importance of this statement and of Martins' is given weight by placing it in an empirical context, as Thompson (1973) does. Having noted that little empirical work has been done on the correspondence between religious symbols and the organisational forms favoured by religious groups, he points out (ibid., 1973: 300) that 'one of the main sources of conflict in religious organisations . . . is the fact that religious symbols cannot in practice be broken down very easily into specifiable empirical conditions without generating controversy'. Thus the strategies, tactics and actions which are involved in achieving and maintaining (which includes changing) social organisation arise from processes which are 'political' (Pettigrew, 1973) and involve negotiation (Strauss, 1978).

Variability in this arena is introduced in a number of ways. First, it should be emphasised that while it is possible to identify agreement about a shared set of core values which refer both to a preferred mode of conduct and a desired end-state within women's movement organisations, it is considered unlikely that participants will share *all* values and cognitions and the potential for conflict, beyond that invoked by the process of translating the core values into action, is maintained. Second, it is also to be expected, as the earlier examples have illustrated, that participants will vary in the skills and commitment which they are able (or choose) to bring to the process of constructing a social order. Third, a longitudinal perspective introduces the variability into the enactment of values which Martins (1974) identifies. At different times different evaluations are made of the most appropriate way to relate values to actions. Finally, Strauss (1978: 259) reminds us that the realm of negotiability is itself mutable with respect to the resources – 'time, money, skill, information, boldness or perhaps desperation' – which are brought to bear on it. However, not all applications of resources are equally weighted, equally acceptable or equally valued in their contribution to the production and maintenance of social order. They must also be identified as legitimate in terms of the core values which characterise the social order in question. For example, two of the women's groups discussed in chapter one considered the possibility of employing paid workers with different outcomes. For one group paid workers meant an inevitable introduction of hierarchy and the idea was therefore rejected, while the other considered that paid workers were essential to their survival and were prepared to put effort into ensuring that this innovation did not unduly affect the nature of their organisation. In these two instances different meanings were attached to similar events. Therefore the political processes already referred to must be extended to include 'politics as the management of meaning' (Pettigrew, 1985: 44) in order to link the value component of social organisation to organising processes within a particular setting.

The emphasis which has been placed on the need to identify the cultural components of, and the negotiative processes inherent in the production of social organisation, has also pointed to the importance of organisational analysis which counters the criticism 'ahistorical, acontextual and aprocessual' (Pettigrew, 1985: 3). This being the case the relatively fragile and temporary forms of organisation found within the women's movement, as with Col's (1981) 'networks', take on a different meaning when attention is shifted from the organisation as such to the notion of a particular ideological per-spective, or set of core values, whose enactment and articulation can be identified in a variety of individual and collective expressions. This approach is indicated by Burrell and Morgan (1979: 311) as one which 'stresses the importance of the *mode of organising* reflecting a particular totality, rather than the importance of organisations as discrete middle-range units' (emphasis in original). Thus by focusing principally on 'organising activity' (Weick, 1979) rather than organisational form, it becomes possible to account for periods in which 'organising activity' is at a high level, while the 'organisation' ceases to exist in the sense of a definable physical location, as occurred on a few occasions during the field work.

This emphasis is most obviously summarised by negotiated order theory (Day and Day, 1977, Strauss *et al.*, 1963, Strauss, 1978). However, typically in the settings (hospitals, medical schools) where this approach to the understanding of social order has been adopted, the situation is seen as one in which different groups of professionals, non-professionals and lay members bring to the same 'locale' different training, socialisation and experience. Faced with a general aim, such as providing patient care, the situation is conceived to have such complexity that it is 'not amenable to solutions by the simple application of the rules of the organisation' (Day and Day, 1977: 131). Thus negotiations arise both to cover the different values which individuals bring to a situation and because of the different contextual contingencies embedded in a situation. It is the second point I wish to emphasise here. Much of the examination of negotiative processes rests on the identification of different (and sometimes competing) perspectives and values (Bucher and Stelling, 1969), but, as Day and Day (1977: 131) observe, 'even in those situations where a remarkable degree of consensus is achieved *vis-à-vis* such issues as etiology, treatment and organisational policy, *the problem of implementation* and the assignment of specific tasks still remains and is subject to the same social pressures' (emphasis added).

In a general sense the arguments of Strauss and his colleagues are a reaction to the inadequacy of bureaucratic rules and procedures to provide sufficient guidance for behaviour in specific instances. In addition they suggest that it is not always possible for individuals to exercise the hierarchical authority which is nominally theirs. The usefulness of this approach to conventional organisations is not disputed, but a caveat must be placed on its immediate applicability to collective organisations. As Rothschild-Whitt (1982: 46) has noted, 'bureaucracy and collectivism are oriented to qualitatively different principles'; in the first case individuals are empowered with authority, while in the second authority is granted only to the collective as a whole. In these terms, 'collectivist organisations should be assessed not as failures to achieve bureaucratic standards they do not share, but as efforts to realise wholly different values' (ibid., 1982: 47). Thus it is argued the themes of negotiated order theory are equally applicable to non-hierarchical and collectivist organisations as to bureaucracies, but the terms of reference must be those which are characteristic of the social order under examination. Strauss *et al.* do not discuss the question of *legitimate* contributions to negotiated order, assuming perhaps that all participants are able to legitimise their conduct by reference to professional codes, structural positions etc. In situations where this is not the case, as in collectivist organisations, the intervening concept of legitimacy as the moral authority of consensus is necessary. The right to make influential contributions to social order is, in some part, dependent on those attempts at influence being perceived as consistent with the shared core values of that order, and it is on these terms that negotiation occurs.

When we come to look at the reasons participants offer for setting up the Women's Centres it will be evident that the initial impulsion is the creation of something which offers an alternative – a previously non-existent facility and/or a counter to previous ways of working. However, these moves to establish 'something else' did not provide a full definition of what this might be; this was to be worked out in conjunction with other participants. The base-line of the organisation could not be assumed but was to be actively created. Burowoy (1979: 6) is one of a number of writers who have argued that, 'organisations do not simply "persist". Like any other enduring pattern of social relations they have to be continually produced.' His use of the word 'enduring' draws attention to the particularly acute position of Women's Centres whose persistence can only be assumed through the continual production and reproduction of social organisation by participants. Such small-scale and innovative organisations do not have sufficient momentum or received precedents to 'persist' without continual inputs of time and energy on the part of their members. The general point here is that participants, both individually and collectively, may be faced with a wide range of choices concerning how to 'produce and reproduce' organisation. As Altheide (1988: 343) has observed 'the context does not automatically direct or lead the actor to one course of action rather than another, there is *always* more than one possible course of action' (original emphasis). These choices are made under conditions of limited energy, limited skills and limited resources. While some of the choices made may include seeking to extend the available energy, skills and resources, it is always true that not all possible areas of attention may be dealt with at once.

At the end of chapter one the concept of organising as a cycle of tasks was introduced. Weick (1979: 3) similarly considers organising as the process by which actors 'assemble ongoing interdependent actions into sensible sequences that generate sensible outcomes'. The means of making sensible – and therefore manageable – the complexity which exists in the world through the assignment of meaning to events and actions are provided at two (analytically separable) levels. At the macro level generalised values may be instrumental in providing simplification: 'so far as effective values emerge ... a field is created which is no longer richly joined and turbulent but simplified and relatively static' (Emery and Trist, 1965: 28). At the level of specific activities a stabilising effect occurs when some component of the structural processes appears as relatively fixed and acquires a taken-for-granted character. Given these parameters the energy of organising is directed elsewhere – to arenas where meaning is uncertain, where resources are inadequate, where behaviour is inappropriate. To quote from Weick again:

> Organising is directed initially at any input that is not self-evident. Happenings that represent a change, a difference or a discontinuity from what has been going on, happenings that seem to have more than one meaning, are the occasion for sizable collective activity. Once these inputs have become less equivocal, there is a decrease in the amount of collective activity directed at them.
>
> (Weick, 1979: 4)

Weick is right in observing the differential attention organising groups give to matters which do and do not (at different times) enter the arena which is subject to negotiation but, in the case of non-hierarchical groups who are almost invariably involved in creating an innovative social order, it is perhaps less easy to detect a ground-line of 'self-evident' happenings than he suggests. The particular characteristics of organising activity within the auto-nomous women's movement are the strong agreement about a set of core values and, at the same time, the relative absence of models or formats for the implementation of these values.

LINKING VALUES AND ACTION: (II) THE MEANS

A number of key points follow from this depiction of the need to link values and action legitimately which, in general terms, have implications for prioritising organising over 'the organisation', and, specifically, in terms of appreciating what is going on within groups attempting to organise non-hierarchically. First, the basic unit of analysis is not the individual or the 'organisation', but what Hall (1987: 2) has termed 'concerted action'. The idea of concerted action focuses attention on situations where actions are *jointly* brought to bear on some object. Similarly Weick (1978) has focused on relationships constructed on interlocking means. Essentially what we are considering is an *interactive* process of search for, imposition of and honouring of a social definition. This emphasis on relationships rather than individuals *per se* makes sense because individuals as whole beings are rarely totally 'within' any particular setting, and instead distribute aspects of their personal resources across a range of different settings which are likely to engender different demands and different styles of participation – a fact which is perhaps more self-evidently true of participants in women's groups than it is sometimes considered to be in more conventional organisational settings, where there has been a tendency to treat participants as if they were not also simultaneously involved in other aspects of social life. Second, the terms of the creation of joint action and its relationship to some outcome depend critically on the communication process through which meaning (the definition of the situation) is established. Once a context of meaning is established through interactions between participants it bounds an arena of action, but again in a temporary and ultimately mutable sense.

As the discussion so far has shown, negotiated order theorists generally agree that at a given point in time or in relation to particular social orders there are limits to what is negotiable. A complete state of flux, where everything is simultaneously available for negotiation, would be 'unmanageable' in Weick's sense, and therefore also a condition of stalemate where no action could be taken. In practice a 'sufficient' degree of routinisation and predicability is a necessary antecedent to action. For a viable and persistent form of organisation the need is for a *flexible* social order (Brown and Hosking, 1986); one which has sufficient continuity to provide a sense of identity but which stops short of complete rigidity which would prevent adaptation to changing circumstances. The latter extreme is perhaps typified by the political group which seeks to achieve total ideological purity and in so doing excises all 'deviant' elements in its membership, obliterating the possibility of renewal. The former situation is also likely to be temporary; if those concerned are unable to establish some basis for repetitive joint action, then, without the development of shared meanings, the situation is that of an aggregate not a social group. These are obviously extreme illustrations and yet examples which are not too far distant from them can be seen in the relatively unformalised organising processes of the women's groups. However, at the same time as recognising that the arena of negotiation will in practice be restricted, it is also true that the factors which may, potentially, enter that arena are numerous, the more so when the social order is nascent and consciously experimental. For example, participants in Women's Centres can be unsure about what kinds of relationships will further their social order, and may thus spend time debating what kind of linkages to form and with whom. Whatever is decided will have implications for what kind of organisation the Centre 'is', that is, its activities will acquire meaning from those with whom participants interact. This kind of example leads to a recognition that conceptualisations of boundaries between 'organisations' and 'environments' can fail to take into account the extent to which boundaries are in reality flexible, permeable *and negotiable*. Altheide (1988) has provided an example of voluntary sector organisations which changed their social order from a participative collective version to a business model through, in his terms, 'enacting a different environment'. His case material clearly shows how reductions in funding triggered, but could not be said to cause, a change in the internal organising processes of the agencies concerned. In an essentially ambiguous situation the agencies selected and enacted a particular symbolic environment which reflected the values and practices of the funding body *as they perceived them*. Alternative courses of action, such as strengthening linkages with other collective organisations, were not pursued. Weick (1978) has also suggested that actors create the environment to which they adapt. Creation here refers to the process of selection and identification through which just some of the possibilities offered by 'the environment' are given meaning and incorporated into the social order. In other words participants make choices about who they associate with and what events they relate to. These choices in turn carry meanings about who they are and what goals they are pursuing. Maturana and Varela (1980) have gone a step further in asserting the notional and enacted quality of the environment. Their argument, developed primarily to have relevance to the biological world, but of undoubted interest to organisational theorists, proposes that living systems are organisationally closed and auto-nomous, making reference only to themselves. Given that the aim of the system is to produce itself, or in the terms used here for social order to be maintained, then the system cannot enter into interactions which are not specified in the pattern of relationships which define the organisation. In this sense the enacted environment is part of the social order and the idea of a boundary between organisation and environment, as assumed in the entitative view of organisations, is exposed as no more than the imposition of an external perspective which does not reflect the reality of actors' perceptions of their world. Morgan (1986: 244–5) points out that when it is possible to 'see' oneself as part of an environment, new relations become possible; that is, other possible identities can be explored, along with the conditions under which they can become realised. This precisely concurs with the situation of the participants in the Women's Centres when they were faced with deciding where to locate and whether to seek external funding. Each identified option was considered in terms of the potential losses or gains to the values of their social order, while it was also recognised that doing nothing and hoping to remain unchanged was infeasible. In this situation the condition of 'sufficient but not too much' social order was achieved.

So, from a negotiated order perspective, the dimensions of organisational life which are brought into higher relief are those of culture and politics. Culture because organising is dependent on the creation of joint meanings and hence concerted action towards some end, and political because joint and collective meanings do not arise self-evidently or uncontroversially, but are negotiated between participants.

SKILFUL NEGOTIATION AND LEADERSHIP

In his discussion of negotiated order Altheide (1988: 343) introduces the idea of the *competent* ideal typical actor; that is, one who is familiar with the meaningful parameters of the situation and is therefore likely to consider such parameters within the course of her action. The idea that competency is definable in relation to working with and for particular social definitions is crucial for understanding how leadership functions are achieved in the case of settings which are pursuing the ideal of a situation characterised by the absence of individual leaders. The competent or skilful actor is able to work with and on behalf of the group through structuring and presenting their contributions in terms of others' criteria for legitimate social order. However, while recognising that some actors may be more skilled than others in this sense, and that situations of non-hierarchy in particular call for a distribution of these skills or competences among participants, we also need to incorporate the idea of joint action to recognise that the central concern is the division of labour in terms of actions, not of individual actors (Hall, 1987: 11). By looking at what people are actually doing it should be possible to avoid overly structured views of joint action which start from the identification of occupants of positions. Hall continues by arguing for the identification of tasks and bundles of tasks around which joint action takes place; 'it is necessary to determine essential activities and how they are structured, allocated, and merged', a directive which reflects Westerlund and Sjöstrand's (1979) urge to explore ways of carrying out basic organisational tasks other than through a system of super- and subordinate relationships. But what are 'essential activities'? Beyond the basic proposal that they are those required for the creation, maintenance and furtherance of a social identity through the enactment of a particular social order, to begin to answer this question it is necessary to look more closely at the skills of competent social actors. Are they in fact the skills of leaders?

The grassroots accounts of women organising in chapter one make strong statements about the centrality for their purpose of creating forms of social organisation which differ from conventional forms in so far as they are not composed of 'leaders' and 'followers'. Instead they emphasise the kinds of tactics which can be employed in attempting to ensure that the interaction patterns through which social organisation is created and maintained promote collectivity rather than hierarchy. Given this stance, it would perhaps be possible to argue that the development of theory which can account for the practices of small collective organisations need not be concerned with the concept of leadership and should rather search for a different form of language to express what is being attempted. However, there are two particular counter-indications to this approach. First, the strong oppositional stance of organisers within the women's movement to 'leaders' and the practice of leadership *as it is conventionally defined* makes this a reference point, albeit a negative one, against which present organising practices are compared and adjusted. Second, given the importance of the concept of leadership in the organisational literature, it would be foolish to propose a new set of concepts which do not relate to those in current use – although ultimately greater understanding of non-hierarchical organisational processes may lead in that direction.

In order to reach a better understanding of the role played by leadership processes in the construction of a particular social order it is necessary to look at the social acts which comprise leadership, at the functions which leadership performs, and at the conditions under which leadership is accepted. In line with the arguments presented so far, all these factors are contingent upon the cultural context within which they occur, and to which in turn they contribute (Brown, 1990a). For example, Smith and Peterson (1988) have argued that our current understandings of leadership are very much tied into the value systems of Western advanced industrial countries, predicated on a culture of hierarchy and the reality of status position, such that leadership is commonly taken to be a description of what one individual (a leader) does to another (a subordinate). We may well add the notion of 'maleness' to their list of identifiers, since the value system to which they refer is, in all its components, in opposition to that promoted by the women's movement. Nevertheless Smith and Peterson are right to argue for greater attention to the cultures and contexts within which leadership acts occur; however, they, as do others, take their alternative examples from Japanese culture which, while placing much greater emphasis on collectivity than most situations in the West, remains strongly and fundamentally hierarchical in its structure. For the purposes of exploring what leadership is, or can be, when it is released from hierarchical constraints and enacted collectively, organising activity with the women's movement provides the best available counter-example.

Given the cues provided by Smith and Peterson and others (for example Brown, 1989, Chermers, 1984), it is relatively easy to see how studies of leadership have been adjudged by many commentators to have reached something of an impasse. In much of the recent literature studies of leadership have become almost inseparable from studies of what managers do or, with the same kind of elision, what those who make decisions do. This approach takes first the individual – identified by status, role or task – and then asks what behaviours are associated with that position. The contingencies of the behaviour of leaders from the basis of particular structural positions have been almost infinitely elaborated, for example in terms of the nature of the task, the skills required for its execution, the characteristics of subordinates, or the appropriateness of different leadership styles in different contexts. Whilst this approach clearly is a reaction against, and of course an improvement on, the earliest versions of leadership theories which sought to identify some essential quality of an individual's behaviour which was distinct from any context in which it operated, the strong structural determinism which characterises leadership theories which take the existence of a hierarchy as their starting position, whether acknowledged or not, leads only to simple behaviouralism. These theories do not relate how leadership is accomplished in any general sense, since the elision of leader and manager, leadership and management prevents the articulation of a discussion of leadership which is not derived from structural definitions. There are other approaches to the understanding of leadership processes which offer more promise, but before considering those it is worth remarking on the fact that this version of leadership, which relates behaviours to position in an organisational structure, has, by its very ubiquity in theory and in taken for granted 'common sense' assumptions about what organisational life is like, become the form in which 'leadership' is conventionally understood and the totem which is rejected by women organising. Katz and Kahn (1978: 526), for example, observe that 'there is an almost universal assumption that even a small subpart of an organisation can operate successfully only if some person (i.e. one person) has been formally designated as leader'. In rejecting this version of leadership the principal objection of the women's movement is in fact to the implied hierarchical structure, where authority to direct and to decide has a fixed and located quality, which does not accord equal value to each participant as a potential contributor to organisation. Consequently much of the internal self-monitoring of their organisational processes is directed towards achieving precisely the opposite situation – one in which there is emphatically no formally identifiable leader, and preferably no informal one either, at least not for long.

Alternative conceptualisations of leadership which have made an explicit separation between status position or delegated task management and influential contributions to organisational processes provide a more useful way of thinking about the nature of leadership under conditions of non-hierarchy. Thus, for example, Katz and Kahn's version of leadership allocates the term to precisely those aspects of organisation which are *not* prescribed by the mechanics of hierarchy, such that leadership is 'the influential increment over and above mechanical compliance with the routine directives of the organisation' (1978: 528). The conditions they attach to the exercise of leadership in this sense of incremental influence – the incompleteness of organisation design to provide sufficiently detailed and appropriate activity specifications, the changing external environment which reduces internal repetitiveness, and the internal dynamics and complex processes that are characteristic of human role occupants – are close to identical to the conditions for negotiated order identified by Strauss *et al.* As with Strauss' arguments, Katz and Kahn recognise that much which takes place within organised settings is neither programmed nor programmable. Neither the formal structure of relationships nor the existence of bureaucratic procedures can make much headway in accounting for or determining the true complexity of organisational life.

If this picture of what organisation life is like is accepted, it becomes difficult to accept the behaviourism of earlier leadership theorists whereby, once a relationship between behavioural styles and outcomes of value to managers was identified, leaders (or managers) could be trained to select and adopt an appropriate style from a menu of alternatives, dependent on their assessment of the contingencies of the situation.[1] The limitations of this argument are perhaps by now self-evident. What is less comprehensible is the limited extent to which the insights that have been produced detailing the complexity of organisational life have been applied to the concept of leadership. The alternative recognition that leadership behaviour is a variety of 'situated social action' places its stress on the identification of leadership acts through observing who is influential in a social system, in what circumstances, and how, rather than starting from the position described above where role, status or task allocation defines 'a leader', and assumes that in order to understand how leadership 'works' we need only observe and categorise the behaviours of such pre-defined individuals in terms of their immediate interrelations.

REMOVING LEADERSHIP FROM THE CONSTRAINTS OF HIERARCHY

Katz and Kahn's (1978) separation of leadership from the power of office provides an important direction for bringing a greater sense of organisational reality into what is involved in leadership behaviour. As they point out (1978: 528–9) those who are designated equal by means of authority structures are, almost invariably, not equal in their influence and contribution to social order. Conversely, there are aspects of power and influence which are not assigned by organisational structures and are therefore available to *all members of the organisation*. These they identify as expert power and referrent power (which refers to influence based on liking or identification with another), drawing on French and Raven's (1960) typology of power. Whilst we will wish to develop their ideas about how power and influence can operate when they are not backed by structural authority, the crucial insight for our purposes is that influence can be exercised between peers, along lateral as well as vertical linkages, and independent of formal designation. The emphasis on referrent power is very much in the tradition of the human relations school (and in particular Likert, 1961, McGregor, 1960) where it is seen as a major contributor to organisational effectiveness. However, here, as we have discussed, the managerialist slant of this tradition views contributions to organisation 'over and above' those prescribed formally and mechanically as a cheap, indeed almost a free, good which may be made available to management. For this reason, having identified the potentiality of this kind of contribution, it is then defined in terms of its additionality, rather than as the central process it more accurately is. The exercise of referrent power, in particular, is the added value to interpersonal relationships and small group work. Thus, while acknowledging that there are wider implications in the later work of Likert, and of Herbst, in so far as they relate a spread of leadership to a reduction in hierarchy, which have been discussed, leadership in the sense the concept is presented by Katz and Kahn is indeed posed as incremental rather than central to the core processes of organising.

Continuing the search for the 'essential actions' or core processes of organising, we have seen that the women's groups whose experiences were described in chapter one do expend a great deal of effort in managing and developing their interpersonal and group skills, but they do more than this. They also dedicate effort and resources to identifying appropriate tasks, carrying them out and managing relations with those with whom they are, or may become, interdependent. This range of activities goes further than the 'double task' of small-scale (laboratory) groups where different individuals may emerge as leaders in relation to the process of carrying out the task in hand, and in relation to managing and nurturing the affective component of the group. The important aspects of leadership which are missing in narrower conceptualisations of the term are those which go beyond the face-to-face, within-group or dyadic interactions. As Hosking and Morley (1988: 92) observe, 'Groups exist in the context of other groups, individuals simultaneously belong to many groups, and group memberships overlap ... Processes of this kind have rarely been contemplated in the leadership literature.' Laying out the field of inquiry in this way has immediate resonance with the situation of the participants in the Women's Centres and the contexts in which they operate. Individuals are only partially and intermittently engaged with this group. When they come together to form a group they are required, for example, to make assessments of the strength of membership and the capacities of participants, to identify tasks which will be attractive and which are consonant with their systems of values, and to maintain a resource base. All these activities are concerned with and directed towards promoting and maintaining what is special and distinctive about this group or organisation. In part all groups, whether overtly 'oppositional' or not, define themselves in relation to their difference from other groups. This sense of difference or distinctiveness is captured by a social identity and social order which is meaningful both within the group and in relation to external others. Leadership in this wider sense is essentially located within organisational processes and is concerned with promoting the values and interests of the social order in question (Hosking, 1988). In so doing it is as much concerned with characteristics of and events in the group's environment as with internal processes. In fact the two are seamlessly linked in so far as leadership processes move ideas, information and meanings back and forth. This permeability and flexibility of organisational 'boundaries' is particularly apparent in the case studies where the pattern of membership of the Women's Centres was analogous to a series of concentric circles consisting of participants who varied in the intensity and frequency of their commitment to and involvement in different tasks and events. The gradation of involvement from a very active core group to those whose involvement was only fleeting is one illustration of the inappropriateness of attempting to fix a boundary line between the 'organisation' and its 'environment'.

A model of leadership processes which takes as its starting point the identification of leadership acts by the perceived effectiveness of their contribution to social order, rather than from their structural position (Brown, 1989, 1990a, Brown and Hosking, 1986, Grieco and Hosking, 1987, Hosking, 1988, Hosking and Morley, 1988, Morley and Hosking, 1984), has considerable advantages for our purposes because it makes no prior assumptions about the form of organisation. This decoupling of hierarchical structure and those individuals who contribute more influential acts of organising liberates the concept of leadership, while at the same time demanding that the researcher give close attention to how potential acts of leadership are legitimated by participants in diverse settings.

Within this model the core processes (or essential actions in Hall's terminology) of organising and of leadership are the negotiations through which issues are agreed, solutions developed and policies put into effect (Hosking and Morley, 1988: 92). Whatever actions are undertaken, to be influential they must be seen to meet the criterion of a legitimate contribution to social order. Leadership behaviour is thus an interactive and negotiated phenomenon; leadership acts, whether they lead to a relatively permanent designation attached to one or a limited number of individuals or whether they are widely distributed among participants, achieve their status as a result of the perceived quality of their contributions. Where leadership acts are seen to come particularly from a limited number of participants (i.e. these people are 'leaders') it is because these individuals make consistent contributions to social order and are expected and perceived to do so by others. In these situations, where minority influence is accepted, leadership is 'focused' (Gibb, 1969). Within the Women's Centres, where 'focused' leadership was not part of the social order, those who are perceived to be too consistently influential are often, over time, delegitimated by other participants. In these situations there is the contrary requirement for a system of *distributed leadership* (Brown and Hosking, 1986) where consistent contributions to social order are expected and valued from all group members.

The special quality which distinguishes the contributions of leaders from those of others is that they are more skilful organisers. Where, as under non-hierarchy, the requirement is for a social order in which leadership acts are distributed among participants the stark alternatives are that either everyone must become a skilful organiser or that the social order will fail, perhaps over time changing to another version which does not accord the same value to distributed leadership. This suggests that for groups seeking to organise non-hierarchically the demand for skilful leadership in order to protect and promote the group's values is likely to be particularly acute.

THE SKILLS OF ORGANISING

We have argued that studies of leadership need to focus not on what people in particular positions do but rather on leadership as process, and specifically processes in which influential acts of organising contribute to the structuring of interactions and relationships, activities and sentiments; processes in which definitions of social order are negotiated, found acceptable, implemented and renegotiated; processes in which interdependencies are organised in ways which promote the values and interests of the social order (Hosking, 1988: 147). But why skilful? Why is it not sufficient to assume that, under non-hierarchy, every participant's contribution must be equally effective since a priori all are equally valid? This is because leadership is an essentially political process, involving complex decision-making and competence in the manipulation of cultural values, symbols and meaning. Decision-making occurs in relation to the unending quest to create a present time situation which approaches congruence with the desired end-state of existence. In the present time participants identify current or anticipated events which are seen to have meaning in relation to their values and interests. These events – that is, those that are identified as salient – are interpreted as potential gains or losses for the social order. The attribution of saliency is important because, from the infinite number of actual or potential events, only a few will be identified as requiring attention. This process of selection is one component of the process of enacting an environment and is also illustration that choices are being made. It is of course quite possible that inappropriate or insufficient identification of salient events will occur, resulting in, for example, a failure to develop an awareness of potential threats. There are several instances in the case studies where participants failed to recognise the extent to which other actors were in a position to damage or even obliterate their endeavours. These failures stemmed from an insufficient exercise of one of the core skills of organising – that of *networking*. In one of the instances referred to above the potential threat was changed to an opportunity by networking; that is, by building new relationships with those who were in a position to determine the future funding of the Women's Centre. These relationships were used to gather information which informed vital choices and to influence opinion in favour of the Centre (Brown and Hosking, 1986: 72). In general participants may be more or less active in building social contacts 'outside' their social order as well as within it. These contacts can provide information and a range of other resources and create exchange relationships which are mutually beneficial. Gray (1985) discusses 'collaborative relationships' in the interorganisational domain which are precisely of this type. Interestingly, among the conditions she identifies for the formation of these kinds of relationships are the limitations of traditional adversarial methods of conflict resolution, problems which are bigger than any single 'organisation' acting alone can solve, and the inevitability of one organisation's actions creating consequences for others. Thus, while she is at pains to point out the specificity of the domain from which her analysis is drawn, in fact there are close parallels between the form of these collaborative relations and those which comprise the networking component of organising skills. Gray (1985: 916) similarly proposes the creation of a negotiated order through which greater understanding of the context is achieved and judgements are enriched. Extreme differences in power between actors can affect effective problem identification and direction setting through inhibiting the interactive processes through which the necessary information is assembled, and instead 'a sufficient distribution of power is necessary'. In order to create, through networking, interdependencies that provide optimum value for each actor the quality of the relationships which are formed should approach a condition of non-hierarchy. Where this condition is not approached trust is undermined and both weaker and stronger parties may be inhibited in the presentation of their views (Walton, 1969: 3). Gray (1985: 932) concludes by arguing that there are many problems in the interorganisational domain which require structuring so that all stakeholders (her term) can contribute to the negotiation of collaborative solutions; 'traditional bureaucratic problem solving methods are maladaptive'. It seems wherever we look there is evidence of the existence and perceived value of non-hierarchical relationships.

Networking then, is about forming peer relationships with interdependent others. It is enacted through transactions and exchanges. Some commentators (for example, Col, 1981, Hall, 1987) see this concept as so central to social organisation that they prefer to use the term 'network' rather than 'group', in order to capture better the complex, fluid quality of joint social actions. Whichever term is preferred, the *process* of networking is crucial as a means of handling the core problems of organising as it is defined here –

working out what is going on and why, deciding what to do about it and translating those understandings into action. Each stage in this cycle depends on amassing information, making assessments about the merit of different courses of action in terms of furthering participants' values and interests, and deploying resources to achieve the preferred action. At each point there are choices to be made. These choices will be better informed if participants (or leaders) 'move around' the decision-making environment and interact with actual or potential interdependent others (Hosking, 1988: 159). In this way events which may by puzzling become clearer as the meaning which is to be attached to them is negotiated in the light of information about others' interpretations. At the same time participants may become aware of contradictions, threats or opportunities to which they will have to devise a response. Influence is achieved 'internally' by structuring the information gleaned from the environment in such a way that it can be understood and acted on by participants, and 'externally' by a similar process of promoting 'scripts' which simplify and codify the understanding others receive of the group's social order. These are the processes by which information is given social meaning and through which leadership emerges; 'leadership acts are those which most influence what information is used and how' (Hosking, 1988: 159). These acts can also be depicted as acts of power, displayed in the design and imposition of paradigmatic frameworks within which the meaning of actions is defined (see, for example, Brown, 1978: 376).

Social organisation, when characterised as it is here, can be seen to involve certain 'decision-making dilemmas' (Kotter, 1982: 76). These dilemmas derive from the need to manage relationships, particularly in the absence of status authority, to manage resources through balancing long- and short-term considerations, to schedule activities in terms of deciding what to do and for how long, and to manage values through negotiating norms concerning modes of conduct and desired end-states, and the relationship between these two (Brown and Hosking, 1986: 72). We have seen how networking is an activity which makes an important contribution to the organising cycle through assembling information, understanding threats and opportunities and negotiating shared meanings. Moving on to the implementation phase of the cycle, organisers (or leaders) also need to devise ways of linking the demands of tasks with the capacities of participants. Capacities refer not only to factors such as skills and competences, but also, and particularly salient within the women's groups, to other kinds of resources, not least levels of individual commitment. Here again choices have to be made and justified so that appropriate and effective action can be taken.

SUMMARY

Negotiation characterises organising processes because meaning is not transparent nor is there any necessary or obvious relationship between values and action. Individuals and groups promote different scripts and influence has to be acceptable. Within different social orders the negotiative processes will be more or less collective, more or less routinised. Because women's movement organisations reject individualised leadership as a mode of conduct and because these 'organisations' are innovative and relatively unbounded, negotiative processes here will be more collective, less routinised than in some other social orders. Nevertheless leadership processes, as they have been defined here, are central to the maintenance of social order and we can reasonably argue that in these circumstances leadership skills will be particularly required.

NOTE

1   It should be pointed out that the range of situations which has been examined and codified in this way is largely limited to interactions in small groups with leaders and in leader-subordinate dyads. See Smith and Peterson, 1988.

Chapter 4

Introduction to the case material

This chapter summarises the discussion so far and introduces a framework for the case material which is presented in the next three chapters.

In chapter one we reviewed a range of examples of organising activity in the women's movement in Britain and elsewhere and, in organisational terms, showed how the stance of the movement is simultaneously oppositional – to conventional modes of organising – and avocational – of something else. This 'something else' is characterised as non-hierarchical organisation – the structuring of relationships towards some end in a way which creates and maintains equality between participants – and it is the clear and emphatic expression of the centrality of the value of this form of organising which makes women's movement organisations an appropriate locus for exploring how non-hierarchy 'works'. Such a specification is paralleled in anarchist approaches to social order, but comparison with accounts written from a feminist perspective illustrates how anarchists have glossed over two important features of non-hierarchical organisation: first, the need to identify an ideology or rationality which motivates such attempts by imbuing them with a value dimension; and second, the need to go beyond assertions of 'spontaneous cooperation' by inquiring into the precise nature of the strategies and tactics which may be employed in the implementation of non-hierarchical organisation. Drawing on a wide range of anecdotal and reflexive accounts from the women's movement the search was for communalities of experience and intention and for the identification of problem areas and proposed solutions.

It appears, on the basis of this evidence, that the pursuit of equality is likely to be constrained by variations in the levels of skill and knowledge, and of power and influence, in the extent of commitment of participants, and by the need to form relations with a hierarchically organised environment. These problems are frequently recognised by participants and some ingenious solutions can be devised, directed towards minimising differentials which are seen to be reducible and/or minimising the effects of differentials which are not seen to be reducible. Different groups may well adopt different solutions to similar problems; for example, the question of whether or not to employ paid workers was differently assessed by two groups, but in both cases there was a recognition that the assessment made had implications in terms of the core values. At the same time, beyond the moral imperative to organise in this manner, a range of organisational efficiencies was proposed including flexibility, innovation, risk-taking, increased commitment and the development of personal autonomy. Thus the main theme which runs through the discussion in chapter one is that the process of attempting to construct non-hierarchical organisation is one which may place heavy demands on participants in terms of the skills and time involved, but which nevertheless is seen as a worthwhile endeavour since it provides a means of enacting a particular system of values which are considered to carry moral weight. The application of these values to the processes of organising carries with it the requirement that contributions to social order are perceived as legitimate; thus the overriding problem facing participants is to devise ways of accumulating and exercising their organising skills in a manner appropriate to the pursuit of non-hierarchy when there are few available models of practice for them to draw on.

In chapter two the review of some of the main themes of the organisational literature noted that, where non-hierarchical or semi-autonomous groups have been observed and discussed, most attention has been given to groups with specific task designations operating within hierarchically structured contexts. Such groups are seen as having the capacity to develop interactions with particular desirable qualities but, within the constraints which circumscribe them, are limited in the range of their activities. For example, such groups may not be required to work out the nature of their task, to attract resources from elsewhere, to form relationships with other groups, and to maintain their identity. As such the activities of these kinds of group fall short of the full range of organising issues addressed by the participants in the women's groups. Work in the human resources tradition offers some extension to the area of interest by proposing that the preferred forms of interaction seen as characteristic of the semi-autonomous group may usefully be adopted by higher levels of the organisation and, as with the examples of feminist organising practice, an 'efficiency' argument is proposed such that increased participation and decreased hierarchy within the organisation are seen as necessary to match the turbulence of external environments. However, in this case there is a concomitant argument (or assumption) that individuals' interests and goals should be congruent with the goals of 'the organisation'; if this is not so 'management' (the people who are permitted to stand outside group processes) is available to make good this deficit by engendering the right kind of commitment.

Without further elaboration it is hard to see how these depictions of organisational processes can be applied directly to women's movement organisations. Two points are important here. First, many of the women organising were concerned with a wider range of organisational activities than simply those concerned with carrying out a defined task with defined resources. Second, there is no one 'outside' the group, perhaps charged with implementing an incentive structure, who is able or permitted to 'create commitment', nor, under non-hierarchy, can any individual member take on this role on an ongoing basis. The entitative view of organisation as an aggregation of role-determined behaviours in particular makes little sense here. The idea of 'the organisation' as somehow superior to organisation as a cooperative of its members denies the evidence we already have that participants are continually and iteratively active in the process of organising. Consequently alternative approaches which have emphasised the importance of seeing participants as active and knowledgeable actors have much more appeal. Moreover treating organisation as activity makes it possible to offer an account for periods when 'the organisation' is fragile or clearly temporary and when the membership varies according to who has made a decision to be committed – to devote some of their personal resources to furthering a particular set of values and interests – and to what extent.

Given the apparent limitations of approaches to organising which derive from assumptions of role-determined behaviour to capture fully the 'processes through which particular organisational patterns are generated and sustained' (Benson, 1977: 8), we have argued instead for an approach which highlights the dynamic and dialectic quality of organisation. Negotiated order theory emphasises the political and cultural qualities of organisational actions and in particular draws attention to the conditional and temporary nature of organisation. This perspective has the capacity to 'explain' what is going on across a wide range of settings, but it is a demanding one. It requires that we explore how participants define their situation, the resources available to them, and the appropriateness of the actions they take. We can anticipate that these definitions will vary over time, but that they will be informed by the content of the core values which describe both the preferred mode of conduct and the desired end-state of the social order in question. Social order refers to the joint creation of a sense of social identity which influences the form and content of interactions and relationships such that they generate behaviours which are appropriate with respect to the core values (Brown and Hosking, 1986: 69). The question of *legitimate* contributions to social order is therefore ever present. We need also to recognise that, while there is always the potential for any aspect of the social order to receive attention and hence enter the arena of negotiation, in practice at a given point some aspects of the social order will be seen as relatively fixed – either uncontentious or apparently immutable – and will thus take on structural qualities.

It has also been argued (in chapter three) that the organising activities which are implied in the construction and maintenance of social order require skill and may therefore be carried out more or less successfully. These skills can be conceptualised as the skills of leadership which, fundamentally, are concerned with managing the dilemma of 'sufficient' social order, to provide a sense of identity and continuity, but not 'too much', which would result in a rigid system, unadaptable to changing circumstances (Brown and Hosking, 1986, Hosking, 1988). Based on the understanding that leadership is identified through specific influential 'acts of organising' we are able to propose that leadership can be decoupled conceptually from the categorisation of the observed behaviours of individuals holding defined status positions. In general terms leadership involves complex decision-making processes through which choices are made, meanings determined and actions agreed and implemented. How leadership acts are sanctioned in particular settings will depend on the core values of the social order; clearly where non-hierarchy is valued a system of distributed, as opposed to focused, leadership is desired.

These observations provide us with a framework for examining the case material. In order to get closer to the 'how' of creating and maintaining social order we need to look at situated action and the way in which it is linked to history and to wider contexts. Rather than presume the existence of entities such as organisations, the focus is on a network of relationships and linkages through which resources are created and allocated in the pursuit of shared goals. The emphasis which has been given to the negotiative processes by which meaning is created through linking interpretations and actions to values draws attention to the contribution of participants as active, knowledgeable actors. Social organisation, as it is conceived here, is a process – always in a condition of becoming, rather than being – but nevertheless a process which is informed by interpretations of the past, the wider context of the present, and the consideration of alternative futures. From this myriad of possibilities participants create more manageable simplifications by constructing narratives which 'make sense' (Weick, 1979). These simplifications may become relatively routinised and uncontested or they may remain 'up front', the subject of frequent revision. More broadly, the particular aspects of the social order which are brought into the negotiating arena will generally show shifts over time, depending on the degree of uncertainty which is identified and seen to be in need of simplification. In the case material we will see how three particular factors – the definition of the group, the definition of the group's task, and the assumption that certain resources will persist without the expenditure of particular effort – were, at different times, taken for granted or the focus of much attention and debate.

Principally, then, the intention of the case study material is to describe and explicate the manner in which participants in Women's Centres interpret and seek to enact non-hierarchical organisation. It is argued that a full understanding of this, or any, organising activity can only derive from an analytical approach which seeks to examine both the interaction of different point-in-time perspectives and simultaneously to consider these as part of a processual flow, such that action is constructed in relation to its context and is at the same time part of the process of creating that context. The processual approach adopted in the case material allows us to see the shifts in structural emphases as the facets of the social order which are 'taken for granted' change over time, and to observe the different influences brought to the process of organising by different participants. We have also argued that the process of organising is most appropriately seen as one of complex decision-making which some participants will perform more skilfully than others. We need therefore to look at who is more influential, how, and in what circumstances, at the activities which foster the social order, and at how participants manage the very real difficulties of creating non-hierarchy through minimising differentials.

However, before moving on a comment about the unit of analysis is necessary. So far we have been at pains to point out that approaches which reify organisations and conceptualise them as unitary actors negate the active involvement of individual participants in creating organisation. This is a necessary argument, but it is not the whole story. The need to find a way of connecting individuals, processes and contexts requires a formulation which goes beyond simply asserting the essential sovereignty of the individual. Whilst we need to retain the importance of human agency, more central is the concern with *joint actions*, that is with the form and content of relationships. However, it is not easy to find a language to express the nature of relationships in brief terms, and for this reason the term 'group' will be used, although it should be understood that this is shorthand for a nodal point in a network of relationships.

METHODS OF DATA COLLECTION

Hall (1987) has argued that the requirement for holistic analysis makes case study research the only valid methodology. Dogmatic perhaps, but there are a number of rationales for the appropriateness of case study research in this context. Case study research has been characterised (House 1980: 40) as 'complex, holistic and involv[ing] a myriad of interactive variables'. Its advantage is that it allows these variables to be studied 'intensely and simultaneously' and is the only method which can reveal the dynamics of phenomena which are 'political' or negotiated (Berg 1979: 32). Another characteristic, instanced by Yin (1984: 23), is that 'the boundaries between phenomenon and context are not clearly defined'. In terms of the multiplicity of factors operating it has been suggested (Argyris, 1979) that some 'noise' – that is, additional, extraneous and possibly obscuring material – is inevitable in accounts, as it is in life. This problem of drawing a distinction between phenomenon and context may be exacerbated if the subject matter is currently underexplored or 'not currently in vogue' (Znaniecki, 1980: 68). The methodological problems in this situation are those of 'setting limits to the inquiry and of focussing on the categories within which the data can be assimilated and understood' (House, 1980: 42).

These points may be illustrated by my experience in the field while conducting the research. The data were collected in two ways. First, by becoming a member of the Women's Centre where I attended meetings, joined in more informal interactions and worked on campaigns, and second, by carrying out semi-structured interviews with other members of the group. However, at no time was I attempting to observe and record 'everything'; the focus of the research was always 'organisation', but my understanding of what this encompassed changed over time. Initially, perhaps, I attended too much to formal meetings taking place within the locus of the organisation, seeing these as the focal point of organising. As time passed I became aware of two points which necessitated a modification of this approach. First, that activities relating to organising were not confined to meetings and occurred in a variety of more informal settings, and second, that participants were presenting an account of their feelings, in terms of their experience of the affective quality of the setting, as a legitimate input into organising activities. In fact I was beginning to identify a transferable *mode of conduct*, a preferred form of interaction implemented across a wide variety of settings, although initially I could not have labelled it in those terms. What I did perceive was a broad spread of interaction throughout a social network of which meetings, as such, were only one of a number of nodal points. The question then became one of isolating out organising activity analytically from this broad sweep of social interaction. Gradually the realisation came that there was a conflation here. The core values and the mode of conduct *were* generalisable for *all* interactions throughout the social network (and as such may be employed to construct a definition of a social movement (Brown and Hosking, 1986)). On the other hand participants themselves appeared to have no difficulty identifying when they were engaging in organising activity. This sense of organising activity can be summarised as a series of agreements to cooperate in purposive groups around issues which are perceived to require attention. In these purposive groups issues are identified, decisions rehearsed, actions initiated and the responsibility for pursuing these actions assumed (cf. Argyris and Schon, 1978). A particular characteristic of organising activity in these settings is that such groupings are likely to have a temporary and fluid nature. Once this realisation had been achieved it was possible to pursue the emerging analysis in terms of the need for participants to hold the skills of organising and to exercise them in a manner which was legitimate with respect to the core values of the social order.

A second feature which influenced the way in which the research was conducted was the fact that these settings were feminist; constructed around the core values of the women's movement which have been detailed here. It would have been foolish and entirely inappropriate to attempt to downplay the importance of this. The last ten years have seen the articulation of both an anti-positivist and a feminist approach to social research which are in many respects identical (see, for example, Reason and Rowan, 1981, Reinharz, 1983, Stanley and Wise, 1983). The alternative promotion of a critical subjectivity, achieved through collaboration, reflexivity and an action orientation, also fits comfortably with the demands of case study methods. Specifically from a feminist perspective there is the additional requirement that the relationship between researcher and 'subject' should not be oppressive, manipulative or hierarchical. In other words the kinds of relationships through which the research is carried out should parallel and be consistent with those which are promoted in the field setting. This is both an ideological imperative and a practical necessity. Certain kinds of data can only be obtained by becoming part of the group studied (Cassell, 1977), and in many ways the process of becoming part of the group is also the means by which the distinctive qualities of the particular social order in question are identified. As a researcher and as one participant among many in the Centres I was particularly conscious of the relationship between these two roles. However, until recently the literature on research methods offered field researchers the choice of a position on a continuum from complete observer to complete participant, with the former implying lack of access to important material and understandings, and the latter carrying with it awful warnings of the danger of 'going native'; an abdication of all critical competence. My own view is that this continuum seriously over-simplifies the reality of field research. The researcher does not adopt a single stance in the interests of data collection, or even, as some have suggested, move between different roles at different times. The real issue is the adoption of different stances and different awarenesses *at the same time*. Cassell (1977: 415) expressed this well when she described her simultaneous positioning as analyst and participant: 'It was the analyst who dealt with the categories although the experiences of the same individual as participant may have helped to generate these categories.' Further, an interesting feature of these particular settings is that participation is generally voluntary and part time, and in these terms the researcher may become as fully a participant as any other, in contrast to much other research in organisations where, typically, there is a choice between remaining 'a researcher', outside the organisation, but able to move freely within it, or taking up a specified structural position which permits shared experience with those similarly positioned, but inhibits free movement.

The question of shared experience was also pertinent to the conduct of a number of interviews, carried out after approximately one year of field work. These interviews were semi-structured, to the extent that there were a number of topics I wished to explore, but the primary intention was to create an exchange in which other participants' own stories, and in particular their understanding and interpretation of events, could emerge. For both myself and others the bounded nature of the interviews made it possible for them to operate as 'time out', when we reflected on a stream of events in which, in most cases, we had both participated. Attention was directed towards explicating participants' definitions and perspectives on their own and others' organising activities. In settings such as Women's Centres where participation is predominantly voluntary and part time, the arenas where organising activity occurs are perhaps less immediately self-evident than in conventional organisations. A focus, therefore, in the field work was to use a mix of observation and participants' reports to identify situations where organising occurred.

In the presentation of the case material the intention is to provide the reader with an amount of data which is adequate for the purpose of achieving an appreciation of the situation, and in particular to use the longitudinal perspective to bring into focus the changing arena of negotiation. Since the intention is not to attempt a global coverage of an area of social life but to 'see' one aspect of it through the interrelation of different perspectives and understandings, there is an inevitable selection of material. I accept that what is presented here is ultimately my own summation, and that others may well place the emphases differently.

It is difficult to make one, or even several, case studies do all the work of exemplifying a theoretical framework, nor in the usual run of events do interesting and illustrative incidents occur to order. Nevertheless I believe it is important to use a narrative format in order to provide a 'bottom-up' processual account. Data were also collected in a similar fashion, although over a shorter time scale, in three other Women's Centres and these are used to provide further illustration of some of the discussion points.

NARROWING THE FOCUS: WHAT IS A WOMEN'S CENTRE?

The illustrations in chapter one were drawn from a wide variety of examples of women organising in Britain and elsewhere. Before presenting the story of Greystone Women's Centre it is appropriate to narrow the focus by considering how Women's Centres are particular examples within the wider range of organising activity in the women's movement. Naturally there are many local variations, depending on the resources available and participants' specific agendas, but two characteristics in particular define a Women's Centre. These are the fact of a definite physical location and the offer of open access to all women. In these respects they form a visible and accessible facet of the women's movement and, in relative terms, show a greater degree of formalisation and continuity than other more fluid and ephemeral groupings.

There are around forty Women's Centres operating in Britain today. The emphasis and details of the facilities which are provided will vary but in general it is likely that most of the following areas will be covered:

- a physical space for the use of women; as a meeting place for groups and more informally for 'dropping in';
- an information and referral point for issues of particular pertinence to women and the locality;
- coordination of activities; discussion groups, educational courses and campaigns.

Those towns and cities which have Women's Centres will vary over time. There are always some projects coming to the end of their life and others which are starting up. It may even happen, as Segal described at Islington, that different groups of women set up a Women's Centre in the same location over a number of years. All population centres have the potential to establish a Women's Centre;

other examples of women's movement activity will occur to a greater or lesser extent, only some will formalise a section of this activity in the establishment of a Women's Centre. Thus Women's Centres represent an endeavour, through the provision of certain resources, to 'pin down' a section of the fluid, flexible and overlapping groupings which constitute a social movement, while at the same time offering access into the movement for those who do not, at present, consider themselves members.

The next three chapters relate the story of Greystone Women's Centre from its genesis as a community project within an inner city community college through a period of transition to a re-established independent Centre. It is not intended as an account of either more or less successful organising in any summative sense, although there is evidence of both. Its primary purpose is as a vehicle to explore the 'how' of non-hierarchical organisation at a micro level, and over time. The immediate context of the action is described in the case study, while the wider cultural context of women's movement organisations has been outlined in chapter one.

The Women's Centre at Greystone began life as a community project attached to a local school and community college. Three years later it was established as an autonomous group, receiving funding from charitable trusts, and in a different location. In the intervening period many participants came and went, while at times a core group continued to organise in the absence of 'an organisation'. The initial situation was characterised by focused leadership which was later rejected as values promoting non-hierarchy became dominant, and participants struggled to devise ways of creating a situation of distributed leadership, which in this instance was exacerbated by the fluid and part-time nature of participation in the Centre. In the course of the three years the shifting arena of negotiation is observable as different aspects of the social order come under scrutiny, as are the conflicts between different interpretations of core values and the differences in the ways in which values are connected to actions by different participants and at different times. Amongst all this are examples of more or less skilful acts of organising.

Chapter 5

Greystone Women's Centre I
A community project

PROLOGUE

Greystone Women's Centre was located in an inner city area. In the 1970s the area had been the focus of a Community Development Project, one of a number of projects established under a Home Office initiative as part of the Urban Programme. As a consequence a number of community projects had been set up and the area had undergone extensive redevelopment, including the building of high-rise blocks and the purpose-built Simpson School and Community College which was designed to provide a focus for local activities. Ann took up an appointment as a community worker at Simpson. After a few months of 'hanging around trying to discover what I was intended to do' she settled on the idea of a 'Women's Information Centre'. The early publicity material made clear the intentions of the project and identified gaps in existing provision which the Centre could fill:

> it became apparent that there was a need to provide additional support to the women and mothers in the area of Simpson School. The idea of setting up a room or Centre came from the Mums' group which meets in Simpson and was responded to by the community workers and teachers concerned. Simpson is involved in a Mothers' group, Mums' and toddlers' group, an Asian girls' group, teaching English as a foreign language and many other community activities. It was felt, however, that a wider need had not been catered for, a fact which had been highlighted in the past when crisis situations emphasised the need for a place or a means to give more time and advice to women involved in these problems, whether it be relationship, health or financial worries. It was clearly understood that such a place had to be outside the

home and outside the official atmosphere of the school or other professional services. From this the idea of setting up a Women's Information Centre was engendered.

The handout went on to outline the range of services envisaged:

The main aim of the Centre is to provide a supportive and easily accessible place to go:
- In times of crisis relating to family or relationship problems (i.e. cases of battering, homelessness).
- To obtain welfare rights information (such as supplementary benefit inquiries, maternity benefits, sexual discrimination, etc.).
- Pregnancy counselling (practical information on pregnancy, adoption, abortion, etc.).
- For information on the facilities or organisations in the area (nurseries, family planning clinics, community groups, day and evening classes, training courses and other groups).
- For free legal advice.
- For advice on accommodation, private or council housing; rights for tenants and landlords.
- For health advice/discussion groups concerning women's health (i.e. drugs and their effects, breast cancer, cervical smears, menopause, miscarriage) and also information on children's health.

The parameters of the project were clear: it was distinctive in that it was to be for women and would offer more time and a different kind of environment from other advice and support agencies. Less distinctive perhaps, except for the emphasis on women's health issues, was the range of advice to be offered.

During the summer Ann worked towards making her project a reality. The community team had vacated a room and she took it over, organised its refurbishment and amassed some of the information necessary to provide the advice service. By the beginning of the autumn term the stage was set; it remained to fill it with people.

THE OPENING OF THE CENTRE

Ann's intention was that the Centre would be run by a group of 'volunteers' (this being the term in use at the time), and individual women were invited to become involved by attending a training course in welfare rights. At the time I was teaching continuing education courses in the school and, following Ann's invitation, started attending training sessions with two women who were members of my sociology class. Most of the other attendees were women living locally who participated in the 'Mums' group'. This first training course emphasised the acquisition of knowledge which was seen as necessary to provide the advice service outlined in the handout. Obviously the scope of this was considerable and there were limits to the amount of usable information which could be transmitted in a short course. In addition, in line with the stress placed on the ways in which this Centre was going to be different from other advice agencies, some time was devoted to sessions which, through role play and other similar techniques, directly focused on the kinds of relationship volunteers might form with 'clients' (again this was the term used). These were run with the help of a member of the drama department and involved the acting out and discussion of likely 'problem situations'. Some six months later there was another course of the same type, but at a higher level of sophistication in that it was run by a lecturer in counselling skills from a local college and involved the use of video-feedback. I found these sessions enjoyable and interesting, but also quite challenging. For some of the volunteers this challenge appeared to be too great and their attendance lapsed. At this early stage there were no general discussions about the nature of the Centre or the appropriateness of the task; the considerable demands of the task were not at that time modified by comparison with the actual competences of potential participants, who were instead placed in a position of deciding whether they could, or wished to, try to achieve the standards of technical competence in advice-giving they were presented with.

The divisive effect of the training sessions was in contrast with the way in which the desired end-state was depicted, with its assumptions of minimum differentials between those who seek and those who offer advice, and, by implication, between advice-givers. To quote again from the publicity material:

> The aim of the Centre is not just to become another Information Centre, but we hope it will develop into a place where women can get a lot of time and support in an informal atmosphere. [The] volunteers are women who have faced similar problems to those who may come to the Centre for help and advice.

It was intended that the Centre would eventually be run by local women who would be able to relate to 'clients' on the basis of similar life experiences, and who would be able to take time over a problem in a way that was impossible for other agencies. The training course was seen as part of a general development towards a 'self-help' mode of organising through the strategy of supporting a group over a period of time until they are in a position to take over the running of an organisation. This kind of approach was, and perhaps still is, a common one within community work. Ann commented: 'I saw it as a very normal part of community work in the sense that you initiate a project, you get people involved, you get them to run it themselves and you move away'. However, this espousal of a self-help model needs to be seen in relation to the volunteer/client orientation of the training course. Although standards were later relaxed, at this stage volunteers were being presented with a role-model of a quasi-professional who was both familiar with a wide range of information about legal and welfare rights and who possessed a high level of interpersonal skills. However, while technical and interpersonal skills were identified as important, the skills of organising were not.

In January the Women's Information Centre (WIC) opened with something of a flourish in the local community. It was presented as something different from any of the existing services – somewhere for women to drop in, share their problems and work things out on a self-help basis. Ann's description of the opening day gives a good indication of the WIC's location in the local social network:

It was very crowded; the whole day there were people in and out. There were all the people from the legal and income rights centre, there were the vicars, there were all the local community workers, lots of local mums, all the people working with local mums' and toddlers' groups, health visitors – all the contacts you have as a community worker rather than as something else.

On the evidence of this network of contacts there is no doubt that the Centre was a community project – like other community projects? The fact that it was specifically oriented towards women did not have salience in terms of distinguishing it from other community projects, and only in the broadest terms could it be said to be feminist in the sense of being women-centred; in fact the early publicity material stated that 'men are welcome too!' Nevertheless, the depiction of the desired end-state contained clear elements of non-hierarchy in its emphasis on minimum differentiation and peer relationships. The next sections look at the mechanisms which were adopted in order to try to work towards this goal.

THE ROTA SYSTEM

After the opening day the Centre was open for four and a half days a week and I began working on the rota on Friday mornings. The intention was, although it did not always work out in practice, that there should always be two people in the Centre and at this time my co-worker was a social work student. The point of this arrangement was to allow one of the workers to accompany a woman to, for example, the social security offices and help her to make a claim if necessary. On two occasions I did this with a woman who was homeless, in that I helped her to sign on for benefit and look for somewhere to live, and later moved her from a hostel to a flat. However, for much of the time I was on the rota very little happened. It is possible that the time I was there was atypical (and other workers did report some very busy sessions), but there is no doubt that a general problem facing volunteers was that the number and type of 'clients' using the Centre on a drop-in basis was irregular and unpredictable. The training sessions had perhaps produced an expectation of higher levels of work activity than was usually the case. What I experienced was long periods of inactivity interspersed with major problems. For example, two I particularly remember having to deal with on my own were a battered woman seeking an emergency injunction and another who, without warning, attempted to cut her wrists with a milk bottle. In both cases I felt quite inadequate to deal with the situation.

The need to manage the unpredictability of having 'too much' or 'too little' to do was one which volunteers dealt with in different ways. Initially the student and I spent a lot of time just sitting around waiting for people to come in; we had a feeling that somehow we should be 'ready'. Later we began to bring in other work to do while we waited. Other volunteers adapted differently. There was usually a list displayed of minor tasks to be done, but very often the time was spent chatting, reading books and making personal phone calls. Thus, although the 'inactive' periods were used by volunteers in ways which were pleasant and productive for them personally, this could only in the broadest sense be seen as useful preparation for the occasional crisis. Moreover, with the limited amount of time each volunteer spent in the Centre, major problems did not occur with sufficient frequency for them to constitute a useful learning experience. The relatively short time spent in the Centre produced other difficulties for volunteers; while the idea of 'talking through' a problem implied an open-ended approach I, in common with some of the other workers, had young children and it was difficult to find a way of saying, 'I can listen to you sympathetically until 12 o'clock, then I have to lock the Centre and collect my daughter'. Certainly I do not think I was alone in seeing my role within the Centre as narrow and bounded in time; volunteers in those early days were not often proactive in relation to wider issues affecting the Centre, and the extent to which we behaved as organisers was limited.

Most often 'clients', for their part, came to the Centre with expectations derived from their experiences with conventional agencies – that is, one of fairly immediate problem-solving, and to some extent this was reinforced by the way in which the Centre operated. For each 'client' a record-sheet was filled in with details of the problem she presented and the action taken. This was done to obviate the distress of having to tell her story anew to different volunteers and as an aid to efficiency in an attempt to ensure continuity of action. Nevertheless it did little to persuade a newcomer, or indeed the volunteers, that the Centre was other than 'just another agency', in spite of the arguments to the contrary.

The realisation that this emphasis on problem-solving and the nature of the procedures which went along with it were at odds with stated goals of the Centre, and perhaps inimical to the development of other aspects of work, led to a gradual shift in emphasis. The room was reorganised to look less like an office and more time and energy were given to promoting group work. The definition of a competent volunteer was one which was subject to continual renegotiation and it was now seen that the original expectations had been pitched at too high a level. Stress was now placed on being able to retrieve and act on information from the filing system, rather than expecting it to be fully learned. The rule of thumb adopted for welfare rights problems[1] was to do no more than you would do for yourself in terms of making phone calls and writing letters. Although this might appear to be a great deal less than the service it was originally intended to provide, in practice it normally turned out to be a great deal more than most 'clients' were able to undertake for themselves. It was also more than some volunteers were able to undertake without support and it was necessary to recognise and accept that there was in fact a 'two-tier' system of volunteers operating. In part this arose because training courses were not continuous and there had to be other ways of assimilating newcomers into the activities of the Centre. This was generally done by putting them on the same rota spot as a more experienced volunteer who was able to show them the ropes, an instance of the basic tactic of skill-sharing, frequently used in attempts to create non-hierarchical organisation. However, there were also other factors operating. The women working on the rota could broadly be divided into two categories: those living locally who had only a basic education and were frequently unused to the routine of working in an office, and those who were 'imported' from outside, normally graduates and chosen for a particular skill they had to offer. Ann was clear about the mixture of women she wanted to attract into the Centre and the reasons for it:

> I spent a lot of time encouraging local mums – going round to the house and having a cup of tea and talking them into coming to the Centre, and coming to the training course and then doing their morning stint and supporting them through that. I spent far more time on that and wanted to keep away, for instance, students and people who just wander in and take over – who've got nothing to do with the area, even though they could be useful, and I used them, but to a limited extent. I didn't want them to take over. And as soon as there are more people like that the local mums wouldn't come anyway; it's not their social scene. Part of the Centre's social – you chat and get on with people, feel comfortable there. If it became more of those kind of people they wouldn't have come. So I was always balancing between those two sides of things.

In this scenario there is a clear intention that the 'more skilled' participants should make an instrumental input into the Centre, but be prevented from assuming a degree of ownership. The skills they were seen to have were necessary in relation to the task of the Centre, as it was then defined, but the culture of the Centre was intended to be that of a local project. In a later conversation with Jo (who was appointed as a part-time counsellor for young women) I expressed the feeling that in the early days I had felt very isolated, and it was not until later that I experienced any sense of working with women. She suggested that a lot of volunteers would say the opposite, and went on, 'I think you, because of your experience and background, were given that role, whereas a lot of the other volunteers were never actually allowed to [work on their own], which was difficult'. She summed up the problem in this way:

Being realistic, someone new coming in doesn't even like answering the phone. All right, fair enough. But I mean it's a bit tricky when you're doing that kind of work. So it'll take them a lot of time and they would need someone with them who's done a bit more till they feel confident. Well, that's OK, but it has implications and we have other women like yourself who know the ropes and can manage. So you've got two tiers whether you like it or not, and the question is what you do with it.

This tension between the avowed aim of a Centre run as a self-help project by local women and the contingent use of graduate 'outsiders' was a continual theme in this phase of the Women's Centre. However, the symbolic distinction between the two groups, which was important, over-states the difference in practical terms; as I have already indicated there were occasions when I felt far from competent and equally some of the local women were far from lacking in skills.

In line with the principles of self-help and personal development it is possible to outline the ideal career of a volunteer who 'makes the grade'. Typical steps in skill acquisition and increasing commitment would run something like the following:

(i)   The potential volunteer would be a local woman and would first approach the Centre as a client.
(ii) Depending on the type of problem she would be encouraged to join one of the existing groups, such as the single parents' group, or to attend a training course.
(iii) Here – and this is essential – she would find enough support and interest in the situation to keep coming back.
(iv) She would then be eligible, with induction and supervision from an established volunteer, to take a place on the rota.
(v)   Through this process she would learn how to make phone calls and write letters, to use contacts and information, until she was considered sufficiently competent to work on her own. In other words, she would still be a 'local woman' but she would have acquired the competences of the 'outsiders'.

Two local women, Gina and Iris, did succeed in this and, at different times, achieved the position of part-time paid worker. A further stage, where a volunteer gained sufficient skills and self-confidence to apply successfully for a job or training course and thus to leave the Centre, was an option taken up by some.

JOINT ACTION: THE BEGINNINGS OF ORGANISING

The early days of the Centre were characterised by relatively limited contact between volunteers who worked on different days of the week and an absence of any designated forum for collective organising. The first discussion between women working in the Centre which had any degree of formality was a meeting set up to receive a report from a student who had been working on placement. Her presentation led to a discussion of the current status of the Centre and some proposals for modifying it. The discrepancies between the current reality and the desired end-state were highlighted and the basic questions raised on this occasion – what kind of organisation should this be and how should we work in order to move towards that position? – were restated and reconsidered at frequent intervals.

Seven people including myself attended the meeting. The others were two teachers from the school, the student presenting the report, two local women (one an ex-client, the other the part-time worker) and a professional working in the area. The student's brief had been to consider the extent of 'social problems' in the area and the role of the Centre in relation to them. Her analysis drew attention to a range of problems such as homelessness, higher than average proportions of elderly people, one-parent families and unemployment which might be found in any inner city area, but her conclusion was that the Centre should offer a social environment rather than an 'official' one; there were already sufficient official and semi-official agencies in existence in that area.[2] The meeting endorsed this view and went on to consider the present use of the Centre:

> Gina commented on the relatively few local women involved in the Centre. Few came to meetings and few were volunteers. This was also commented on by most people present. It was decided that the new committee should look into this in detail and that perhaps one solution was more field work in the area.

This statement amounted to an acknowledgement that, while the generalised goal of creating a Centre of and for local women remained, the tactics which had so far been adopted to achieving this end were not particularly successful and that some rethinking was necessary. The shortfall of volunteers was related to the original decision to open for four and a half days a week, which meant that Gina was doing a great deal of filling-in and that it was rarely possible to have two volunteers at each session as had been intended. In retrospect it was felt that it would probably have been better to start by opening for only two days a week and to expand from there, but as the opening hours had already been publicised it was better to try to persevere with them. Arguably the current emphasis on problem-solving discouraged casual drop-in use of the Centre, and perhaps it was not possible to provide for both these activities at the same time. But there was strong agreement about the need for some form of decision-making committee, and in particular an emphasis on the need for a format which broke down the distinction between clients, volunteers and professionals. Participative and non-hierarchical forms of organising were identified as valuable features of the way the Centre should be operating, not just as an expression of a desirable principle, but also as a practical move towards increasing the number of women willing to work in the Centre. The minutes recorded:

> General comments were made by all volunteers on the need for people who worked in the Centre to see it as a corporate venture rather than as a Centre run by one or two 'professionals' with volunteer helpers. It was thought that a more open approach to decisions on the Centre was needed so that everyone had a say on important issues. If this happened it might encourage the volunteers who appeared to have dropped out of late.

Following this discussion a management committee was established. However, as constituted, it did not conform closely to the intentions of the previous meeting being primarily a representative body rather than a participative one. In a later conversation Ann indicated that she had already spent some time thinking about how decision-making should be structured:

> Before the Centre opened I'd spent quite some time on my own working out very closely what the decision-making structure should be. I'd actually worked out how many should be this, how many should be outsiders – I think there were four outsiders. They were chosen from the various agencies in Greystone which would be the most help to the Centre. Then there were so many

volunteers, they of course would have predominated. And then there were the so-called staff which was myself and Jo. I actually worked out a voting system and when the volunteers can totally overthrow the management committee.

The voting system was never made fully explicit, or ever used, although the membership of the committee was the mix of Centre staff, volunteers and professionals working in other agencies which Ann had envisaged. The nature of the meetings did not lead to the presentation of clear-cut proposals on which either/or decisions could be taken. Instead, in the main, they consisted of discussions of issues which led to suggestions for implementation or further exploration, and reporting back on what had happened since the last meeting. That this particular style of meeting became the norm (and as time went on the emphasis moved more towards reporting back and less initiating took place) must be related to the intervals between them and the differing nature of participation for the various members. As meetings took place roughly every four weeks it was necessary to differentiate between 'policy' and day-to-day decisions. The former were clearly the domain of the management committee, but residual decisions or those that arose in the implementation of policy were not so clearly located. That such decisions would almost inevitably come to rest amongst those who could make the greatest inputs of time and had the best access to information – in essence the paid staff – was not acknowledged explicitly, although from time to time there were short-lived attempts to place this kind of decision with a smaller sub-group meeting at more frequent intervals.

Placing both the ideological imperative to develop some form of collective management of the Centre and the aim of maintaining and extending networks of other relevant agencies within the same organisational mechanism resulted in a situation where neither objective was satisfactorily achieved. For the professionals management committee meetings were just one more meeting to be slotted into an already busy schedule, and it was apparent from the level of non-attendance that in general it was not one which was given particularly high priority. On the other hand the fact that similar meetings were a normal part of their working life meant that when they did attend it was easy for them to use the occasion to articulate a viewpoint which would influence any decision-making or to direct the discussion into areas which were of concern to them. Their familiarity with this conventional, semi-bureaucratic mechanism was in contrast to its unfamiliarity to many of the local women; thus it served to increase rather than decrease differentials between the two groups by inhibiting the latter's participation. Jo's reflection on her first management committee meeting after taking up her post illuminates this dissonance:

> What appealed to me [when I was appointed] was that it was this very locally based project, and then we had this thing called a management committee. To me management committees mean local authority structures which means formal paid employment. It meant something quite frightening even then. To the local volunteers the management committee was something they would never envisage having anything to do with.

An alternative to this view of the management committee as a very traditional (and alienating) organisational structure came from the school. Here it was seen as radical and innovative. Ann said that in terms of her ideas on self-help, 'I was trying to put control out of my hands into the hands of a management committee, and I fought with the Head about that constantly. He doesn't believe in self-help.' There were conflicts too in the process of moving towards an independent community project. Ann recalled, 'I was always trying to put it across to them [the school] that the management committee had the decisions', but in a later conversation she described the situation rather differently:

> The management committee in its true sense could be seen more as a consultative body, with the ultimate aim of preparing the volunteers slowly and gradually to take over more responsibility and perhaps eventually to take over the Centre when it was able to become independent. So, in a way, though I set the management committee up as a decision-making body I saw it as only half that in many ways; it wouldn't become that until it became independent.

So was it the chicken or the egg? I suggested that this view of the management committee should be read as one which benefits from hindsight, when the difficulty of constructing an appropriate decision-making forum was clearer. Certainly at the time I was not aware of its quasi-token nature. However, Ann contested this view and drew my attention to her statement of development aims, from which I quote:

Unlike many similar projects the setting up of the Centre was not based on an already existing cohesive group of people. A number of different women volunteered to work in the Centre (some from the Mums' group, from other contacts within the school, students and other agencies) and cohesiveness as a group has now to be worked on and takes time. As the community worker responsible for setting up the Centre, I have always seen my role as one of encouragement, providing the resources for such a Centre to come about, a link with the school and other community workers and agencies – one of development. I have always been well aware that the Centre should in no way depend on my work – from the beginning I have been working towards establishing a core group of volunteers, the idea of participation (through volunteers' meetings and the setting up of a management committee) and a means by which all volunteers can take part in what the Centre is doing. This is not an easy task – new volunteers in a new project demand guidance from someone else; their short session in the Centre and their home commitments do not allow them much time to take on extra work and tasks.

Here an identified aim – the production of a cohesive group – is seen as a necessary antecedent to an independent Centre. The means by which this aim might be achieved are also indicated: through the support and encouragement of Ann and through the management committee. Some of the difficulties inherent in this approach have already been suggested, namely the diverse membership and the alienating effect of this format on some of the members, and the relative infrequency of meetings. The first pre-management committee meeting had also identified the need for the Centre to be seen as a 'corporate venture', but on this occasion the suggested means was 'a more open approach to decision-making'. It is doubtful whether, as constructed, the management committee could fulfil this requirement, but some considerable time was to pass before the problem could be stated in those terms.

The minutes of the management committee for this period show the focus of activity and discussion to be directed fairly narrowly. A series of health talks was set up and the process of publicising these, and the Centre in general, was given importance. This was done by leafleting, talking to local mothers' groups, advertisements in the local press and a public service announcement on television. A great deal of work was done by Ann to find sources of funding which would enable the Centre to employ its own workers. In this she was successful to the extent that a local charitable trust agreed to fund a part-time counsellor for young women for three years and Jo was appointed to this post. Small amounts of money were raised from other sources, but the larger applications to bodies such as Urban Aid were unsuccessful. The progress of these applications was brought to the management committee, but the question of whether or not they should be initiated was not. At the same time it was known that the present premises had a short life and there were ongoing explorations of other possibilities. The other main item which recurred in management committees was discussion about how the Centre and the management structure were operating, the contradictions which appeared to be inherent in the situation and suggestions for their amelioration. The fundamental questions of 'what is the appropriate task?', 'what direction are we moving in?' and above all 'how is this going to happen?' were implicit in these discussions. The following extracts from the minutes are illustrative of the dilemmas which were identified:

> When asked whether the Centre was operating as a social centre or a place for 'women with problems' Ann replied that the Centre ... could be an informal drop-in place for women to come, but that we couldn't encourage it to become a busy crowded place [and] that in order for the Centre to succeed on a self-help basis this must be kept as its focus. This is threatened if the Centre takes on too much or becomes too wide in its concerns.

At the next meeting it was noted that:

> The idea of a Centre running on a self-help basis is a difficult one to make work. Many of the volunteers lack confidence – the Centre is important not just for people who come in with queries, but for the volunteers themselves. The volunteers and the situations they have to deal with are so varied that it is impossible to say why they stop coming.

The solution to low attendance at meetings proposed on this occasion was to move the meetings from evenings to lunchtimes.

At this point two staff changes took place. Gina, the part-time coordinator, left to take a full-time job and no funding was available to replace her. Ann reduced her working hours to allow herself more time to pursue her other interests and, although the hours she did work were now spent wholly in the Centre, the minutes recorded, 'because of these changes it is now more important than ever that volunteers and members of the management committee take a greater interest in the Centre'. It was suggested that:

It might be a good idea to have a small group of four or five people who would meet regularly, perhaps once a fortnight, to keep up to date on what the Centre is doing. This group would make proposals to the larger group, i.e. the management committee which could make the final decision, but the smaller group would be able to present clearly what the choices were on any particular issue.

By now management committee meetings consisted almost entirely of reporting back on current activities, and this proposed move towards devolution can be seen as a response to feelings of tokenism on the part of its members. Interest and attendance had reached a low ebb; meetings were used to ask for ratification of existing activities and, in the case of members who were representatives of outside bodies, for dissemination of information about these activities to their client groups. Thus the proposed restructuring can be seen as an attempt to move some members closer to the information base and to enable them to acquire the kind of knowledge which would facilitate more authentic participation in deciding the kinds of activities undertaken. However, there is something of a double bind operating here; in order to gain this kind of knowledge it was necessary for a volunteer to spend an amount of time in the Centre which approached that of the paid staff. On the other hand there was no impetus to do so unless this greater participation carried with it some benefits, such as the right to have a greater influence on the shape of the future. Some of the unemployed women who did spend an amount of time in the Centre found that their sense of direction was too much at odds with the community work perspective to be contained within the same setting and left.

The establishment of the 'smaller group' was short-lived. A couple of months later it was stated at the management committee that the 'main form of participation should be through this committee and that therefore there will be no steering committee'. The structural emphases remained unchanged: 'Two volunteer members are to be replaced as they no longer work in the Centre. It was decided that the place of [a professional who moved to another job] remain open for her replacement.'

During that summer a small group of women, including myself, began to meet in order to try to identify the reasons for the low level of participation and to consider what could be done to counter this. The question was raised as to whether the ideological objective of shared decision-making was in practice unworkable because of the wide variation between women in terms of such factors as skill, knowledge or length of involvement. However, before this question could be fully explored events outside the Centre meant that other forms of action had to take precedence.

THE SCHOOL AND THE LOCAL AUTHORITY

The speed with which the WIC was set up was, to a very great extent, due to Ann's initiatives in commandeering resources from the school. This meant that, in addition to the free use of a room and the inputs of Ann herself as a community worker, the Centre also enjoyed free postage, printing and telephone calls. These benefits did not, of course, come free of all costs. For the Centre to continue undisturbed it was necessary to avoid 'upsetting' the school – that is, whatever activities the Centre undertook, they should not appear to be controversial. To this end it was written into the formal statement of aims that the Centre would not engage in any form of direct political action.[3] Some time later this accession to the demand for an apolitical stance produced its own costs in that the Centre came under attack from the nearby Benefits Centre who considered the failure to take a campaigning approach as an abdication of moral responsibility, and hence refused to endorse the WIC's application for Urban Aid funding. There were costs too in the loss of volunteers who wanted to develop areas of work which were considered too threatening for the school to countenance and from which they were dissuaded.

Although the extent of it was not apparent to many people within the Centre, a great deal of Ann's energies went into negotiating the relationship between the school and the Centre. She later described how she saw the situation:

> I always saw myself in the middle between the volunteers, the people on the management committee and the school . . . and it's like on the one hand I was always fighting the school for more freedom for the Centre, so I was going in like that and saying, 'leave it alone and just let it be', and stopping them interfering in any way and at the same time in a sense holding back the Centre

or people in it who'd want to strive outwards more explicitly, which I knew just couldn't be, 'cos I saw what could be and couldn't be in that situation. So to keep [the Head] happy – I saw what we could get out of it – it also meant we couldn't do other things. I was very much in the middle.

I asked her whether she considered that the compromise which was struck was the 'right' one, and there was no doubt that she did. 'Obviously I didn't like the compromise very much, but when you saw the benefits – no other Centre would have free premises. No, I think the benefits were enormous – it just couldn't have happened any other way.'

The additional factor which did lead to a reaction from the school related to the premises which the Centre was occupying. It had always been known that the building which housed the Centre, as well as a youth club and some teaching rooms, was designated 'unfit' and would eventually be demolished to make way for a bus garage. When this happened it was intended that the activities in this building would be transferred to another close by which was in the process of refurbishment. Indeed the first set of plans for the refurbishment of the Annex included a 'shop front' for the WIC, and represented a considerable improvement in accessibility over the present location. However, five months before the planned date for the move the news broke that the Magistrates' Courts had requisitioned the present building and were going to take it over in the very near future. As this occurred just as the Centre was about to close for two weeks and many people were about to take their summer holidays, Ann phoned the homes and properties department of the council to make sure nothing was going to happen in the next couple of weeks:

They assured me we wouldn't be affected – they weren't going to touch the Centre. One of them gave me the date of October 29th as the day they would have to come in and start work on the toilets – but not until then. On August 19th, while everyone was away, the removal vans came. [Two members of the community team] were left to pack up all the information, books, files and furniture in the Centre and put them in temporary rooms. They were given permission to put them in a room in the Annex by [the Head]. On September 2nd I returned from holiday to find the Centre was a load of boxes and chairs stacked in a small room in the Annex. The Annex itself looked like a bomb-site.

OTHER ACTIVITIES IN THE CENTRE

Besides offering advice and support on individual problems a major activity in this first phase of the Centre was the development of a range of group work. As well as engaging with the individual women who participated in the groups, this activity also increased the level of interaction with other agencies in the locality. Two different, although not necessarily exclusive, approaches to developing group work were in operation here. On the one hand the impetus to engage in a particular activity would come from the identification of a 'client group'; something would be organised in relation to their perceived needs and they would then be persuaded to become involved with it. Alternatively the women within the Centre would organise primarily for themselves, and the activity would be sufficiently attractive to outsiders to draw them to it. *Ideally* there would be no discrepancy between these two approaches – local women working within the Centre would organise activities related to their experiences which would also be of relevance to other local women who would become involved on the basis of 'shared life experiences'. An early series of health talks was a successful example of this model, giving rise to a group for single parents and a menopause support group.

An adaptation of the first approach was for community workers and other professionals to act as brokers between the Centre and the client group to which they had particular access. Asian women were one group who were seen as likely to benefit from involvement with the Centre, and in the early days two Asian community workers attended management committee meetings. Through these contacts the first series of health talks was publicised among the Asian community and the possibility of providing interpreters was considered although in the event there was insufficient interest to warrant this. At one meeting 'it was stressed that Asian women would only come to the Centre if there was something to do, they were unlikely to come just to talk'. The next meeting minuted, 'There is a need for an activity to which Asian women can be invited, either one to be started here, or the Centre could liaise with an ongoing group. [The Community Relations Council worker] may be able to help with such a group.' The next move was to arrange two health talks in Asian languages. 'We need to work out what we can and cannot do in terms of working with Asian women . . . an Asian health worker is willing to take over talks if and when they get off the ground.' After that there were no further references in the minutes to working with Asian women and the Community Relations Council worker ceased to attend meetings. This failure to engage with the local Asian community to any great extent is best understood when it is appreciated that there were already other well-developed centres for social activities in the area. Notably there was a Family Centre attached to another school which was well used. It seemed that the Centre had 'identified' and was attempting to respond to a need which was not, in fact, reciprocated by the intended recipients.

In other areas activities did take off, although not always in the intended direction. Jo's job title was 'counsellor for girls and young women', and her working hours were arranged for the late afternoon and early evening so that she could see women by appointment at times when the Centre was otherwise unused. Jo described how she felt about having to go out and tout for customers, and the problems which ensued when her 'clients' turned out to be different from the intended ones:

> It's OK if you're employed by the Social Services or a school or whatever, but when I did the ground work going round local agencies saying I was employed by the Women's Information Centre to be a counsellor for young women – nothing! I had next to no credibility, and this problem developed whereby I actually began to have women coming in for counselling and therapy and I enjoyed that. I felt it was valuable, you know, but they were very definitely middle class intelligent feminist women, and the women I was supposed to be working with were the 16 to 25 year olds, a very different group of women altogether, and there was this feeling by some people that I shouldn't be doing that sort of counselling. If I did they should come at some other time and they should pay, because this was not the role of the WIC. That was difficult because the bit I enjoyed most was the work with those women, because they knew what they wanted, they came to do it and we did some good work. The rest of the time I felt I was trying to sell something to people who didn't particularly want to know.

The counselling service provided was one which was comprehensible and accessible to the women who used it but, without endorsement by and referrals from statutory agencies, it was unlikely to be perceived as appropriate by its intended 'clients'. The way in which it operated was also some distance from the expressed commitment to developing self-help forms of work, since it was clearly an example of a client/professional model of work.

The wide range of services offered by the Centre at this time made it inevitable that there would be many outside contacts, and extensive lists of names and telephone numbers were kept in the Centre. However, while the training courses directed attention to the contacts which were available they included little discussion of how these were to be handled. Some relationships, notably those with the school and the local authority were, as we have seen, negotiated almost totally by Ann. Others, with agencies such as the British Pregnancy Advisory Service and local housing associations, were largely unproblematic since, in the main, they consisted of referring on appropriate women. The two agencies with which the most difficult relations were experienced in the early days were the Benefits Centre mentioned earlier and the Social Services area office. In both instances the difficulties arose through a reaction to the feeling that amateurs were attempting to set themselves up in competition with established professionals. Mediating the situation with the Benefits Centre involved a considerable withdrawal from its field of expertise. The modification in the case of Social Services was rather different; when it was made clear through discussion that the role of WIC could be complementary to their work by creating a space where women could talk at greater length than was possible within the statutory service, they became increasingly supportive. One member of the area office was on the management committee and continued to be involved as a member of the collective which was later formed.

It is clear from these examples of the activities developed by the Centre that there was a parallel need to develop working relations with other agencies and relevant professionals in the area. Thus, from the perspective of the various 'relevant agencies' different forms of interaction with the Centre can be identified. Relatively uninvolved relationships occurred when there was simple referring on, as in the case of housing associations, or where a key worker decided that the Centre had little to offer, as the Asian community worker appeared to do. For those who did interact more closely with the Centre, the involvement would persist as long as the Centre was seen to provide some useful supplementary service or as a location where the agency workers themselves could work on alternative forms of service provision. The former may be seen in referrals from Social Services of women who 'need time to talk'; the latter is exampled by the Probation Service's setting up of a support group for women who were ex-offenders and by the work developed by Karen, a clinical psychologist.

CHALLENGING THE FORM OF ORGANISING

Karen had recently moved to the area and was looking for ways in which she could develop new kinds of practices with women who had drink and drug related problems. She had seen the publicity for the health talks in the Centre and came to see what was going on:

> My reaction was just very confused, afterwards hanging about talking to Ann, explaining that I'd just arrived in the area. I said I was interested in what was going on and Ann was saying 'that would be really interesting if you were to get involved'. It came at a time where I had made a decision that, rather than just talking about politics, I would act them out.

This meeting seemed, at first sight, an opportune way of meeting a need that had been identified in the management committee:

> Ann suggested that the Centre needs a consultant in psychiatric care to act as a consultant to the Centre for those cases with which we need more expert advice. It was suggested that we make contact with the Psychiatric Unit as they may have resources or advice to offer.

However, the fit is less than perfect; Karen was interested in setting up self-help groups, an activity which she described as 'political', whereas Ann's concern appears to be in terms of seeking support for individually difficult 'cases'. Karen was able to get permission from her superior to start working with groups of women in the Centre. At first this was her main concern and she did not see it as appropriate to be involved herself with the organisation of the Centre:

> I think my role was very much seen as having a set of skills which could be put into the Centre, so all the structural bit, all the thinking through where this fitted, all those issues weren't my responsibility... The thing it boils down to was my role was that I was dealing with the potential of one aspect of the Centre which was somehow in contrast with what was going on at [the hospital] and mental health generally; that could be something very positive

and very different offered for women, and it could be done within this particular Centre.

However, in the process of setting up these groups Karen found she 'was getting more involved with Jo, involved with other things and somehow using my initiative more, and just accepting the collective aspects of the Centre and not checking out with Ann so much'. So, in the course of developing her own work Karen, perhaps inevitably, discovered she had shared interests with other women and the simple fact of spending time in the Centre forced her to look more closely at the disjunction between her assumptions of a collective form of organisation and the current reality. A number of other women who came in with similar assumptions chose not to attempt to work with this disjunction and left. Jo later suggested that there was one overriding aspect of working in the Centre which could account for women dropping out:

> It was called the WIC so some women came along who were feminist and they expected to find a feminist centre. And what they found was this rather strange thing which aimed to give advice and support, rather nebulous, and always talked about being careful not to offend the school governors and they couldn't make sense of this, so generally went away, but some stayed around ... The constraint not to cause offence to the school was that bit too heavy and in the end it was offensive.

So, while Ann was doing her best to negotiate a compromise between the expectations of the school and those of some of the participants in the Centre, in a sense the 'wrong' pictures were being painted to each audience. The fact that those in the school were presented with a picture of a Centre moving rapidly towards independence may well have been a factor in their later decision to withdraw support, while, as Jo described, the constant damping down of any activity which could be construed as political alienated some potential participants.

By now it was known that the Centre would have to move and because of this, as Karen remarked, 'the sense of stability – oh we'll just go on as before – was changing'. There was an emerging sense that the initial setting-up period was in danger of becoming the status quo and that it was time to take stock of the situation. It will be remembered that the original intentions arose from a community work model of development; that over a period of time there would be a change in organisational style from focused leadership by Ann to some kind of collective organisation. No timetable for this change had been made explicit, rather there was a sense that in some way a state of readiness would be perceptible to Ann who would take it as her signal to withdraw:

> There was a time when [the head of the community team] said, 'What would you do if you moved out now?' and I said, 'It's not ready to, you know. I've got to set more things up and more people up before I can do that'.

The mechanism through which the change from one form of organisation to another was intended to take place was through the management committee. Here, it was envisaged, participants would learn the processes of taking and sharing responsibility to an extent which would eventually lead naturally to Ann's redundancy. However, the attempt to impose collectivity by fiat only served to make more apparent the strength of the leadership. Ann remarked at the time, 'I've tried to get them [the volunteers] to take things on, but they won't'. This reluctance to assume responsibility may be related to the style of the management committee meetings which have already been described as consisting largely of information trans-mission from Ann to other participants, and which also frequently included requests for people to take responsibility for organising certain activities. The passivity induced by the first type of interaction was reflected in the second – volunteering to take on tasks was rare within meetings and women had to be approached individually. There was also a process of reinforcement here; because many of the volunteers were not normally party to decision-making and did not have access to some areas of information, they were uncertain what would be required of them and whether they had the skills to do what was required. Hence only a few had the confidence to take on a task, and these women were more likely to have some relevant experience already on which to draw. On the other hand some initiatives were stifled because they could not meet the requirement to be apolitical.

The series of meetings which took place in the early summer, before the Centre was 'dumped', was ostensibly set up to design a new volunteers training course for the autumn. They became, however, a 'garbage can' into which was tipped the problem of volunteer drop-out, disquiet about the workings of the management committee, reaction to the constraints imposed by close association with the school and the question of poor relationships with some of the other community groups in the area. One of these meetings identified the following pressures on the Centre:

- from the school and the local authority – to be non-controversial;
- from other agencies – to be as competent as them or to keep out of their territory;
- from volunteers – to have enough but not too much to do;
- from 'clients' – to do everything, to be reliable.

Although no resolution was reached, solutions were suggested in the form of alternative structures intended to give a broader base to decision-making and to facilitate task- and skill-sharing. When the break for the summer came some progress had been made and the situation was left with 'one more' meeting to be held. The action of the school in closing the Centre had the effect of bringing the issues under discussion more sharply into focus, moving the action out into the community and of precipitating the train of events which led to Ann's decision to resign.

SUMMARY

Throughout most of this first phase in the story of Greystone Women's Centre Ann's strong commitment to a community work approach and her important 'gatekeeping' function in relation to the resources provided by the school were influential in defining the kinds of activities which could be undertaken within the Centre, the mix of the participants and the form of the decision-making processes. A statement of the need for an 'open' decision-making process was made at one of the first meetings, but Ann's position enabled her to resist this demand until she decided to resign.

The vision presented of the eventual end-state was of a situation in which professional input would become redundant, and the Centre would be run by women who would be able to relate to the problems of others on the basis of similar life experiences. A central problem faced during this period, when the needs of 'local' women were seen as having primacy, was to find a way of moving from a position where 'outsiders' were used for their skills, but discouraged from 'taking over'. Ann's response was to spend much of her time encouraging and supporting 'local' women, but as Jo pointed out the nature of the work, and thus the skills required to perform it, placed heavy demands on many women.

An early meeting had proposed that some format for decision-making which would facilitate a reduction in the distinctions between different groups of women be adopted. This, it was intended, would ease communication and skill-sharing and also increase the level of involvement of members. However, the management committee which was formed instead included a number of representatives of outside agencies and as such could not operate as an effective vehicle for developing a self-help form of organisation. Nevertheless the criterion which Ann intended would signal the appropriate moment for her withdrawal was the establishment of a strong and cohesive core group of participants.

The description of the attendance at the opening day makes quite explicit reference to the fact that the Women's Centre in Greystone was located in a community work network. In terms of continuing relationships the agencies invited to send a representative to the management committee were those who were seen to 'be of the most help to the Centre'. Not all the agencies developed strong associations with the Centre through this mechanism and the extent to which the additional facility offered them was taken up was limited. The Social Services department referred some clients and in the areas of health, mental health and probation after-care new initiatives were established. In areas where there was already adequate provision, as was the case for Asian women and welfare rights advice, the intended developments did not take place. In general where agencies perceived that their area of competence was encroached on by the Centre's work greater difficulties were experienced in developing a working relationship and in some cases, notably that of the Benefits Centre, the objection was more fundamental. Throughout this phase the close association with the school was a constraint; it was necessary to comply with their definition of 'non-political' and this definition was not acceptable to the Benefits Centre or, later, to some of the workers in the Centre. The main rationale for cooperation from the school – free premises and services – ended abruptly not long afterwards when the school was placed under pressure by the council and it was made clear that there was no question of the school supporting the Centre in the face of this opposition.

NOTES

1 A few hundred yards from the Centre was a well-established and competent agency which specialised in this field. Relations were poor for a long time

and it was not until the WIC had reduced its aspirations in this area that they improved. Attacks were levelled at standards of competence: on the one hand, Centre workers were accused of making too many mistakes which had to be cleaned up; on the other, that they were incapable of distinguishing between simple and complex problems.

2 One after-effect of the Home Office-sponsored Community Development Project in the 1970s was that this area was better provided with advice agencies than other parts of the city.

3 This had particular pertinence at the time since an adjacent building was housing a sit-in of parents protesting at its closure as a nursery school.

Chapter 6

Greystone Women's Centre II
Moving out

CLOSURE AND CAMPAIGNING

After the Women's Information Centre was reduced to a pile of boxes in a dirty room there was a general rallying round to re-establish the Centre as quickly as possible in the Annex so that the proposed programme of activities for the autumn could take place. The people concerned were responsive to the crisis and those in the school were helpful. Ann's contemporary account read:

> We set to building the Centre up again, volunteers spent hours cleaning the rooms, putting up posters, putting down carpets etc. It took enormous effort from everyone to set the Centre up again. By September 21st the Centre had set itself up as before, the telephone had been installed and we had spent limited funds on changing our address on all the stationery and leaflets. A new publicity programme had been set in motion and leaflets had been printed. [The head of community work and the school administrator] had helped all they could to provide all that was needed. We were told that we had to remain in these rooms until our new premises on the other side of the building had been renovated. As agreed a new wall was to be built and we were told that this had been given priority, and would be the first part of the building to be completed.

So far all was well. To some extent the urgency stemmed from a feeling that the Centre had created a degree of momentum which would be lost if action to preserve it was not taken. Ann's retrospective assessment recognises this, but also notes that there would have to be some changes if the potential was to be fully realised:

The summer before [the Centre] was closed I think it was one of its most active. It was on a high then, there was lot going on. It's like a lot of the old work had started filtering through, and if it had carried on at that level I think it'd have a lot more strength, a lot more contacts. Just given more freedom and it would, I think, have gone on to lots of different things.

The minutes of the first management committee held in the new premises did, in fact, show more potential for action than action itself. Three of the groups had come to the end of their life; the single parents' group 'needs someone to coordinate it', the menopause support group 'has served its purpose', and people seeking legal advice were to be referred elsewhere, recognising that this service was available in a number of other locations in the area. Three projected groups were overtaken by events and failed to start, as did the new volunteer training course. It was agreed that a local women's group could hold their meetings in the Centre 'although some explanation would have to be made about the difficulties which could arise if the Centre's name was associated with campaigning'. In the event this group did not start meeting in the Centre until it had relocated in independent premises where the restriction on campaigning did not apply. The point that the move, in itself, did not lead to any questioning of the mix of activities or the organisational form of the Centre is illustrated by these items from the minutes and also by two other statements made at the same meeting. It had been decided to make an application for a full-time worker under a government scheme (the Community Enterprise Programme (CEP)) and the job description for this post read, 'Such a person would be responsible for single-parent groups and especially the baby-sitting service'. In other words it was assumed that the person appointed would slot into a vacant position within the Centre as it then was – there was no suggestion that she might be involved in a discussion of the scope of the job. The second statement was about the move itself: 'Nothing can be done now but it is important not to just let it happen without protest.'

As it turned out the move was only the beginning of a series of events which were far-reaching in their consequences. Two days after the Centre had reopened Ann attended a social event at the school. Here she was told by the head of community work that the Centre would have to close. An alternative use for the Annex as a centre for unemployed people was proposed by the city council, and it was part of a deal that the school would only receive the funding for this development if the Centre ceased to exist. Ann recorded:

He [the head of community work] could not say who made the decision or why. All he understood was the either/or blackmail of the situation and given that the school would drop the Centre like a hot coal in favour of the new project for the Annex and they were very sorry about it.

Events at this time and the period immediately following it were fast-moving and confused; there is variation in individual accounts and it is difficult to reconstruct an exact sequence of events. The political facts of the situation were not clear at the time although it was later suggested that one member of the city council was opposed to the WIC and was prepared to veto the refurbishment grant unless the Centre ceased operation.

The following evening an emergency meeting of such members of the management committee as could be assembled at short notice took place. The announcement of closure had come totally without warning and much of the meeting was taken up with trying to work out who was behind the move and why, and to find a way of making sense of the situation. As there was so little information available – reflecting perhaps the very limited extent to which members of the Centre had so far developed relationships with influential others outside their immediate orbit – the best tactic for the moment appeared to be to stay put and attempt to carry on as usual, if this were possible, while exploring the extent of support for the Centre among other local agencies. This proved to be an interesting and revealing exercise. The main preoccupation of the senior staff of the school was with securing the funding and ensuing prestige attached to a large-scale project; for them the Centre was a minor irritation standing in the way of this. Within the team of community workers reactions were mixed. Some saw it as a project which had grown too big and too obviously political, others described it as the only really successful and exciting piece of community work which had been done. One consequence of the closure of the Centre was to stimulate considerable debate within the community team as to the proper direction of their work. These reactions were, perhaps, predictable. More support had been anticipated from other groups and welfare agencies in the area. It turned out that this was not the case; support from this quarter was at best muted and the reaction from the

Benefits Centre was overtly hostile. The criticisms stemmed from a perception of the Centre as poorly integrated with other related areas of work and, conversely, it became apparent that many aspects of the Centre's work were relatively invisible to outsiders. In order to discuss these responses it was decided to hold the 'last', deferred meeting of the series of discussions started in the summer. These meetings had started as an offshoot of the management committee, but by this time it had become clear that the main discussants were Ann, Karen, Jo and myself. The intention was to devise a new form of organisation for the Centre which would increase the commitment and involvement of others and would also take into account the criticisms being made of its way of working and thus to anticipate a better basis for support from other agencies. Essential to this was the proposal that the Centre was redefined as a collective so that the 'management committee' would operate in future as a participative body rather than a representative one. However, this proposal was unacceptable to Ann and there appeared to be no possible compromise solution. After a long and painful meeting she decided to resign from her position in the Centre and ask the school for redeployment in another capacity.

Ann made this announcement at the next meeting of the management committee where she also reported that she was being threatened with suspension or sacking if she became involved in any form of protest over the closure. However, the rest of the participants at the meeting were not subject to the same sanctions and there was a general feeling that we had worked for long enough under the constraints of the present situation. It was agreed that the best possible outcome would be if ways and means could be found for the Centre to become independent, but two other options were also considered worth exploring – the school was reportedly trying to arrange accommodation for the Centre in a nearby church's social centre, or it might be possible to remain in the Annex and be subsumed within the Unemployment Centre.

Later the same day Karen, Jo and I met in a pub and found ourselves reaching a decision to protest at the closure and to mount a campaign in an attempt to save the Centre. As Karen remembered it:

The decision was – do we fight this as an issue with the Council, which would involve things like petitions, and do we try to go independent? And that seemed like an incredible leap, just unobtainable. And I think what we decided to do was to do it just for the hell of it.

Jo's recollection, from the perspective of a paid worker who had been spending a lot of time in meetings arguing unsuccessfully with the school, was less enthusiastic:

> I was very low, very fed up. And Karen suddenly saying, 'Well, what are we going to do? I think we ought to picket the Council House and do this and do that.' I felt got at at the time because if anyone was to do that bit – well it was being directed at me and all that stuff was so contrary to my nature. But someone had to say it, that was the other side of it, or else we would literally have died.

The next morning in the Centre I duplicated and distributed copies of a petition. We had also taken on the tasks of lobbying other community groups for their support and through this process of making contact with relevant organisations a great deal of previously unavailable information about the social standing of the Centre was collected in a short time. In fact it is truer to say that this information was available, but until the changes brought about by recent events the group of women in the Centre had not defined themselves as people for whom it was useful or necessary, and had therefore not sought to acquire it. In particular, a conversation Karen had with White (a member of another community group in the area) proved crucial. He referred to a previous application the Centre had made to the Cadbury charitable trusts:

> Last time we'd applied for Cadbury money they'd asked round other groups and the other groups had given us the thumbs down, because of the connection with the school, because of the political aspect of it, and because we weren't really part of anything else, just sort of existed. And I was asking what the chances were, and so really if you like it was White who got us the money. What he was saying was, 'If you put it in again and emphasise those changes this guy will come round and ask the other groups, and if he gets a favourable report then the chances were we would get the money'. That was really significant because at that point we wouldn't have applied to Cadbury again because we'd been refused. So we put in the application again and by that time, because of the work we'd done, the other groups said, 'Yes, we think this is a really good idea and should be supported'. And that was where the money came

from. It was that lunchtime I think – it suddenly seemed it wasn't just doing it for the hell of it.

Until that point none of us had been aware that charitable trusts made these kinds of inquiries when assessing an application for funding. The importance of developing good working relations with other agencies on the basis of a shared political perspective was only now fully appreciated.

The promise of Cadbury money arrived in December. The four months of activity which led up to that point involved a number of changes in the organisational style and the emphasis of activities from the previous period. The most immediate of these was that the campaign to protest against the closure of the Centre moved the action into a much more public arena, engaging with the council and the local press.

The first report to appear in a local newspaper included the school's point of view:

> College administration officer said, 'I have the utmost respect for the Centre. I think it is one of the best community development projects that has come out of the school.' But he confirmed that the Centre had been told to leave as it did not fit in with the 'overall conception of the Annex project as a 16 plus training centre'. He added, 'I do not think the Centre will have to close down its services. It is presently up for discussion and we are negotiating for accommodation close by.' But another worker at the Centre accused the school of disowning the type of people it was intended to help. 'We're determined to fight this', she said. While discussions are taking place the women are searching for new premises.

During the week that followed a great deal of work went into raising the petition, exploring possible support among local councillors and discovering the procedural aspects of presenting a petition to council. Karen reported her conversation with a sympathetic councillor. 'What he said was, "Well if I support it it'll be the kiss of death", and told us who to try and get on our side.'

In other aspects of the campaign, however, our behaviour was less informed and at times it was downright naive. On one occasion the group of women attending the council session where the petition was to be presented became embroiled in a fundamental discussion of tactics and arrived at the Council House too late to engage in any effective lobbying. This state of affairs arose because one woman arrived with new information from the school administrator, namely that if a demonstration took place we would be thrown out tomorrow. Could it then possibly do any good? The fact that this was something of a red herring since the petition would be presented to council whether the group turned up or not did not prevent the question being given time-consuming consideration. In part this was because of the forceful way in which the argument was presented, but it also reflected a significant change in the style of discussion between group members. Dissension and difference were taken seriously and explored for the possibility of compromise or accommodation. The fact that this internal discussion was allowed to take up time which might more usefully have been spent in the public arena did not, I think, occur to anyone until we finally arrived at the Council House to find other petitioning groups had been waving banners and handing out leaflets to members of the council as they arrived.

The presenting councillor talked about the petition for perhaps two minutes, giving a list of the Centre's activities, drawing attention to the fact that Social Services were increasingly relying on voluntary bodies and pointing out that no demands were being made on council beyond a request for premises. He 'hoped a way could be found to accommodate this service'. The matter was referred to the 'appropriate committee'. It was something of an anticlimax. Given the formal nature of the proceedings it was unlikely that any action at this time would have made any difference to the outcome. However, while this view can be only conjectural, what seems clear is that the amount of activity taking place at this time together with the 'non-aligned' location of the Centre were important in securing the funding from the Cadbury Trust. Jo recalled:

> When I think of it it all feels very accidental. How we got the money from Cadbury is because it was just at the right time. In the beginning if we'd wanted to go independent we would definitely not have got it because they wouldn't have been interested. Also if we had been a fully-fledged Women's Centre on a feminist basis they wouldn't have touched it with a barge-pole. But because we were in between, we'd been chucked out by the local authority – which had its own appeal – we were a local, community based group. OK, it was just for women, but it was a locally based thing. It was ideal, so we got it.

This account describes a position which it would seem almost impossible to engineer by design. What it does refer to by implication is the importance of the collective which formed in response to these events and which held together despite a number of setbacks and disappointments during the period the Centre was non-operational and the successful networking with other local agencies. Jo also commented, 'I think that was why Cadbury gave it to us, because we were seen to be a living organisation'.

THE FORMATION OF THE COLLECTIVE

An important part of the lobbying activity which was now taking place was a conscious attempt to broaden the base of community involvement in the Centre. While other women active in the community were aware of the existence of the Centre, for the most part their links with it had been rather tenuous. One social worker with whom I discussed this said that she had seen the Centre as 'fiercely independent' in its early days. However, it was now clear that for the Centre to continue to exist in any form it was necessary to build support for it within the locality and to reduce the distinction between 'insiders' and 'outsiders'. In other words, to increase the 'ownership' of the Centre by encouraging more women to become involved in its future development, and thus at the same time to increase its level of support by increasing the number of women for whom the question of its continuance was of some importance. To this end a meeting was organised outside the usual run of management committee meetings. It was held at Jo's home in the evening and efforts were made to get as many women to attend as possible. At this point negotiations with a vicar were moving forward, since the previous management committee meeting had considered that a move into the church's social centre was the only immediate option. The move was expected to take place within the next few weeks when the details of rooms and phone lines were worked out. The 'extraordinary' meeting considered the implications of this move in greater detail and attempted to understand what the formation of an independent and collective existence for the Centre would involve. Twelve women attended this meeting. All had had some contact with the Centre before, but for five it had been slight or recent in origin, and for one it represented a return after an absence of several months.

The application for the Community Enterprise Worker had been approved but, in the interval before this worker could be appointed, it seemed in some sense obvious that Jo, as the only paid worker, albeit a part-time one, would step into the gap created by Ann's departure and take on a coordinating role. However, she was very clear that she did not want to be involved in a simple change in personnel without a concomitant change in the way the Centre was organised. The minutes of the meeting record Jo as saying:

> She was not prepared to take on Ann's role, as she was employed as a counsellor and wished to carry on that work based at the Centre, alongside other groups and individuals who would also use the Centre as a base. Each of these individuals or groups would have a say in the management of the Centre and take some of the responsibility for, for example, the appointment and supervision of paid workers and volunteers in the Centre.

This statement clearly expresses a different approach to organising and to leadership from the one that prevailed in the first phase. None the less it is also a statement which reflects the sentiments about the desirability of a non-hierarchical format which had been expressed by some participants for a considerable time, although never enacted. In the next stage in the Centre's story, when it was effectively homeless, Jo's presence was an important factor in maintaining a fragile continuity. At the same time her adamant refusal to take up a central position was crucial to facilitating the development of the collective.

In this meeting there was heated debate about whether the move to the church's social centre was advisable, even though the previous meeting had identified it as the only viable short-term option. This, in part, involved a consideration of how the physical and social environment could affect the range of activities which could be undertaken, which in turn raised the question of what kind of organisation the Centre was, and in part arose from a feeling that this was effectively 'selling out' to the school and would mean an end to the protest campaign. In particular the fact that it was a religious organisation was talked through – to what extent would this in itself affect the definition of the Centre? Those who had had personal contact with the vicar were inclined to think that this aspect was less important than might be supposed; the vicar was described as very open to community activities and very keen to accommodate the Centre. However, there was no doubt that the setting would be constraining in some way, and that simply in terms of the amount of space available the Centre would probably be little more than an office. It was unlikely that there would be any capacity for group work and for some participants this was of crucial importance. Karen, in particular, felt that an inability to engage in group work would mean that it would not 'really be a Women's Centre'. The alternative course of action suggested was a sit-in in the current premises, although some participants felt that the cold reality of spending nights in the Annex demanded more energy and enthusiasm than actually existed. Eventually a vote was taken and it was decided by five to three (with some abstentions) to move into the church's social centre, but to view it as a strictly temporary base from which to work towards independence.

Accordingly a campaign was launched to protest at the treatment of the Centre and to fund-raise with the intention of re-establishment on an independent footing. Letters were sent to a large number of local contacts asking them to write to the council recording their protest, and the following report appeared in the local press:

WOMEN'S HELP GROUP FIGHT CLOSURE CUTS
Workers at Greystone Women's Information Centre have launched a fund-raising campaign in a bid to save it from closure. They say the Centre which is being forced to quit its offices in the Annex must be self-financing if it is to survive. At the moment it is financed by the city council and charities.

The Centre is being moved to make way for a youth unemployment scheme and the workers say that the new premises which have been found next door at the church are inadequate. One of the workers, Iris, said the Centre would have to close because there was not enough space to run all its activities.

Jo, a counsellor, said in the past two years the Centre had provided support and advice and set up self-help groups for women and their families. 'We see the church as a temporary base and we will use the time to strengthen our resources and work towards independence.' She said the Centre was hoping for grants from firms and charities to help it pay for better premises.

An open invitation was sent out to all women 'interested in the future of the Centre and the possibility of working as a collective', and the subsequent meeting was attended by about 15 women, including some who were working in other community groups. There was a good deal of support for some kind of cooperative venture and the possibility of shared premises with one or more of these groups was seriously considered. Meanwhile, the move into the church's social centre was delayed because of 'some problems with the erection of partitions' in the space the Centre was supposed to occupy. In the event these partitions were never erected and the Centre was never established in that building. It continued to maintain a presence within the Annex while alterations to this building for the new project went on, and the women who went in and out expected from day to day to find access denied to them. All the planned developments and the group activities ceased for the time being.

In other areas, however, positive progress was being made. The effect of the publicity campaign was greatly to enhance the visibility of the Centre and this was rewarded with strong support from community groups and individuals. A working collective was now established, following the open meeting, and the meetings were well attended. When I talked later with Jo about them she remarked:

> There was quite a mixture of women, some of them we've never seen again, but they were there for quite a few weeks. And I think, 'Why did they come?' Because it was important to them that there should be a Women's Centre or because they got something out of being with other women.

A further effect of this increased community support was that encouraging feedback was being received from the two charitable trusts to whom reapplication had been made, and the CEP post was currently being advertised. It appeared that the one large task remaining was to find suitable premises to rent. When this was discussed the possibility of a city centre location was considered, but it was felt that this could have the effect of changing the nature of the Centre into something more like a Citizens Advice Bureau, and that it was preferable to try to remain within the local area.

While deliberations about the future of the Centre were continuing within the council another event occurred which, although it had no direct connection with the Centre, had a major effect on what happened in the following weeks. A strike of the National Union of Public Employees (NUPE) closed the school buildings and involved us, with others, in a decision not to cross picket lines. Thus, although it was still physically possible to gain access to the Annex, nobody wanted to break the strike and so meetings of the collective were held in the church's social centre. Jo and others tried to use this building as a base to keep the Centre going, but it was almost impossible since the school's community team had also taken over this space and were overflowing from it themselves. One morning I went in and found it impossible to find anywhere to sit down – and so the Centre was more effectively closed by the strike than by any of the actions taken so far by the school or the council. On the other hand a strong collective of interested and involved women had evolved with considerable facility. This was an interesting contrast with the low level of volunteer support which had been a persistent problem in the recent past. When I discussed this phenomenon later with Karen she suggested that, 'rather than the collective creating cohesion, the cohesion was already there'. In this sense it can be argued that the way in which the Centre had been structured previously had had the effect of suppressing a collective consensus which was there, ready to be activated. Two other points are pertinent in this context: first, these events took place from a base-line of nothing – a situation where the Centre was expected to fade quietly away – so that any improvement from that position was a real gain, and second, because there were no guidelines or prescriptions for appropriate behaviour in the situation, people were able to operate in ways which were most comfortable for them – it was all useful and welcomed. Sally was an example of this. She worked in the school and had been very active in the early days before dropping out completely. She now reappeared and put in a great deal of effort searching for suitable premises. This took a long time but was eventually accomplished, after which she again faded from the scene. As well, since nothing specific was expected of anybody, individuals found they were able to take on tasks without feeling they were necessarily expected to succeed. Karen talked about how her experience of the feeling of cohesiveness provided the support for her to take things on and to take risks. She also recognised how her own commitment to the idea of the Women's Centre was an essential ingredient in the activities she engaged in; that she was able, because of this, to engage with and convince people with whom she had only minimal contact before. Throughout this period there was a feeling of excitement and improvisation. These facets of action were often referred to as 'accidental' or 'fortuitous'. For example, Jo talked about the way the Cadbury funding was obtained in these terms:

> It all felt very accidental. Karen got this piece of information and said, 'Why don't you contact so and so?' Well it was worth a try, we

did, and that was what it was like. None of the tedium of getting an application form.

In fact, it is more accurate to argue that the members of the collective were now deploying their skills as networkers and influencers effectively, since the restriction on taking action and behaving politically was nullified. Above all there was no ambiguity about what needed to be done.

The collective meetings which took place towards the end of the year showed a number of differences from the earlier management committees. They took place more often and were better attended, with up to 15 women. It was also noticeable that there was a change from women attending as representatives of other agencies to attending as interested individuals who might or might not also be involved with other community or women's groups. In other words the commitment of the individual women who participated in this period of organising had a large element of personal choice. Of necessity the prevailing theme in the discussions was also different. The former activities of the Centre – drop-in and group work and counselling – had ceased, and instead the practicalities of premises and funding were uppermost. Contacts with other individuals and groups were being explored to see how far mutually useful interactions could take place. This was particularly apparent in the number of different combinations of shared premises with other groups and agencies which were proposed and considered. What was taking place at this time was a testing out of the various forms reconstruction of the Centre might take and what meaning could be attached to different choices. Thus, for example, what could be inferred about the future nature of the Centre if it was located in association with one group or another? What implications were there in applying for charitable status? And so on. The need to explore more fully how these issues could be worked out and translated into action led to a decision to hold an all-day workshop in January.

NEW PREMISES AND A NEW WORKER

By December encouraging responses were being received from two of the charitable trusts to whom applications for funding had been made. In particular it now seemed very likely that a substantial sum of money would be provided by one of the Cadbury charities. The

Gulbenkian Foundation had also made a positive response and, in relation to this, discussions with the Social Services area office indicated that, while there was little likelihood of money from them, they were prepared to give support to the Centre's application. All this, together with the fact that the new worker's post had been approved and was currently being advertised, was sufficient indication that, in some quarters at least, the nature of the work *and* the collective style of working of those involved in the Women's Centre were recognised as appropriate and legitimate. There remained the question of suitable premises from which to develop the potential which now appeared to exist. It is probably impossible to estimate whether more time and energy went into searching for premises or into securing a financial base – both were obviously demanding activities and both were essential for the achievement of an independent existence – but at times it felt as if persuading charitable trusts to part with money was easy compared with the process of finding somewhere to set up shop. Eventually the lease of a council-owned shop immediately opposite the Annex became available and the collective decided that its size and position were close to the ideal. There were also many drawbacks, including flooded cellars, and a great deal of time and work was necessary before the Centre could be described as re-established, but there is no doubt that the identification of these premises was important in keeping enthusiasm and action going.

By this time it was known that a Cadbury Trust would provide funding over two years to cover rent and running costs and to employ a part-time coordinator. At the next meeting of the collective there was general agreement that this post should go to Iris; there was no question that there should be an interview process, rather it was now possible to acknowledge more tangibly the work that Iris was already doing. On the other hand there was a great deal of discussion about how the interviews for the other post should be conducted and what sort of woman we wanted to appoint. In this case, because of the qualifying conditions,[1] there was no internal candidate. The post was termed 'Project Coordinator' and the job description which was circulated carried with it the legacy of the Centre's antecedents in community work:

> The main work of the Project Coordinator will be to take responsibility for the coordination and organisation of new projects within the Women's Information Centre. The underlying

aim of this role will be to set up new projects or groups, and to encourage volunteers to take over the eventual running of these projects, in line with the Centre's aims of self-help. The main areas of work will involve working with single parents, unemployed women, informal adult education with local mothers and the training of volunteers. The applicant would be expected to be able to work on her own initiative as well as with other people, and to show enthusiasm towards the aims of the Centre which is in the process of reforming itself as a collective.

However, as members of the collective planned the selection process, it emerged that, rather than requiring any specific skills or interests from the candidates, emphasis would be placed on personal style and commitment to the project as a whole. One member in particular was adamant that we should not consider experience in community work sufficient qualification without also requiring some evidence of a commitment to feminism. This discussion was in effect an encapsulation and codification of the altered value system which distinguished this phase of activity from the first. The Centre of the future, in which this new worker would play a key role, was now seen as a feminist organisation with all that implied in terms of non-hierarchical organisation and the sharing of tasks and skills. Linda was appointed to this post because of her previous experience of feminist organising and her considerable interpersonal skills.

SUMMARY

In the first phase of the story at Greystone the existence of a physical location for the Centre could be taken for granted, but there was variation, and some confusion, in the definition of the task of the Centre. In the second phase, during which the Centre was without a secure physical base for several months, the task of the group assumed a simple clarity – to establish an independent Women's Centre – and to this end organising activity was at a high level. The second phase also marked a change in the criteria for membership of the group. The 'managed' mix of local and non-local women advocated in the early stages gave way to a more open policy of welcoming all interested individuals.

After Ann's departure Jo's refusal to place herself in a similar central position was important in the subsequent emergence of the collective. Jo was still being paid during this period of uncertainty and thus carried much of the work, but the fact that this work was done with the backing of a collective and in the light of collective decision-making was important to her. Both the emotional and practical support she received and the fact that the Centre, such as it was, was organised in a way which was congruent with her own values were important in enabling her to persevere through different circumstances.

The collective was formed by the simple process of inviting as many women as possible to attend a meeting to discuss the future of the Centre. At this stage the perceived need was for a broad base of interest in the community as a counter to the relatively isolationist position in the first phase. It is probable that, to some extent, the crisis facilitated the formation of the collective as a 'cause' around which to organise; on the other hand the argument put by Karen that a collectivity of interest already existed which had been effectively suppressed by the way the Centre was structured is a useful insight. By the time of Linda's appointment the importance attached to collective and non-hierarchical organising was such that evidence of her commitment to this was the prime consideration in the decision to offer her the post.

When, in the wake of the closure, agencies outside the Centre were canvassed for their support it became evident that the lack of support was more extensive than had previously been appreciated. Criticisms were directed both at the overly independent stance of the Centre and at the form of its organisation. The success in obtaining funding from the Cadbury Trust appears attributable to the extent to which these criticisms were successfully answered. In order to achieve this it was necessary for members of the group to acquire information which they had not previously sought and to exercise skills which had not previously been required.

In all the discussions of alternative futures which took place at this time the extent to which it was felt the Centre might be shaped or influenced by one association or another was an important consideration. The reluctance to accept any constraints on the work of the Centre was reflected in the amount of time and energy expended in the search for independent premises. The building which was eventually found was in a poor condition but this was seen as insufficient to detract from its other advantages.

NOTE

1 Applicants had to be registered as unemployed for six months if they were under 25, for 12 months if they were older.

Chapter 7

Greystone Women's Centre III
Moving on

A NEW BEGINNING

In spite of the progress which had been made the saga of the new premises was far from over. The shop had already been surveyed and some major building work identified, but before the repairs could start another hurdle was discovered. As the shop had been a second-hand business a request for change of use would have to be made to the council in order to use it for anything else. This appeared to be far from a formality and the available information indicated that once again councillors would have to be persuaded. A collective meeting discussed whether it was possible just to move in and hope for the best, but decided that too much attention was already directed to the Centre and that there was no option in this case but to play it straight. Accordingly Jo went to see someone in the planning department and met with an unexpected response:

> She said, 'No, don't apply for change of use, you'll not get it. You'll waste £40 on the application and you won't get it.' The collective had decided we should just go ahead and apply for change of use, we didn't realise it would be £40. So I go on this collective decision and there was this woman saying you don't stand a chance. So we applied and we got it and if we'd obeyed everyone's advice we wouldn't have got it.

In this case the risk-taking was justified, since the change of use was granted, but the incident was one example of the difficulty of maintaining the vision of the Centre in the light of conflicting messages from different external actors. Jo also talked about the strain of simply keeping going during this period, and the role the collective played in maintaining her motivation and commitment:

What I remember about the last twelve months, especially the winter months, is just keeping going. A couple of weeks going to collect my pay packet thinking, 'Perhaps I should resign, this isn't right'. I wasn't doing work because I couldn't get in [because of the NUPE strike]. There was nothing, waiting to hear about the money, premises, thinking 'This is stupid'. But there was always just enough hope, just enough maybe, to keep going. I think the other part of it was that we had reformed as a collective and when we did meet for me that felt good.

The day-long workshop held at the end of January was one of the more positive and enjoyable occasions. It was held with the intention of trying to find out how much support for the new Centre there might be, and from this to work out ways of achieving the kind of Centre women wanted. Particular emphasis was placed on discovering the range of contacts which already existed and thinking about ways in which these networks could be developed and extended. Some 30 women attended the workshop and 11 already existing user groups were identified, with another 15 possibilities. It is worth quoting at length from Jo's report on the day since it captures admirably the numerous contradictions contained within the aims and expectations expressed:

We talked about what sort of Centre we wanted and we came up with two main answers. In the first place we wanted a Centre which would feel welcoming, where women could drop in for a cup of coffee with no more complicated reason than wanting to meet and talk with other women. The emphasis was on contact, communication, a meeting place. Secondly, being realistic, many of us felt that we often need an excuse, a reason to call into a strange building peopled by unknown women, and therefore we wanted a place where things would happen in a structured and timetabled way. We came up with a long list of possibilities.

Our assumption that we wanted to be non-hierarchical involved us in a long discussion about the difference between participating in the Centre by being a user and participating by being an organiser and decision-maker. We decided this was and would continue to be a problem. Practical difficulties of baby-sitters and not overly sympathetic husbands would make it difficult for women to come to collective meetings, even if they felt motivated to do so. Alongside acknowledgement of this fact was the statement that we did not want to perpetuate the 'serving' role of women by having a system which resulted in one group of women clearing up after or taking responsibility for another group.

Children should be welcome and be made to feel welcome, as only in that way will women who are mothers feel welcome. At the same time a woman who has carved out a space in the week for herself, free of the demands of kids, should not then be expected to run a crèche. We thought there might be some difficulties in meeting both these needs.

There was some concern about how we would 'attract' women to use the Centre. It was pointed out that there was always this mythical group of women for whom the Centre exists, and they're always 'out there' and never in the Centre. As we had, at this time, 30 women in the Centre, it was true to say that if we were all in the Centre at one time it would be full. It is more realistic to start from the women who do show their interest by turning up and hoping that the life and activity these women create will, in itself, attract other women.

Should the Centre aim to offer specialist knowledge and advice or act mainly as a referral agency in advice-giving? Past experience has made us wary of setting ourselves up as 'experts' in any field. Nevertheless it is also true that some agencies which offer very good professional advice do not and cannot specialise in areas of particular relevance to women. It was felt that while the Centre should not take upon itself the role of expert in, for example, legal matters, it should nevertheless concern itself with gathering information and evidence on matters of law and the social security system directly related to women. Furthermore, now there were no ties with the local authority, the Centre should be concerned with campaigning when and where appropriate.

Our energy and enthusiasm were somewhat curtailed by the knowledge that we do not have a definite 'yes' for the premises we want to move into, but we have money for two years, one full-time and two part-time workers, plus lots of women . . .

REAPPRAISING POLICIES

The success of the workshop, in terms of the number of participants and the amount of energy it produced, gave a much needed boost to the women most closely involved with the difficulties of keeping the

Centre in existence. In particular, it was encouraging that so many busy and over-committed women felt it important enough to give their support and, through their contacts with other community groups, the implied support of greater numbers. Moreover, in spite of the contradictions identified in Jo's report, there was a broad consensus about the direction the Centre should take in the future, differences being more ones of emphasis and implementation than of fundamental values. However, the basic assumption of non-hierarchy as the preferred mode of organising was tempered by the knowledge that women would, in practice, engage with the Centre in different ways, bringing different skills, expectations and degrees of involvement. Thus the general homogeneity of opinion which was manifest at the workshop must, in part at least, be seen as a consequence of the self-selected nature of the participants. It became clear in the following weeks, when attempts were made to implement the suggestions put forward at the workshop, that it was an essentially theoretical consensus and a commitment at a distance. Many of those in this group of women were able and very willing to be involved in the Centre on an occasional basis, but typically they were already in work situations which did not allow them to spend time developing the Centre in a day-to-day sense. This point was made very clearly at the next meeting of the collective where it was found that there was no one present except the paid workers who could work regularly in the Centre.

This meeting was informed that the council had passed the application for change of use and that therefore the Centre could open as soon as the lease was signed. This was expected to take place within the next couple of weeks. The remainder of the meeting attempted to deal with matters which would affect the future running of the Centre. The question of how, exactly, volunteers could be involved with the Centre was discussed yet again. It was reported that there were a number of women who were able to devote some time to this, but who were not able to be present at evening meetings. It was therefore suggested that another meeting be held during the day specifically for them, indication of the fact that the women who would be working in the Centre were, by and large, a quite different group from those who would be attending collective meetings. Other differences were also apparent. It was decided that in future collective meetings would be held alternately at 6.30 p.m. for those who preferred to come straight from work, and at 7.30 p.m. for those who had children and preferred to come out later, and also that there should be a separation between meetings which considered policy and general principles and those that dealt with the 'nitty-gritty' of the everyday work. By no means all these suggested changes were implemented for very long but the discussion of them was important in the way that it focused on the different ways different women engaged with the Centre and attempted to institute mechanisms which would increase the possibility that women in different circumstances could contribute to it.

The process of modifying the social order, which had begun with the formation of the collective, was further influenced by the contributions of the newly appointed worker, Linda. She brought with her experience of working in a Women's Centre in another town and, consequently, some viewpoints and perspectives which she had already developed in that situation. For example, she suggested, and it was agreed, that in future women who worked in the Centre would be described as 'workers' and not as 'volunteers', removing, in name at least, the distinction between paid and unpaid workers, and, in the same vein, that the Centre should simply be known as 'Greystone Women's Centre' – dropping 'Information' from the name. Both these changes were indicative of the move away from the earlier agency model of 'staff' and 'volunteers' who dealt with 'clients' towards a format for organising in which these differences were less clear cut and which was intended to signal a reduction in differentials. These proposals were welcomed and agreed at this point, although the process of actually working out how they were best made operational and put into practice was less straightforward. Nevertheless, the fact that there was a strong consensus about trying to work in a more democratic and participative way provided an important reference point for the way in which future developments were assessed.

A consequence of Linda's interventions was to open up discussions of policy and to challenge some of the ways of working which had not been examined previously. At this particular meeting she was very concerned about the way confidential records were kept, feeling that these records meant that women who used the Centre for advice were treated as 'clients'; the practice was therefore demeaning to them and not consonant with the activities of a feminist organisation. The other point of view (and the one which had prevailed in the past) was based on a more pragmatic approach; that if a woman came to the Centre on several different occasions it was likely that she would see different workers and keeping records of these interactions would save her the distress of repeating her story from scratch each time. In this instance two equally well-intentioned principles were being invoked as a basis for action. The fact that the action outcome of one principle was contradictory to the other made resolution difficult and it was decided to defer the issue for longer discussion at another time. This discussion did not in fact take place in collective meetings. When I talked to Linda about it some time later she said:

> To me still the most important thing, if women come in looking for something and they walk through the door and say, 'Are you social workers?', to be able to say 'No', and see the relief on their faces is just really important. And I'm so glad we don't have any of this sort of documentation of case records any more; it gave me the creeps when I first arrived.
> *When did they finally get dumped?*
> About three months ago when Jo and I threw them all in black plastic sacks.
> *Did you and Jo make that decision together?*
> Yes, more or less. I was the one pushing for it, but Jo agreed.

This form of decision-making is one illustration of the difficulties which arose in the working out of the relationship between the collective and the workers, both paid and unpaid. The collective could have continued to debate matters of principle at length – those actually working in the Centre faced a constant reminder of the issues at stake.

The question of whether or not a Women's Centre was necessarily or inevitably identical with a feminist centre was one which had always been implicit in discussions and practices, but was only now debated openly. For example, Linda was very surprised that no discussion had ever taken place or policy worked out towards the occasional men who came into the Centre. Indeed the question had never arisen in that form; men had in the past come in, typically for benefits advice, and had been dealt with. As Ann saw it:

> The fact that it was called the Women's Information Centre obviously meant that it was for women. Only those men who felt they had to give support, or there were a couple of men who came in with their wives, and that was it. It didn't have to be an issue.

This is perhaps an over-simplification of the situation. While the Centre was closely associated with the school some men, such as the head of community work, assumed a right to come into the Centre whenever they felt it necessary, while others, such as the community photographer, were accepted as part of the local network and came in for 'chats'. In the new premises the concept of 'women only' was much more consciously adopted, but there were still circumstances where pragmatic compromises were necessary, such as the period when a male builders' co-op was carrying out repairs and alterations to the building.

Even when a clear policy towards non-essential men had been agreed the process of operating it at a personal level with women and men to whom the idea was new was not without difficulties. Jo described an incident where the boyfriend of a new worker was hanging about waiting for her:

Linda said, 'You take her on one side and say this is women only'. And I felt awful. She would feel embarrassed that she'd let him in here and I felt it's my fault because I didn't say to her, 'By the way it's women only here because there aren't many women only spaces and we feel it would be useful if this was just for women'. I'd literally just forgotten to say this. But I think we do have to do this, we do have to state the case, you can't just stick a notice on the door; that way we'd just get hassled.

This incident illustrates the general problem of moving from an agreed value statement to its implementation in a particular context. The substance of the concern is an example of a continuing issue which was managed in various ways at different times, but never fully resolved. Among the women who used the Centre were those for whom feminism was an accepted and important part of their lives and those for whom the ideas were new and possibly threatening or irrelevant. Moreover, while there had been a reaction away from the 'client' model which had typified the early days of the Centre, the problems which this had raised had not gone away. The differences between the 'middle-class' and the 'local' women identified by Ann in the first phase were in many ways the same as those between the feminists and non-feminists (or perhaps potential feminists). Many of the women involved, while differing in their analysis of the situation and their suggested solutions, were aware of this as a central dilemma for the Centre. Linda's view was that:

In any sized town you'd expect there to be a reasonable number of unemployed feminists, and I've increasingly come to the viewpoint that it's necessary for feminist women to be involved in the Centre. To be even talking about attracting other women – in inverted commas – I mean it's a bit of a farce really. In fact, a Women's Centre can be OK just to provide a service for feminist women, and then hopefully other things will happen. It doesn't have to be the other way round. I think the Women's Centre's fine to be a resource for the women who use it.

Jo had a rather different perspective:

I think what feminism hasn't managed to do is to carry working-class women along with it, or to speak in a language which has relevance. Or perhaps it has relevance but those women don't pick it up consciously except on very specific issues such as violence. What I see as a potentially big issue is how the new Centre actually involves all sorts of women and not just the feminists. Karen said something the other day which I hadn't thought of in those terms. She said she wanted it to be a *women's* Centre, not a feminists' Centre, which I thought was very clear. I thought, 'Yes, that's what I'm committed to'.

These two perspectives are not necessarily conflicting in the long term, that is in relation to the desired end-state, as Linda was ready to acknowledge that, 'hopefully other things will happen', 'other things' being the involvement of more local women. But there is a divergence between the two views in terms of time scales and tactics. Linda was prepared to set aside the involvement of 'other women' as a long-term goal which might be attained just as well by working primarily with feminist women as by other means, while Jo was concerned to achieve the involvement of 'all sorts of women' from the beginning, although she was uncertain as to how best to go about this. A tactic that was tried out at this time was the setting up of workers' meetings in an attempt to cut across differences by giving primacy to the group of women who spent most time in the Centre. These meetings were consciously different from the collective meetings, being held during the day and established with the intention of creating a cohesive group who would be informed about and involved in the day-to-day activities. If this could be achieved it would also have the effect of reducing some of the pressure on the paid workers. However, at this time the protracted difficulties with the premises were still paramount, preventing the development of new work and the workers' meetings ceased after a while.

PROBLEMS OF BEING 'A WORKER'

The building into which the Centre was to move had been left in a very dirty and dilapidated condition by the previous tenant. There was a good deal of enthusiasm for cleaning and redecorating but it was soon discovered that far more substantial repairs were needed and that there would be a considerable delay before the building was ready for use. The lease could not be signed until the work identified by the surveyor, including treatment of the flooded cellar and rewiring, had been carried out. This period was characterised by well-attended meetings where significant numbers of women showed their willingness to work towards making the Centre viable and, at the same time, continual difficulties and uncertainties to the extent that there was still discussion and investigation of other possible premises. Apart from the poor state of the building the greatest difficulty arose because the council, unlike the Cadbury Trust, refused to deal with the Women's Centre as 'an organisation' in that they would not accept a corporate signature to the lease, but instead were attempting to insist that two individuals signed and thereby accepted personal liability for keeping the premises 'in good repair'. The council had obviously not sought to enforce this clause with the previous tenant, but there was a feeling that the antagonism which still existed towards the Centre in some quarters would make it more likely that they would take action in the future. A solution proposed by the collective was that a much longer list of women – up to 15 – would sign the lease and thus spread the liability more widely. Eventually a compromise solution was reached whereby the council agreed to accept six signatories and another, informal, list was drawn up in the Centre of women who were prepared to share the liability if the need arose.

It was also at this stage that Linda was beginning to feel that her job was not turning out to be the one she had been appointed to do, and wanted to do. The state of crisis had been going on for so long that it had become normal in terms of everyday work and, while it was seen as important to define it as temporary in order to look forward to a more stable and rewarding future, the reality was that so much time was taken up with administration and fund-raising there was very little left for anything else. What had not been appreciated at the time Linda was appointed was the extent to which there would be a continual need to negotiate with the council and other outside bodies and no mention of this kind of activity had been included when the job description was drawn up. Arguably this omission was a reflection of the lack of attention given to networking and liaison with other groups in the first phase.

Both Jo and Linda talked about the difficulties they experienced in doing their jobs, and how they found that what they actually did differed from what they had expected and how they would have wished to spend their time. Jo said:

> I find it very difficult working here. You're pulled in lots of different directions, plus a responsibility to someone who comes in and says, 'I'd like to work here unpaid, what shall I do?' That, plus being part time. I sometimes long for just one task, one direction. It's problematic on lots of levels really. The pragmatic one of just getting what needs to be done, done. I'll get the accounts out one morning and half an hour later a woman comes in – even if I'm point-blank rude to her she will *still* talk to me about whatever she's talking about, or I might decide I want to listen to her anyway and the accounts don't get done that day. I could hand it to someone else but nobody has amassed the knowledge that I have to do those bloody accounts. Practical problems are even things like the Centre is for women to meet each other, but with some women there's just silence and they don't talk to each other and then I feel this awful responsibility to be this catalyst, this caring person.

This statement can be read as an expression of the need for a flexible social order – the requirement for sufficient predictability and stability to manage the necessary administrative tasks with, at the same time, the capacity to adapt to changing circumstances. The particular difficulty Jo found herself in was that she needed to create and maintain an appropriate social order almost entirely by herself and for herself. The necessary task and skill-sharing with others, in this case in relation to doing the accounts, had not taken place. Linda arrived at a similar viewpoint after some months of working in the Centre:

> I had hundreds of plans when I first started the job that I would get out and about different places. I suppose in a way it's the tyranny

of the telephone, and also if the Centre says it's open then I think it has to be open because otherwise women are going to come down and find it closed and not come again. I suppose what I didn't comprehend when I came to the interview was what being the only full-time worker in a place is . . ., and perhaps being on my own for long stretches of time, and if women did come in they were women I had to support rather than it being a two-way thing. I would now never take a job where I was the only full-time worker, because it does feel that a lot of responsibility falls on me. That's not to say it's not wonderful when Jo's there, but she's not there all the time and her place isn't filled by other women. That had not occurred to me.

She had discovered that although, strictly speaking, there was nothing to prevent her going out to visit other groups with the intention of creating more interest in the Centre, as with Jo the need to maintain the establishment of the Centre, through doing administrative work and simply by being there, severely restricted other activities. The other women who did come in regularly were often reluctant to be left on their own to deal with callers and to answer the phone, and were also very dependent on her or Jo for direction. Thus a situation developed where those women who were interested in and capable of discussing policy and initiating activities actually spent a very limited amount of time in the Centre, while those who were frequently there needed support from the paid workers and tended to behave in a way which assumed a hierarchical structure. In this context Linda described how the position of Iris had changed because of changed circumstances:

> Since we've lost the typewriter we've actually lost what Iris saw as her main skill, in her own terms and possibly in other people's as well. But we don't do any typing any more. She can do lots of things, but she somehow assumes that because there's this group of us who've got degrees we should be deferred to. It's really difficult to overcome – I think it's our problem to take on, not hers. But I'm not prepared to answer questions like, 'Linda, what shall I do?' I mean not for ever.

I asked Jo how she responded to women who came in willing to help but without any previous experience of working in a collective organisation:

> I find that very difficult, and I think Linda is quite good at that,

because I get so exasperated when they say, 'Tell me what to do'. I suppose partly – and this is the bit I don't like – I'm thinking if I ask them to do that will they do it right? But then it's also exasperating if I say, 'Would you like to do this?' then I have to spend time showing them and the afternoon's gone. Perhaps that's my job, but then we need more people to do it.

Both Jo and Linda wanted to work in a way which would emphasise and enhance the collective aspects of the Centre, but found that doing so was time-consuming to the extent that at some point a decision had to be made about 'getting on' with other things or continuing to pursue their support roles. They were continually torn between developmental work outside the Centre, the essential administrative tasks and working with women who might in the future be able to take on some of these tasks. The workers' meetings were one way they attempted to broaden their support base but at this time the continuing 'temporary' existence in the school's Annex made it difficult to establish this group.

WHAT IS A COLLECTIVE?

A meeting in late May tried to assess the shortcomings of the present situation and to suggest what positive steps should be taken as soon as it was possible to move into the new premises. Much of the discussion focused on what might be described as the 'atmosphere' of the Centre. In spite of the difficulties and unofficial nature of the present situation some women were still finding their way in, but concern was expressed that the image the Centre had in the community was still as a place for people with problems; in spite of the changes which had taken place not enough time had been given to communicating these to others. Linda said she felt the physical setting in itself structured the kinds of relationship which were created, that it was hard for women to come in without a specific problem and on her part hard to know whether she was striking the right balance between being welcoming and overwhelming. It was difficult to put ourselves in the position of newcomers, but everyone knew that spending much time in the present building was not particularly pleasant. The vision of the new Centre which was collectively constructed was essentially a reiteration of the discussion at the January workshop, focusing on a much more open, welcoming environment which would make it easy for women to spend time there and which would emphasise 'fun' activities as much as problem-centred ones. The other important dimension of this vision of the future was that the Centre should be *busy*, used by a wide range of individuals and groups and as a focal point for information and contacts. In this situation the role of paid workers would be different from the present one. 'The paid workers shouldn't be running the Centre, they should be there to facilitate other women to run the Centre.'

This picture was very much in contrast with the present rather reduced group of women. None of the workers was coming to collective meetings and the workers' meetings had now ceased. Two of the regular attenders at collective meetings said they had begun to ask themselves why they were there and 'making decisions' since they weren't actually doing anything in the Centre. However, both Jo and Linda said that they welcomed their support and the chance to discuss issues with women who shared their feminist assumptions. In parallel to the way they sought assistance with bookkeeping and filing, they valued a reference group which allowed them to examine the ideological questions which arose in the course of their work. Nevertheless, the basic unease that two such distinct groups existed remained a matter for concern. Jo summarised the situation:

> There is a very big difference between a Women's Centre which has grown out of a local community and a collective which has grown out of committed feminist women. What we have is a pool of some committed women who are mostly in paid employment plus other women – who are what the Women's Centre is about – who come in for a multitude of reasons, and you cannot assume a base-line ideology.

Could you or couldn't you? It would seem to depend on who you asked. The January workshop had illustrated the importance placed on participative decision-making as an ideal during this phase of the Centre's life. The desire to create a social order which would have the capacity to be responsive to the wishes and needs of participants was clearly stated, while also acknowledging that there were no clear means of resolving the dilemmas which could and did arise. Most notably the dilemma raised by the wish to operate in a non-hierarchical way and the different versions of participation inherent in the nature of the Centre, as it was then defined, remained unresolved. On the other hand the view that the Centre should aim to attract a particular group of women and exclude others, as in the past, was challenged, and instead the stress was placed on accepting whatever interest was shown and working with this to create a situation which would, in turn, prove attractive to outsiders. The different forms of participation identified at the workshop were later enacted in a range of meetings at different times and with different agendas. The aim was to increase the level of participation by making it possible for the maximum number of women to become involved in some way. However, this modification did not remove the fact of two distinct groups or the perceived need to find some way of identifying and making operational the distinction between 'policy' and 'day-to-day' decisions.

During the summer these discussions continued but the problems with the building came to an end when the lease was finally signed and it became possible to move in and begin decorating. This, at least, was something which could be enjoyably shared, but when the first meeting took place in the Albert Street building it was clear, from the point of view of the paid workers, that this sharing was not extensive enough. Both Jo and Linda said that they were finding meetings depressing and that they were just reporting back decisions which had been made anyway. As such, they found them largely a waste of time and they suggested they could be improved by restructuring along more conventional lines with a formal agenda, minutes and so on. Their request for a more bureaucratic form of interaction can be seen as an antidote to the lack of predictability in much of their work and a felt need for some structure, some routine. However, for some people, including myself, the advantage of this kind of change was not so obvious. Here the emphasis was on the affective dimension of meetings and there were expressions of how nice it was to have these meetings as a focus for seeing other people and keeping in touch – if there were any contentious issues it was assumed that they would be talked through with the collective before any decision was made. With the advantage of hindsight I now consider that many members of the collective failed to recognise just how clearly they were being told that this kind of general support was not really useful at the present time, and that 'decision-making' was not normally something which could be deferred, if required. It happened all the time and if you weren't there you weren't a part of it. As a strategy for the future it was decided once again to alternate business meetings and issue-based discussions and, in an attempt to increase the number of women who had a more intimate knowledge of the Centre's workings, to have a rotating chair who would be responsible for producing the agenda.

When I talked with Jo and Linda later they made it clear that they valued the collective and wanted it to continue, 'because it was the body *we* could come to'. On the other hand it was not sufficient for the collective to be simply a source of ideas or a means of keeping alive a vision of a better future. For it to work well for them it would also have to be a source of energy which they could bring to bear on the day-to-day work. For Jo, the commitment to creating and maintaining non-hierarchy was, in itself, a considerable drain on the available energy. From her perspective the social order was 'too flexible', to an extent that threatened to become untenable:

> With no models, it's a continual struggle to work out what a collective is ... The point about being pulled in six different directions is true. I thought at the beginning that's how we must operate and I thought perhaps collective working was partly about that, but now I think I would be more into being very specific about people's responsibilities because – well I just don't think you can run anything on that basis.

It is arguable whether this desire to introduce more bureaucratic elements into the mode of organising was only a response to the difficulty of devising models for collective working, or whether there was also a question about the degree of skill and purposiveness which now characterised organising activities. Karen pointed out how, from her perspective, the style of the collective had changed from the heady days of the campaign:

> Collective action before had been very much, 'We need to act, we need to work out plans of action, to work out how we can achieve the goals we set ourselves', and that I found fine, really energising. Then I had a lot of problems and I remember bringing them up along the lines that I felt uneasy actually being directive and suggesting things, but why I had to was a sense of – you know, meetings wouldn't start, they would drag on. There was no sense of, 'This has got to be done, we're going to do it'. As long as we were doing things collectively the question of whether we were doing them effectively using all the resources we had didn't seem to be there.

Another incident highlighted the lack of clarity surrounding the status and functions of the collective. Two women, attending for the first time, had dominated the meeting in an aggressive and overbearing manner. This led to an examination of a question which had so far been given little attention – just how open were these meetings? In the past newcomers had always been welcomed, but this had carried with it the assumption that being *interested* also implied *doing* something. And simply turning up at a meeting and expounding one's opinion was not seen as 'doing something'. There was an emerging feeling that participation in collective meetings needed to be legitimated by active involvement. This modification to the social order signalled an attempt to deal with the imbalance between those who assumed a right to enjoy the interactive 'goods' provided by the Centre and/or to put forward their views without taking on a corresponding responsibility to contribute to the maintenance and development of the Centre, and those who did do this work. The potential cost in raising what had always been very low barriers around the Centre was the exclusion of women who, in the short term at least, assumed neither rights nor responsibilities.

The Centre was now ready for an 'official' reopening and a week of events culminating in a day workshop and a long-postponed party was arranged. The workshop, which was attended by about thirty women, was intended to publicise the new Centre and to explore its future directions and activities in terms of the needs and interests of women in the community – in essence the same agenda as the first workshop six months earlier. However, this discussion was overlaid by disagreements between sub-groups within the collective about the nature of appropriate involvement and commitment. These disagreements were essentially the same ones which had been explored in collective meetings in recent months, but the added sense of occasion served to heighten and intensify feelings. As I was clearly identified with one of the sub-groups I can, at best, only do partial justice to the views of some of the other participants whose perspective was different. The group with which I was associated consisted mainly of women who had been involved with the Centre for some time and who had been active in securing the funding and had signed the lease on the property. However, recently our involvement with the Centre had reduced and only a small proportion of our working week was spent there. The other group comprised the paid workers and other women who had begun to work regularly in the Centre.

In the afternoon of the workshop the planned session which was to have been led by members of the first group was replaced by a more general discussion of 'who would do what' in the new Centre. The sense of being ousted was strong but, meeting afterwards, we felt it was necessary to try to unravel our personal reactions from a serious examination of whether it would be better for the Centre for us to withdraw. Hence much of the discussion focused on trying to understand the values being articulated by the second group. For example, the visibility and viability of different kinds of work in the Centre appeared to be of crucial importance. Interestingly, Jo, who was associated with the first group historically, had not shared the discomfort of the others – her first reaction afterwards being that, 'It had gone quite well really'. Her main contribution had been to read out a long list of administrative and clerical tasks 'which have to be done before anything else can happen', and it was this emphasis, together with the assertion that decision-making should rest with those who were most frequently there which called into question the kind of inputs which were made by the first group. On examination they realised that their inputs typically were made at times of low visibility such as Saturday mornings, or involved the kind of work which, superficially, seemed to imply the kind of client/professional relationships which had been rejected in the past.

The group also felt it necessary to consider whether their behaviour did constitute a concentration of power which should therefore rightly be rejected. The general feeling was that it was not possible to answer the question definitively. Perceptions of power concentration must depend on one's own perspective, and at this point both 'sides' could be said to be accusing the other of power-grabbing. However, in one matter at least it was felt that there could be no argument about the extent of commitment; this was the signing of the lease – and there had been no mention of it at any time during the workshop. Whilst the women concerned did not want to feel that the fact of having signed the lease conferred any additional rights to them, nevertheless the act of signing had been an important one, both symbolically and in terms of any real financial liability it might bring. It was therefore particularly upsetting to realise how little meaning it carried for some of the other women. On the other hand it was later put to me by one of the 'other' group that the failure to mention the lease at the workshop had not been wilful avoidance, rather it had been seen as a simple 'administrative detail', lacking the symbolic value accorded it by the other group. The discussion ended with a sense that each woman needed to work out her response to the events for herself but that, importantly, she did have a choice about whether to re-enter the fray or to withdraw at that point. For myself, I felt it was appropriate to withdraw. It was true that my involvement had become more marginal recently, and I decided I needed to recognise the extent to which I was prioritising other commitments and that, for the foreseeable future, I was not prepared to devote any more time to the Centre.

However, perhaps not wishing to leave the situation in such an unresolved state, I decided to attend one more collective meeting. This decision, although arbitrary, was important in that it left me with a much more optimistic view of future possibilities than I would otherwise have had. Although initially awkward, this meeting did develop into a forum where an open exchange of views was possible. The fact that the new members of the second group knew nothing about the lease was rectified, and the seemingly narrow focus on administrative and clerical work within the Centre was restated as an attempt to remove it from the 'totally invisible' area. Arguments were put forward as to whether it was more appropriate to organise the Centre around a closed or open collective, communality of experience and the safety of familiar faces being ranged against the impossibility of unequivocally defining 'work' and thus distinguishing between workers and non-workers. As the discussion proceeded it became possible to examine more calmly the issues raised by the workshop and eventually the woman who had been the strongest advocate of a closed collective remarked, 'I seem to be out-voted'. However, in conclusion, it cannot be said that one side or another 'won' but that the principle of dialogue had been reinstated and with it the possibility of a dissolution, rather than a transference, of power.

A few months later Linda's funding came to an end and Jo resigned as well, feeling that being the only paid worker was an untenable position. The Centre was kept open by a small group of women who were successful in acquiring funding to support five workers.

SUMMARY

When Linda was appointed she had already acquired experience of working within the women's movement. This meant she was able to bring to her work a more consciously feminist orientation than had prevailed in the past. One effect of this was, by the changing of the name of the Centre and the abolition of personal files, to remove the remnants of the community work model which still existed. The January workshop emphasised the value attached to participative decision-making and non-hierarchical organising, while also detailing some of the problems inherent in trying to enact these values.

As time went on the simple fact of the collective was no longer enough to justify its existence, as it had been in the second phase. It was becoming clear that the interest which had been welcomed during the second phase no longer provided a strong enough support for the work of the Centre. In part this was due to the persistence of the 'crisis' which increased the scope of the work, but even under less stressed circumstances Jo and Linda had difficulty accommodating the demands placed on them within the available time. Linda's view of the role of the paid workers and her efforts to establish workers' meetings place more emphasis on those who participated over those who were merely 'interested'. Whilst both Jo and Linda continued to acknowledge the value of the collective in terms of the general support it provided for their work, the increasing distinction between the collective and the workers' group served to reduce, both on pragmatic and ideological grounds, the legitimacy of the collective as a decision-making body. However, the view that the paid workers should act essentially as facilitators was hard to enact when the majority of the women who were able to spend time in the Centre lacked experience of collective working, and in many ways the earlier distinction between 'locals' and 'outsiders' is congruent with the later distinction between feminists and non-feminists.

The vision of the new Centre which had served as a motivating force throughout the period of transition was now losing its power. In the sense that funding and premises had been acquired the future had arrived and with it came a decreased sense of purposiveness. Moving from the turbulence of phase two to the relative stability of phase three meant that there were fewer interactions with the environment and more attention was given to internal processes within the Centre, both in terms of the appropriateness and viability of short- and long-term goals and the tactics which could effectively link the two. The need to consolidate this new position led Jo to question the viability of continually having to negotiate a path through a totally open decision-making structure, and the domination of a meeting by two 'outsiders' further reinforced this view. The November workshop effectively focused the tensions of the third phase, and was able to do so because finally a 'within Centre' group, closely approximating to the intention behind the workers' meetings, had been established.

Chapter 8

Creating non-hierarchical organisation

The story of Greystone Women's Centre should have removed any lingering doubts that characterisations of non-hierarchical organisation as 'spontaneous' or 'natural' are in any way adequate depictions of what is involved. Instead we have seen how participants are engaged in a creative struggle to build a desired future through their actions in the present. This is done through a continual process of innovation, review and modification, in the course of which some participants become skilled organisers. The remaining three chapters will draw on this, and other, case material to explore the processes of organising and leadership in relation to specific and generalised accounts of non-hierarchy, to suggest how organisation theory can accommodate and use such insights, and finally to consider some implications for practice in terms of the particular situation of Women's Centres.

NEGOTIATING ORDER

The fundamental question which was continually addressed by participants is a reflexive one: what is the Women's Centre like now and how might it be modified to resemble more closely the Women's Centre we would like it to be? Thus the initial impulse is commonly the creation of something which offers an alternative – a previously non-existent facility and a counter to previous ways of working – responsive to and created by the needs of participants. However, these moves to establish 'something else' do not provide a full definition of what this might be; the requirement for participation by all demands that this is worked out in conjunction with other participants as the following description of the genesis of the

Women's Centre at Whitefield illustrates. As at Greystone the trigger was a reaction against the then current style of community work as Jill, the community worker, related:

> Those people who were around and Jane and I sat down and worked out our feelings for that kind of thing, about what a Women's Centre would be, what it was for – it wasn't there to help women with their problems as such. Not that we wouldn't help them with their problems, but it wasn't like an alternative social services.

The picture this group painted of what the Centre was, or could be, was both clear and imprecise:

> Somewhere for women to be with other women where you had space as women. It was in terms of day schools and so on, but just saying more positively there's a way of coming together other than in separate little women's groups and separate women who aren't involved; to actually have the resources, space and everything to make the sort of things you wanted to do more effective. It was fairly vague in general, and what we felt apart from anything else was that we weren't sure what we were letting ourselves in for, and that we could only work it out gradually as we realised what sort of women were coming in, what they were looking for ... We just weren't sure – whether women who would come in would be women who were already in women's groups, involved in feminist things, academic as well! Or whether you may get lots of women who just had no contact with any sort of women's movement, who wanted more practical things to do with their lives. We really had no idea. I think it's probably gone along with a mixture of things. You're never quite sure; there are competing claims on a Women's Centre – you're never quite sure how to resolve the conflicts.

Here, there is a sense that the particularities of day-to-day activities will be continually under negotiation, depending on who is using the Centre and the needs they express, and there is an acceptance that there is unlikely to be a once and for all resolution of the task of the Centre. At the same time, underpinning these negotiations, is a sense of the importance of creating a certain kind of setting which facilitates the enactment of a preferred mode of conduct as a base-line on which to build other activities. Jill summed this up as, 'The feeling, "well, we've got something here", to feel that it was there even if it wasn't doing much. I think everyone just enjoyed having their space in the building to sit and chat to each other – that was nice in itself.'

At Greystone some of the same features were present in the first phase; the project was for women and aimed to offer a different kind of environment from other helping agencies in that more time would be available to discuss problems and those in the 'helping' role would be acting on the basis of similar life experiences. However, there were also a number of differences. At one level the value for participation by all was expressed, but it was qualified by the attempt to give primacy to the needs of local women such that the ethos of the Centre would reflect 'their social scene' rather than that of other, arguably more middle-class, women who did not live in the locality. This dimension of the social order was not seen as negotiable while it was accepted that Ann controlled the resources provided by the school. Her vision of the Centre as one run by and for local women was a major influence in the structuring of relationships, both internally and externally, and it was not until some time later that the Centre was defined as 'a resource for the women who use it', in parallel to the statements made by the women at Whitefield from the beginning. Nevertheless, given the goal of providing advice to local women in a sympathetic manner, some aspects of the social order were modified in the course of the first months. The demands of the training course were reduced to match better the capacities of those who undertook it and, in response to criticisms from other advice agencies, the technical content of advice-giving was reduced. At the same time the room was rearranged to appear more welcoming, 'less like an office', although case notes were still kept of 'clients'. In particular the distinctions between 'clients', 'volunteers' and representatives of other agencies were meaningful at this time and, although some participants expressed a desire to devise a format which could break down the implied differentials in these statuses, the most that was on offer was a process through which a woman could move from apprentice to advice-giver. Other mechanisms, most noticeably the format and style of management committee meetings, were inimical to furthering the desired goal.

This version of the Women's Centre espoused non-hierarchy and collectivism as a desired end-state, but restricted the operation of these values as a mode of conduct because of the concomitant requirement to restrict full participation to local women.

Consequently some women who held more strongly feminist values came expecting to encounter a different culture and left disappointed, but some stayed and were influential in modifying the social order. Karen and Petra were both professionals (working in mental health and the probation service) who saw the Centre offering them an opportunity to work in more innovative and feminist ways with groups of women. What they also 'saw' was a Centre which fitted their assumptions of what it was and they interacted with others in a way which was predicated on the assumption of a collective and non-hierarchical mode of conduct. Thus when the crisis with the school provided the trigger for rethinking the fundamental questions 'what task?', 'what direction?', and 'how?', Karen was right to claim that, 'rather than the collective creating cohesion, the cohesion was already there'. It was evident there were already a substantial number of women working in and around the Centre familiar with the parameters of feminist organising and prepared to work together on that basis once a revision of the Centre had been articulated and resources committed to achieving that goal. The major modification in the social order between the first and second phases at Greystone became possible when the increased dissonance between expectations and perceived reality for one group of women made it possible to see that some aspects of the present social order were in fact mutable, not fixed.

It has been part of the argument so far that, from the vast range of potential factors which may enter the arena of negotiation, only a few are dealt with at a given time. The limits to negotiation vary according to what factors are given most saliency at a given time. Among the women's organisations investigated in this research there were some interesting variations in which aspects of their social order were 'taken for granted' and which were prime consumers of energy and resources. For example, Kington Women's Centre was run by a stable core group of five women who had formed a good relationship with their local authority and were thereby given access to a series of short-term accommodation. They did not seek to recruit other women as individuals, but instead maintained a resource which was available for other women's groups to use. The core group had come to a sufficient agreement about what they were doing and how to maintain that sense of order that they now held few internal meetings. Beyond maintaining the resource and providing welfare rights advice, the energies of this group were directed towards local and national politics. They did not, however, have an open decision-making process and described themselves as 'less feminist' than other Women's Centres. By contrast, at Arlington, the value for non-hierarchy was so strongly held that an elaborate management process was devised with the intention of making it impossible for any sub-group to 'take over' the Centre, and participants there had decided it was unacceptable to employ paid workers. However, they also had secure funding to rent premises for five years. With this as the 'taken for granted' factor, requiring no input of energy or resources, a mode of conduct prevailed characterised by stormy, antagonistic meetings and refusals to compromise on principles and policies. At the time I talked to participants their view was that the Centre was in decline, having failed to nurture a core group or to manage their differences. In yet another group, this one producing a newsletter on behalf of the women's movement, the clear task provided the taken-for-granted feature around which other aspects were structured.

During the second phase at Greystone autonomy and self-determination were the primary goal, a reaction against the circumspection of the 'old regime'. The acquisition of funding and independent premises was seen as the means to this end (after other possibilities had been explored), but the search for premises also took on a strong symbolic value, representing independent action and the opportunity for less token self-management. It is probable that the symbolic value of independent premises later became attached to the lease on the building, signed by a sub-set of participants and perceived as representing the strength of their commitment to the endeavour, such that some of the acrimony at the later workshop may be attributed to the failure of others to acknowledge this commitment. The prevailing mode of conduct was modified too in this phase; dissent and difference were explored with attention and vigour (as when the dissenting voice in the meeting before the lobby of the Council House was heard out) such that those who undertook to act did so secure in the knowledge that they had the backing of a consensus. The mutual empowerment of individuals in relation to the larger group occurred because the agreed task was one which was given salience by all who chose to participate in this phase. However, once this task had been achieved those who had seen this as a sufficient goal withdrew, leaving those who remained to work out again a sense of vision of the future and the means of connecting the present with the future.

The appointment of Linda brought the reminder that if one of the projects of the group was to construct a more feminist social order, it was not yet completed. She was instrumental in expunging one of the last vestiges of the community work model – the case records – and urging other participants to adopt a more rigorous policy towards men coming into the Centre. While these innovations were accepted it was not clear whether a Women's Centre and a feminist centre were one and the same thing, or whether it was desirable that they should be. On the one hand, in terms of participants it was argued that:

Women come in for a variety of reasons and you cannot assume a baseline ideology.

Whereas, in terms of the task: what we were doing, even if you decided it wasn't feminist, *was* feminist. There was no way you could say being involved with working with women who were beaten up, homeless, who have social security difficulties – there was no way you could say dealing with those women wasn't a feminist issue – it was.

Which definition should prevail was never finally resolved and the debate continued. Perhaps on the far horizon was a desired end-state in which all women are feminists and these distinctions are meaningless, but in the interim tactics were needed to connect the present time with a reasonably attainable future. Again different definitions of what was reasonably attainable were in evidence. Either:

A Women's Centre can be OK just to provide a service for feminist women and then hopefully other things will happen.

Or:

The big issue is how the new Centre actually involves all sorts of women and not just the feminists.

The next section will explore in more detail how values are connected with actions. In terms of the present social order it appeared that what was most valued was the quality of interaction, such that when two 'outsiders', whether feminist or not, disrupted a collective meeting by using a mode of conduct which was contrary to the status quo and hence unacceptable to others, the incident triggered another modification of the social order. The protection of the prevailing mode of conduct was one issue but it was also connected with the view that some members of the original collective had outlived their usefulness, since they were now primarily consumers of the environment offered by the Centre rather than contributors to the work. The legitimate form of participation was thus reframed as being open to those who worked in the Centre rather than to all-comers.

VALUES AND ACTION

The participants in the Women's Centres are simultaneously in a position of receiving an ideology (from other examples of similar settings, from their previous experience and from movement literature) and of re-creating it through their actions. The examples provided here have illustrated the importance of shared core values for non-hierarchical forms of organising, skill- and task-sharing and participation by all; they also show that not all values are shared, but centrally it is clear that the identification of core values is insufficient to determine what action is taken (Brown, 1990b). To take one example: Ferree (in press) has conducted case studies of the women's movement in the United States and in the Federal Republic of Germany and described a number of differences. She concludes:

> differences in issues do not follow from the abstract principles of feminist ideology which are similar in both countries. Feminists in the US and in the Federal Republic both talk about the need for equality and the importance of autonomy, but when it comes to expressing these principles in concrete policies, differing points of emphasis arise from the political culture of each nation and the resulting mix of opportunities and roadblocks facing feminists in practice.

(Ferree: in press)

Thus in general terms the sense of social order which is constructed by participants with respect to this system of values is one in which all organisational acts are required to be distributed. That is, any exercise of power, any instance of leadership behaviour, should not *over time* reside with a particular individual or group. However, what cannot be argued but must be understood contextually and processually are the specific examples of value enactment. As MacIver reminds us:

> [V]alues are values only as calling for attainment or maintenance – there would be no values in a static world; conditions and means

are such only as they make for or against the attaining or maintaining of values.

(MacIver, 1964: 257)

Thus, it is not suggested that leadership acts etc. do not occur in settings seeking to implement non-hierarchy; what is necessary is that these are enacted in a manner which is perceived to be consistent with the shared core values. However, what *are* variable and negotiable are the perceptions of temporality and task specificity and hence the arena of negotiation between action and its symbolic or value referents should be understood in terms of the perceived salience of the issue and the resources participants are able or willing to bring to it. It is possible for situations which, in the view of some participants, deviate to a considerable degree from the desired end-state to persist for some time; the time period involved being that which is required for those who are not able to make influential contributions to the social order to acquire the skills which enable them to do so. For example, at Greystone when the workers' group was established (after a number of false starts) the nature of legitimate influence in collective meetings was challenged. On other occasions simpler and more immediate interventions, such as changing the timing of meetings, may be all that is required to redress a perceived imbalance in participation. The general point to be made is that, while there is always some motivation to move closer to the desired end-state, some situations may take more resources and greater skill to influence effectively. In addition, the negotiative processes through which current situations are assessed and demonstrably linked with a preferred mode of conduct and a desired end-state are dependent on participants' ability to manage the 'meaning' of particular tactics or strategies (Pettigrew, 1985) and hence make influential contributions to social order. For example, as the quotations above illustrate, debates about what a Women's Centre is and whether this is necessarily or inevitably identical with a feminist centre formed a recurrent backdrop to other activities. The balance of this debate changed over time, in part dependent on the particular mix of participants who engaged with it and in part on their ability to influence the definition in use. At Greystone the terms of the debate were expressed in decisions about who should participate and in what, such that the timing of meetings was frequently altered or alternated in order to facilitate the participation of different groups of women who appeared to be under-represented, either in terms of a definition of the 'right' balance of participants or in relation to 'full' participation. It was also recognised that different kinds of decisions were needed: those which set broad direction and policy and those which dealt with the details of day-to-day work. Since it appeared to be infeasible to create a situation where all decisions were made by the same group numerous formats for a 'dual system' were devised and sometimes enacted. That these devices were seen to be necessary did not remove the desirability of an end-state in which they would be redundant, but did postpone its attainment. At Whitefield one participant described the situation when, in her words, the Centre was 'working properly':

> It was run on a rota basis and you'd have eight or possibly ten women going in regularly on a sessional basis, and then every Monday afternoon we'd have meetings at which Ruth [the community worker] would sometimes be involved and sometimes not. And that seemed right – that the women who were running the Centre would meet once a week and discuss what was happening, where it would go, what was to be put on.

This in her view came very close to the ideal situation. Perhaps unsurprisingly this ideal state was later disturbed by the loss of some members to paid employment and other activities and those who remained were faced with finding a way to re-create it. By this stage those involved had become disillusioned with the rota system (whereby women undertook to spend a morning or afternoon in the Centre), finding it a boring and unrewarding way of spending time. They then engaged in a discussion which considered both whether there was a better way of operating a rota system *and* whether a rota system was intrinsic to the creation of the kind of Centre they wanted; could it be organised in a way which made it more rewarding for participants, or was there another tactic they could employ which was equally appropriate in relation to the desired end-state? In this case members of the group eventually decided to campaign for independent premises and funding, identifying the restrictions of operating from within a community centre as a primary obstacle to be overcome. These observations point to the particular significance of middle range goals. It appears necessary for participants to define their 'task' in terms of intermediate (and relatively achievable) goals which can be defined as appropriate steps along the road to the desired end-state, since without these intermediate constructs the gap is too large and the route too uncertain. As the example above shows these interim goals may be abandoned as unobtainable or unworkable, or they may be achieved as at Greystone where independent funding and premises were acquired, leaving the group with the need to construct another interim goal to pursue.

SUCCESS

> If we're obsessed with rating our success by the degree that local women use the Centre, then I don't think it's going to be a success for a long, long time. But I think it's a success that it's there.

How then is the success of Women's Centres to be understood? Obvious criteria of success and failure such as size or persistence have some relevance, but cannot be taken as the whole story. As Abrams and McCulloch (1976) observe in their research on communes it is necessary to ask 'persistence of what?' This study has not attempted to engage with debates which are concerned to assess the success or failure of the women's movement in an entitative sense;[1] instead the focus is at the level of the group and its social order. Here, it is suggested, two different modes of identifying success criteria are identifiable, one based on the capacity to negotiate differences between members through a process of consensus and the other based on the identification and articulation of communalities amongst members. In terms of communalities – the shared core values – we can further differentiate between success in terms of the achievement of the desired end-state and, in the shorter term, how particular strategies and tactics are linked to the desired end-state on the basis of assessments of the current position and its relation to the direction to be pursued. Shorter-term assessment criteria will then be applied to the implementation of a particular tactic. Over time different tactics may be introduced in pursuit of the same end-state; their success will be understood in terms which are specific to that strategy or tactic, as well as in relation to an end-state. For example, the importance given to this ideal impelled the short-lived attempt to set up a steering group in the first phase at Greystone, the several attempts to set up a workers' group in the third phase, and contributed to the rejection of the management committee in favour of a more collective form of organisation. At another time the employment of paid workers or the operation of a rota system may be subject to the same dual assessment.

Thus the organising activities of groups can be evaluated in terms of the relationship between the core values of the social order and (a) modes of conduct and (b) end-states. This implies that, for Women's Centres, assessments are made in terms of the extent to which participants are successful in enacting their egalitarian values. It follows that an important 'output' of their social organisation is the very nature and style of the organising activity itself. So, in assessing the success or otherwise of such organising activity attention should not simply be directed narrowly to its longevity, its ability to influence the external environment or its ability to retain members. All these, and other similar factors, must be seen in relation to the need continually to create and re-create a sense of social order in accordance with participants' shared core values. Abrams and McCulloch (1976) come to a similar conclusion when discussing the problems of success in communes. In their view it is a matter of 'creating a setting in which multiple values can be at least partially and fleetingly realised' (ibid., 1976: 155), and they argue that 'a commune is a success insofar as its members seem able to negotiate their way towards a society of equals' (ibid., 1976: 161). In these terms success is transitory – the enactment of a mode of conduct which must be continually reiterated – and is also to be understood in relation to the desired end-state. This duality of success criteria is clearly captured in the quotation above.

Success in more conventional terms – the acquisition of premises and other resources – is nevertheless, at times, very important and in their absence considerable energy is expended in pursuit of their achievement. This, however, describes the *establishment* of a Women's Centre; the existence of a defined physical location. The presence of this facility is essential if the Women's Centre is to be able to fulfil the function of a 'shopfront' of the women's movement; it is not essential for organising activity to occur, as the energetic efforts of the 'crisis collective' at Greystone demonstrate. The absence of a physical facility will usually be seen as a matter requiring attention; its presence will permit energy to be released for attention to other aspects of the social order.

Success as the enactment of a particular mode of conduct may be illustrated by considering the nature of meetings which take place in Women's Centres. Meetings are often seen, both by participants and analysts, as decision-making forums. Thus Rothschild-Whitt (1982: 27) refers to a 'process in which all members participate in the collective formulation of problems and negotiation of decisions'. That this occurs is not disputed, but we must add two further observations in order to comment on the 'sub-text' of collective meetings. It has become something of a truism to assert, as Mansbridge (1973: 355) does, that in participatory groups 'decisions take longer to make'. This can depend, it is argued, on how far the antecedents of a 'decision' are traced back and how the nature of decision-making is understood. As Brunsson (1982) has pointed out decisions are not end products and the move from decision to action is not straightforward. These observations are borne out by the field work experience. Looking at the collective content and context of decision-making *processes* makes clear the fact that decisions are often made and remade without any necessary connection with action, while taking action involves a temporary closure to negotiation. Meetings are frequently used to maintain a state of 'decision readiness' by reviewing and assessing potential solutions or tactics which may be legitimately connected to problems at some future date. They also, quite simply, as women-only spaces, operate as arenas where a mode of conduct which is not widely available may be enacted. Thus success in the shorter term – 'the fact that it's there' – refers to the creation and maintenance of an arena in which participants may express their commitment to the shared core values through the enactment of a preferred mode of conduct.

Success in the longer term – the achievement of the desired end-state – is unlikely to be attained, as the opening quotation indicates. Nevertheless, the collective construction of the desired end-state is important in strengthening motivation and providing direction – a crucial future reference point for present-time assessments.

Women's Centres are successful to the extent to which participants succeed in creating a social order which enacts their egalitarian values. In these terms instances of success are transitory and must therefore be approached contextually and processually. In practice, in these settings efforts towards successful organisation are constrained by the need to assimilate members who may lack appropriate skills or who do not share the values of the social order. More generally, the difficulties are those of innovation – of creating and maintaining a particular social order in contexts where it is rarely fully legitimated and where there are few models on which participants may build.

SKILFUL ORGANISING

It has been argued that success in this sense of maintaining and furthering the social order depends on the application of organising skills and on acts of leadership. Notwithstanding the relative fragility of the 'organisations' described here there is ample evidence that organising activity occurs. This, as has already been indicated, is activity directed towards 'solving' (although in a partial and temporary sense) the core problems of organising; working out what is going on and why, what to do about it and the translation of those understandings into action. Solving these core problems requires the deployment of a set of social skills which comprise the recognition of threats and opportunities, matching capacities with the demands of the task, the management of key dilemmas associated with the achievement and maintenance of social order, and therefore the ability to protect and pursue the values at stake. It is important to emphasise that these activities are difficult and require skill. The fact that the difficulties facing participants in Women's Centres have been explored in some detail should not lead us to suppose that things are necessarily accomplished more satisfactorily in conventional organisations. In this section the 'core processes' of skilful organising are examined. In part the discussion here is drawn from earlier work on organising skills by the author and others (Brown, 1989, 1990a, 1990b, Brown and Hosking, 1986, Hosking, 1988, Hosking and Morley, 1988).

Threats and opportunities: the importance of networking

Building relationships with others with whom one shares a degree of interdependence is important in acquiring information about the environment – about the 'messages' being transmitted to others, and about the possibility of threats or opportunities. Skilled organisers will appreciate the need to gather this information and, if necessary, to seek to adjust the messages received by others if these are unfavourable or inaccurate (Brown and Hosking, 1986, Stewart, 1976). By talking to people and moving around the environment actors are active in information search and interpretation. They are therefore better able to organise their knowledge of the environment and to recognise when interpretations and choices require revision. The clearest example of the exercise of this skill was at Greystone Women's Centre when, after the withdrawal of support by the school, the group decided to seek alternative sources of financial support. The process of networking with other community groups revealed that the picture they held of the Centre was essentially negative, and it was necessary to provide new descriptions of the nature of the Centre's activities in order to influence these other groups in their favour. This was done successfully and as a result closure was turned from a 'threat' to an 'opportunity', that is, financial independence. In this instance the importance of networking is indicated not only by the need to convey different messages to other groups, but also by the fact that the members of the Women's Centre did not, at first, appreciate that these community groups were able to influence the outcome of any grant application. In other words they had not collected the information which would enable them to construct a sufficiently detailed 'map' of their environment to identify the location of potential threats or opportunities or to take steps to ensure that the right messages were being received. At Whitefield Women's Centre, although the group was ultimately unsuccessful in acquiring the lease of the premises they wanted, they were well aware of the need to attempt to ensure that local councillors who would make the crucial decision had an accurate picture of the group's intentions, systematically providing them with briefing material and talking to as many as possible. Less effective was the management of the relationship between the school and the Centre in the first phase at Greystone where each received a negative and potentially threatening picture of each other; as Batstone et al. (1977) have observed more effective performers build relationships which are essentially collusive, designed to prevent the other from getting into difficulties. Thus skilled actors make their own task easier by making things easier for others through, for example, the exchange of (semi)-confidential information which has the function of a resource. Skilful networking thus facilitates the development of a knowledge base, providing the information which allows the choices and interpretations of others to be structured in ways which further the interests of the social order.

We know too (Steinbruner, 1974) that actors form strong categorical judgements even though the available evidence may be inadequate or ambiguous – and this should be seen as the normal state of affairs – and that people have limited capacities for information processing (Welford, 1980). Given this, the process of sense-making by which uncertainty and complexity are made manageable and comprehensible involves the creation of 'scripts'; simplifying stories which can be told or pictures of how things are which can be described. Scripts bring some part of the totality into relief at the expense of others, reducing ambiguity and facilitating communication, and are motivating in so far as they engage central values and suggest ways in which participants should mobilise their resources. In talking through an issue many scripts may be proposed but only a few will be adopted. Those that are are those that make most 'sense', in terms of the available knowledge *and* their demonstrable relation to core values. As Smircich and Morgan (1982: 262) have argued, 'effective leadership depends on the extent to which a definition of the situation [or script] serves as a basis for the action of others'. Under conditions of non-hierarchy, where focused leadership is unacceptable, it is especially necessary that the proposed script has widespread salience.

Capacities and demands

Resources are always limited. Whether we are talking about time, money, skills or information there are never enough. Given this, there is always a need to decide on the best deployment of the available resources and to seek to increase the resource base or, at worst, ensure it does not diminish. The question of maintaining the resource base, particularly in terms of numbers of active women, is a major concern for Women's Centres and is discussed further in chapter ten. The ways in which resources are linked with the demands of the task is important too; that is, the way in which 'the task' is defined so as to make the most of the capacities of participants and, conversely, the way in which capacities are effectively channelled towards 'the task'. As the inverted commas indicate there is a prior question here – what is the task of a Women's Centre? At various times in the stories of the two Women's Centres participants showed that they were uncertain what they should be doing although they were often sure what was *not* appropriate in that 'it wasn't an alternative social services'. In so far as there was a requirement to find a collective definition of the task in conjunction with other participants, at times when there were no immediate threats or opportunities to be dealt with, there was some difficulty in describing a task more specifically than the broad aims of keeping the Centre going and increasing the level of participation. For example, for a time at both Greystone and Whitefield staffing and organising the rota was a task to which resources could be directed; later when this had been tried and found inappropriate it was not clear how those women who wanted to work in the Centre should spend their time, beyond being a resource or facilitator for whatever demands might be made on them. The exploration of a range of legal statuses at Whitefield as a preliminary to seeking independence was a 'task' which appeared to be outside the competence of those who tried to do it, and was inappropriate in terms of furthering the values and interests of the Women's Centre. However, given the difficulty of collecting the kind of information which would allow them to build a bridge between where they were and where they wanted to be, it is understandable that the first step was to try out (and discard) more immediately accessible organisational forms.

This kind of activity was in marked contrast to the energetic, focused and competent activity which took place in both locations when a task had been identified which was both appropriate to the capacities of participants and had relevance in terms of furthering their values and interests, namely the pursuit of funding and premises. It should, however, be noted that this activity was predicated on an adequate level of agreement that this was the *right* task. There were a few dissenters who withdrew their participation. Others increased their level of participation, and it was this endorsement of the task which both spurred on the key actors and increased the available resource base.

Managing key dilemmas

Social organisation, as described here, involves certain 'decision-making dilemmas' (Kotter, 1982). These derive from the need to manage relationships in the absence of formal position power, to balance long- and short-term considerations, and to negotiate a relationship between the values which describe the desired end-state and present-time activities (Brown and Hosking, 1986). Taken together these considerations amount to a general dilemma for all organisations; that of how to achieve a 'sufficient' degree of order to provide a basis for action, but not 'too much' which would result in a loss of flexibility and an inability to perceive and respond to threats and opportunities. In the latter case greater attention to solidary-affective aspects of internal relationships can enhance group cohesion but at the cost of a failure to explore alternatives, seek out resources or recognise the potential of other actors to have positive or negative effects on the group. One example of attempts to handle this dilemma is provided by the collective meeting which took place in the third phase at Greystone where both Jo and Linda proposed that the format of meetings be changed to have a rotating chair who would be responsible for producing an agenda. Other participants failed to see the need for this change and showed that they valued meetings as an occasion for 'seeing other people and keeping in touch', indicating that the solidary-affective aspects of participation were of greater importance to them. However, as we have already seen, the paid workers spent a lot of their time maintaining a 'sufficient' basis for action through the administrative work they did for the Centre. The particular force of this dilemma for groups who are attempting to organise non-hierarchically is that maintaining sufficient social order without at the same time taking on bureaucratic forms is difficult. As Freeman (1975: 102) has observed social movement groups have to 'keep from degenerating into solely consummatory activities on the one hand, or rationalizing . . . into too rigid a structure on the other, and in so doing alienating . . . members'. The answer seems to lie in the introduction of a mode of conduct where every participant has both the right *and* the responsibility to contribute. Non-hierarchical organisation means standing back from taking up a pivotal role, as, for example, Jo did when the collective was formed at Greystone; it does not, however, mean standing back so far as to preclude any effective contribution to the creation and maintenance of social order. Skilled organisers recognise the importance of this mode of conduct and understand the difference between consensus and 'complacent unanimity' (Likert and Likert, 1976). They know that their value for equality does not mean a lack of engagement or that conflict should be devalued.

The dilemma of flexible social order is perhaps especially vivid in social movement organisations. Groups which adopt what may be seen as radical postures can be more tempted to take on a fortress outlook, resistant to networking activity and cut off from information about potential threats or opportunities. In these circumstances, akin to Janis and Mann's (1977) 'groupthink', the *present* social order is maintained, but at the price of failure to search out new resources and to recognise when changes are appropriate. Too little social order can prevail when it appears that everything is continually available for negotiation. Here again an inability to create enough stability in the social order prevents action being taken and over-emphasises internal group processes. Conversely, the complex decision-making processes which are central to skilful organising and to leadership are triggered when participants understand that the current situation is changing, is likely to change or is in need of change, and take action on that basis. In essence the skill lies in creating a social order in which certain kinds of change are seen to make sense (Hosking and Morley, 1988: 106). The flexibility to change is given content by the core values at stake, and contextualised by environmental factors.

Distributed leadership

These issues are relevant to all situations where organising takes place. The skills which are required to handle them are often seen as attributes of leaders but it is more accurate to conceptualise them as 'leadership acts' which must be accomplished by some means, whether by one, a few or many participants, depending on the values which inform the social order in question. As Douglas (1983: 3) has observed there is 'no such thing as a leaderless group, there are only groups with different degrees of leadership residing in the actions of one person or of several'. The values of the women's movement proscribe some ways of carrying out organising activities and advocate others. The term 'distributed leadership' has been used (Brown and Hosking, 1986) to describe the requirement that, in some settings of which women's movement groups are examples, contributions to organising are only acceptable when they are not the prerogative of one or a few participants. That is, leadership acts which are perceived as other than temporally or task specific by other participants will be unacceptable. The evidence which has been presented here should be sufficient to counter Freeman's (1984) 'myth of structurelessness' which argues that a lack of formalised (focused) leadership leads inevitably to a situation where there can be unrestricted exercise of power. On the other hand the argument has not been that non-hierarchy comprises a situation where leadership is redundant (cf. Kerr and Jermier, 1983) and instead instances have been described which show the application of organising skills and the consequences of a shortage of such skills. Thus, in the course of constructing social organisation, participants negotiate over the conditions of influence and their acceptance. This is particularly true where participants share a value for equality since, as the examples have shown, equality cannot be imposed by fiat, but must be negotiated over time. The intention is to create a social order which permits organisational tasks to be accomplished but which does not create a hierarchical system. Thus leadership acts must be accomplished in a manner which constitutes acceptable influence. This process involves managing the differences between participants with the intention of achieving, ultimately, a situation wherein all participants are able to contribute to organising activity on an equal basis. For this to be possible in the sense of a fully enacted system of distributed leadership, *all participants must become skilled organisers.*

The work of Likert and Likert (1976) has suggested the possibility of an inverse relationship between the degree of hierarchy present in a social organisation and the distribution of leadership skills. On this basis it can be suggested that the investigation of forms of task allocation and of collaboration other than super- and subordination which have been identified as underestimated within organisation theory (see, for example, Westerlund and Sjöstrand, 1979) should involve a recognition that organisation may be successfully accomplished in settings where 'consistent contributions to order are expected and valued from *all* group members' (Brown and Hosking, 1986, emphasis in original). Conceptualising leadership as a set of organising skills leads us to see that leadership may be more or less distributed within a social organisation to an extent which is sanctioned by the core values which characterise a particular sense of social order and are successfully enacted by skilful participants.

NOTE

1 See Dahlerup (1986) and Coote and Campbell (1987) for useful assessments of this question.

Chapter 9

Organisation theory and non-hierarchy

Writing in 1985 Reed argued that organisation theory has 'been unable to maintain sufficient theoretical space for the essential ambiguity of organisational life and the need to construct interpretations of it in dynamic rather than structural terms' (Reed, 1985: 117). This book is an attempt to work with an acknowledgement of the ambiguous and dynamic quality of organisational life to explore a particular form of organising. It has not been an easy task, particularly to find a language to convey the dialectic of structural processes and the forms of relationships which are central to an organising perspective. Nor, as Reed (1985: 176) points out, are research methods straightforward. What is demanded is a 'painstaking reconstruction of the conceptual frameworks through which actors make sense of their strategic and tactical interventions in particular situations'. On the other hand, while non-hierarchy as a specific form of organising has received scant attention, there is no shortage of organisational literature which proposes and develops the framework of negotiated order and situated social action adopted here. Moreover, it is evident that participants themselves can amass a wealth of practical knowledge about what is involved in creating and maintaining organisation.

The strength of an approach which stresses organising activity as its central concept, in contrast to the identification of 'an organisation', is its generalisability across all situations where organising occurs. Through exploring the activities of participants seeking to organise non-hierarchically in relatively unformalised and fluid organisational settings, it has been possible to show that the extent of and competence in organising are quite separable from the degree of establishment of a formal organisation. At one level, then, we can liberate the concept of organising from its enactment in any particular setting, but we need also to recognise, as Reed (above) does, that there is an immediate alternate requirement to discover the system of values and perceived context which give it form and content in a particular setting. The core processes of organising are general and generalisable; their form depends on the values which describe a particular social order, and their specific enactment is dependent on the evaluations made by participants of individual events.

The concept of negotiation is central to the arguments which have been presented here. However, the language of negotiation is sometimes seen to imply a process of bargaining between 'combatants', a situation where each actor seeks to achieve maximum benefit for his or her own ends while recognising that this process is likely to involve exchange and trade-offs. Negotiation as exchange and trade is also depicted through market analogies in which a finite good is distributed in relation to the effective exercise of influence and power. By and large these are win–lose games, but this version of negotiation does not capture the full sense of what is entailed. In the earliest expositions of negotiated order theory (Strauss *et al.*, 1963) negotiative processes were also conceived in bargaining terms. For example, in describing the way they see non-professionals creating their working conditions in a hospital, they state:

> They must stake claims and counterdemands; they must engage in games of give and take. *Among the prizes* are: where one will work, the colleagues with whom one will share tasks, and the kinds of patients with whom one will deal.
>
> (Strauss *et al.*, 1963: 154, emphasis added)

In this version of the world there are only a limited number of 'prizes' and there must therefore be winners and losers; the winners are those who succeed in pressing their claims and denying those of others. While this version of what negotiation entails persists in some perspectives today (see, for example, Bartölke, 1988) in the intervening years negotiated order theory has moved on from the specific and grounded inductions of Strauss and his colleagues to a quasi-general theory of situated social action in which negotiation is the crucial central process through which meaning is iteratively and reflexively created. This development has entailed a parallel modification to the way in which negotiation is understood, although the fact that this modification is rarely explicitly identified is a potential source of confusion. We can go some way towards making good this deficit by tracing the development of negotiated order theory and adding some further observations.

A starting point is Mead's (1936) fundamental 'Problem of Society': how is it possible for change to occur while still preserving social order? The response of Strauss and others, as we have noted, is that order should be seen as a series of temporary agreements which are periodically reviewed and revised. While this feature is not underlined in their argument, it is also clear from their case material that participants are active in these processes; they initiate actions and interactions, make choices about how to deploy resources or acquire new ones, and may be more or less skilful in negotiation. In terms of the framework used here they are organising, rather than experiencing, the condition of 'being organised'. As Strauss et al. see it freedom of movement for participants in the hospital setting derives from the limitations of rule-defined behaviour – both in the sense that rules are inadequate to cover all eventualities and that rules are not always enforceable. Order is improvised, but within limits. These limitations are observable in the way in which the hospital appears to be 'more or less' the same organisation from day to day and week to week. More the same because some agreements deal with the relatively routine and therefore become more strongly patterned, especially when viewed over time, and less the same when the micro patterns of interaction which adjust in response to any event that impinges on them are brought into focus.

During the 1970s a dialogue with critics of negotiated order theory led to a number of developments and refinements. Criticisms came particularly from structural theorists and Marxists who argued that insufficient attention was given to large-scale institutional arrangements and historical contexts. In the words of one critic, 'the *important* things are always non-negotiable' (Strauss, 1978: 248, emphasis in original). With the benefit of hindsight it is now easier to see that the basis of this criticism rested in part on the presentation of negotiation as an activity performed by individual negotiators, thus apparently confining the scope of the theory to what takes place in day-to-day (and probably face-to-face) encounters. Viewed in this light there is an immediate parallel with our earlier criticisms of theories of leadership which derive from the identification of 'leaders' and how these people behave in small-scale interactions;

these approaches are incomplete without a parallel examination of the terms on which influence is accepted and an extension of the scope of negotiation to encompass interactions with other social orders, at 'the boundary' and in the macro domain.

Restating Mead's question about the relationship between order and change, Strauss sees the problem as one of finding some mediating position between unrelieved structural determinism and unconstrained individual autonomy, but this apparent dichotomy arises from the use of a point-in-time perspective. While there is no social order without negotiation, at any given time the scope of negotiation is restricted. Thus in seeking to explore the limits of negotiation it is important to insist on the adoption of a longitudinal perspective; in the long term it is possible that everything may become negotiable, in the short term it definitely isn't – as a consequence of actors' limitations as information processors and the need to make some assumptions of predictability in a persisting social order. In this, 'structure' arises as those aspects of the social order which appear (over time but not eternally) as taken for granted factors, acting as 'dominant stabilities' (Brown, 1986) and outside the arena of negotiation. But there is another side to the coin whereby the observation of 'structure' becomes the label attached to larger-scale and/or longer-term processes. This version is stated by Gerson:

> My approach rests on the assumption that both social order and individuals arise in and through a process of negotiation about who shall be whom and what order shall pertain. These negotiations may take place on relatively small scales or on large scales (through the activities of many people over a large area over a long period of time). In fact, we have a general situation in which small scale negotiations are continually taking place in very large numbers *within* the context of larger scale arrangements which are changing more slowly and less visibly to participants.
>
> (Gerson, 1976: 796, emphasis in original)

Writing this a year after the Berlin Wall came down it is difficult to accept a version of societal change which appears to claim that actors cannot actively contribute to large-scale events, or that if they do so the processes are seemingly opaque, except to analysts. A challenge for organisation theory is to find a way of integrating these apparently distinct perspectives of observer and actor. For example, Strauss

(1978: 254) sees the limits to negotiation in terms of larger-scale 'structural' properties of organisations and societies, reflecting the then dominant entitative view of organisation, but these are more accurately viewed as contextual factors, amenable to negotiation but dependent on their perceived saliency to participants, the assessment of the level of resources required to effect change, and the outcomes of choices made about net gains or losses for the social order. What has not yet been explored systematically are the limitations of the capacities of actors for dealing with the ambiguities and uncertainties which are intrinsic to organising. We know that skilled organisers are better able to work with situations demanding complex decision-making, where the effects of a given policy are likely to be mixed, some beneficial, some not (Hosking and Morley, 1988, Steinbruner, 1974), and that whatever is done will in some sense be 'wrong', and that such people carry out wider scans of the environment and have better 'maps' than others, including different accounts of the same events. And at least one major company requires its managers to become competent at 'helicoptering' – standing back from the immediate situation to take a wider perspective. These skills all indicate the need to be able to work with the simultaneity of multiple perspectives and realities. Those who hold them are able to operate as both observer and participant,[1] and to recognise that it is necessary to do so.

Some of the further criticisms of negotiated order theory are misreadings, but they are common ones. For example, Day and Day (1977: 131) consider that emphasising negotiative processes suggests that interactions are usually cooperative, create little disturbance and do not engage with power imbalances. Strauss' (1978: 250) response is simply to point to evidence of conflict in his case material, but we can push this point further. The creation of shared meaning and joint action through negotiation does not imply that the processes involved must be either coercive (i.e. the uncontentious enactment of pre-existing power differentials) or 'cooperative', in the sense above, accomplished without invoking disagreement or dissent. Through exploring the kinds of interaction processes which take place in groups seeking to organise non-hierarchically it has been possible to highlight the desirability of a mode of conduct in which consensus is the outcome of a process in which differences are expressed and views may change. That is to say, the choice is not only between the imposition of definitions or bland uncontentious agreement (which may amount to the same thing); negotiation at its most effective relies on the active participation of those who have a stake in the event and its outcomes.

Ten years after Strauss was writing (for example, Altheide, 1988) negotiation is clearly conceived of as a constructive and interactive process, but crucially it is additive, the mutual creation of relationships which add value – at any level of action, whether the dyad, the group or in the inter-group domain. Negotiation in this sense describes a win–win interaction; some new good which was not available before is created through the formation of relationships. Individuals and groups negotiate over both the form and content of their interactions. We can see from the case material that this operates both in terms of affect and task. At one level Women's Centres act simply as locations where a form of social discourse which is not widely available may be created and enjoyed. At another level the relationships thus created need to have content as well as form, and we can observe the more easily identifiable process of inter-locking means to carry out tasks which are beyond the capacities of individuals acting alone. In general the processes through which the goods of interaction are created may be more or less symmetrical, depending variously on the skills, resources, influence or power which different actors are able to bring to the situation. However, as we have seen, one component in these negotiative processes is the establishment of the legitimacy of whatever resource base is deployed. Central to feminist organising practice is a requirement for relative symmetry in joint actions. This means that, whatever the resource base, its utilisation will be mediated by the coterminous requirement to approach symmetry through a process of enablement or, to use a term which is currently out of vogue, empowerment. In chapter one we saw the lengths to which women organising are prepared to go in order to attempt to create parity of skills and knowledge within groups. These accounts of women organising showed how they understood the fact of differentials in knowledge, commitment and skills between participants and attempted to find ways of reducing or eliminating them, with the aim of creating within-group processes which are symmetrically distributed and approach a condition of non-hierarchy. The notion of structural process then is more than just a gloss; it should convey the sense that certain kinds of processes create certain kinds of structures *and vice versa*.

In other settings differentials exist between participants and are played out in the recognition or imposition of one definition of the situation over another. The process of creating the recognition of one definition over another can be regarded as acts of power, but we need to clarify the distinction between the situations of 'power over' and 'power to' since they differ in their implications for structural processes. In both cases the idea of legitimacy is present, but in attempts to create non-hierarchical organisation 'power over' is not afforded the legitimacy it has in hierarchical contexts. It is therefore not sufficient to attribute power to differentials in, for example, knowledge, status or access to decision-making arenas. The primary source of legitimacy under non-hierarchy is the capacity to demonstrate that meanings and definitions are consonant with the social order in question and have salience for all participants. The idea of 'power to' introduces a different dynamic into group processes; the question is less one of a free market exchange where each individual struggles to create legitimacy for his or her own resource bases, but rather one of the collective empowerment of each participant, based on understanding of and investment in the social order. Neumann (1989: 184) captures this sense of linkage between individuals, groups and wider contexts by defining participation as structural processes 'for organizing individual autonomy in the context of group responsibility and linked to system-wide influence'.

Arguably, there is more at stake here than the ideological altruism which can, perhaps, be read in the efforts of women organising. Numerous researchers and commentators who demonstrate no particular commitment to a political position have observed and described their perception of the *efficiency* of relatively symmetrical relationships. In particular Bennis and Shepard (1965) have catalogued the characteristics of the 'mature group' which also describe the self-identified characteristics of group processes within women's movement groups (Brown, 1989: 236). Similarly we have noted Lickert's (1961) 'principle of supportive relationships' in which the inefficiencies of hierarchical relationships in terms of the goal of creating maximum mutual value from interactions are addressed. Both these and other similar observations are made on the basis of what takes place within small groups. However, one of the arguments here has been that for successful organising these processes must also take place at more macro levels – between groups and in larger contexts. Gray's (1985) work, in what she terms the inter-organisational domain, is therefore interesting. Her point of departure is to identify the conditions which facilitate inter-organisational collaboration. The starting conditions are: (i) issues which are beyond the capacities of one organisation acting alone; (ii) acknowledgement of the limitations of traditional adversarial methods of resolving differences; and (iii) recognition that the activities of one actor create consequences, sometimes unanticipated, for themselves and others. Collaboration is then the pooling of understandings and/or more tangible resources by two or more stakeholders to create solutions to problems which cannot be solved on an individual basis. In other words there is a situation of interdependence to which, as Emery and Trist (1965) have argued, collaboration is the only viable response. In line with our arguments about the importance of networking for skilful organisers, by pooling perceptions among stakeholders greater appreciation of the context is achieved, and a negotiated order is created (Gray, 1985: 916). Gray continues by outlining a three-stage process model of collaboration: problem-setting, direction-setting and structuring. We can equate this model with the model of organising presented here: figuring out what is going on and why, what to do about it, and translating those understandings into action. In the first stage of interaction the focus is on the identification of the issue which joins actors. This includes reaching a consensus about who has a *legitimate* stake in the issue and what precisely the issue is. It will be remembered that a consensus process is one in which differences are expressed and examined for the possibility of accommodation, and thus at this stage in the process the terms of legitimate involvement are negotiated and the relevant interdependencies identified. The second stage, figuring out what to do, involves the articulation of value-referenced goals as each actor expresses his or her desired end-state within a format which facilitates the emergence of a common purpose for the collaboration. Finally, action outcomes are created as interlocked means are structured in a way which systematises the processes of exchange and negotiation, thus developing a social order which has value for all actors.

   This general process of organising through the structuring of joint action is one which can be done more or less skilfully. On the basis of her own case material Gray identifies a number of conditions under which collaboration (or joint action) is likely to be more effective. Although she does not make the connection these conditions parallel those for effective group behaviour. Effectiveness in this sense may be defined as achieving the maximum benefit from the pooling of understandings and resources for the maximum benefit of the shared social order – what it is argued leaders or skilful organisers do. First collaboration is enhanced when participants have the skills to appreciate the position and values of others and can act as networkers. Second differences in power can prevent the construction of a shared social order through inhibiting both weaker and stronger participants' contribution to the process of consensus formulation. Conversely a 'sufficient' distribution of power ensures that all participants influence joint processes and create synergies. Finally, however large the domain considered, it is always necessary for the actors within it to be aware of and manage relationships with their contextual environment. At all levels of action there is a need to build relationships with actors outside the immediate domain in order to ensure the maintenance and furtherance of the social order in question.

The efficiency arguments for 'flatter', more participative organisational forms appear to be strong. But are these forms achievable? At the start the mythical quality of collective and non-hierarchical organisation was noted. To a considerable degree the concept retains this quality because, at the level of practice, it is frequently observed that groups which start out with the intention of operating collectively and non-hierarchically are more or less inevitably 'forced' to become more bureaucratic with the passage of time (for example, Newman, 1980) as the survival of the group appears to depend on an increased level of interaction with bureaucratic institutions in their environment. What we may term the 'contamination thesis' argues that a combination of the need to attract external funding and support, the lack of acceptance of an innovative organisational form, and the corresponding need to create a phony façade to appear acceptable to potential funders leads, almost inevitably, to increased internal differentiation and hence hierarchy. Similar external factors were in evidence in Greystone's negotiations with the local council over the lease of the shop, and at Whitefield where workers in the Women's Centre were required to write reports for the management committee of the community centre where they were located. As one worker said:

> Even if the management committee doesn't comment at all on what's gone on there [in the Women's Centre], there's still the threat, that it's basically accountable, you're supposed to write

reports to go to the management committee. You can write what the hell you like in them, but you're supposed to write something. And they could turn round and say, 'Well we know that's not what's been going on. What has been going on?'

Newman's solution to the problems of the groups she investigated is to counsel against forming relationships with bureaucratic institutions in order to avoid contamination. However, since this course of action does not allow access to new resources or to the understandings of others, contrary to the requirements of skilful organising, it would seem also to lead to the extinction of the original group by other means. Her case material suggests that there may be other reasons for the fact that these groups fail to maintain their collective social order; processes within the groups were such that a mode of conduct was introduced which made it unacceptable to voice problems and difficulties and differences were not articulated. By contrast participants in the Women's Centres did not restrict their interactions in this way and instead dissension and differences were expressed and explored. The facilitation of the introduction and maintenance of a value for a mode of conduct, in which every participant has both the right and responsibility to contribute regardless of whether they disagree with other participants, plays a role in securing high-quality decisions and the commitment of those who participated (Brown and Hosking, 1986: 73–4). This process is also central to achieving a consensus which has salience for all participants. In addition, by moving round their environment they were able to identify influential others who could provide support for their social order as well as those who opposed it. At both Whitefield and Greystone Women's Centres participants lobbied their local councillors at one time or another and were able to ascertain who was prepared to offer support and on what terms. Citing a similar example of the 'bureaucratisation' of a community group Altheide (1988) suggests that the change in social order is best understood as the enactment of a different environment. This alternative conceptualisation has the advantage of removing the determinism implied by Newman's account, by retaining the sense that participants make active choices about who to form relationships with, in the knowledge that these choices will have implications for their future actions and goals. But what we need to be able to ask (and the data provided in both these examples does not supply all the answers) is what kind of change made sense for these groups, which values and goals were prioritised, and did participants have sufficient organising skills to create and maintain an appropriately flexible social order? The conditions for successful non-hierarchical organisation which have emerged from this study point to the need for all participants to be, or become, skilled organisers, thus creating a condition of distributed leadership, that leadership involves competence in building interpersonal and inter-group relationships which comprise a flexible social order, and that these relationships should lead to structural processes which create consistency between actors, processes and contexts.

Given the evidence we have so far it appears that goal-directed motivation *may* be instrumental or value-based, but it is less certain that values promoting the necessary mode of conduct are found in many settings outside feminist or other radical groups. It is likely that the oft-documented difficulties of social movement or community groups occur because they perceive that (i) their beliefs, norms and values differ from those of other groups, (ii) they face 'threats' from other groups, and (iii) they have more radical values and/or more radical decisions to make (Hartley *et al.*, 1983, Janis and Mann, 1977, Tajfel, 1981), and that these factors will place especially heavy demands on the skills of participants (Brown and Hosking, 1986: 73). We should not suppose that these perceptions are wrong; Emery and Trist (in 1965) and Morgan (in 1986) both saw the widespread adoption of more cooperative values in organisational life as a project for the future.

The role of values is therefore important in considering whether bureaucratisation of non-hierarchical groups is either inevitable or a necessary and reasonable choice for survival. At Greystone Jo described how the varying and unpredictable demands of her job led her to see the attraction of a greater degree of bureaucratisation. This change did not, however, take place. While there are a number of reasons for this, including the unavailability of other women who were prepared to take on the same range of tasks, the fact that more bureaucratic structures and processes were not sanctioned by the core values was an important countervailing tendency. Within social movement theory the assumptions of the classical approach to organisational transformation (usually referred to as the Weber-Michels model, and reiterated by Newman, 1980) have now long been challenged. In place of the general prediction that social movement organisations will become more conservative, displacing their original goals in favour of maintenance activities, more complex and contingent transformation processes are proposed (see, for example, Zald and Ash, 1966). In particular the advent of the modern women's movement has led Katz (1981: 142) to recognise that his earlier (Katz, 1957) 'natural history' of organisational transformation requires revision, and specifically that women's movement groups appear to 'eschew the stages of leadership emergence and formal organisation'. Elsewhere (Brown, 1989) I have argued that the key to understanding the resilience of non-hierarchical forms in women's movement organisations is to appreciate how central this value is to the definition of the movement.

Rothschild-Whitt's (1982) conceptualisation of substantive (or value) rationality remains one of the few systematic examinations of the differences between this and formal rationality (the essence of the bureaucratic organisation). These two ideal-typifications are presented as polar extremes, designed to encourage the exploration of the 'limits of organisational reality [which] appear to be far wider than students of organisations have generally imagined' (ibid., 1982: 46). Thus, in her analysis, the polar opposite of formal bureaucracy is a fully collectivised democracy. On a number of dimensions this ideal-typification is similar to the generalised form of non-hierarchy within women's movement organisations. Thus:

- Authority [is] resident in the collective as a whole; delegated, if at all, only temporarily and subject to recall.
- Ideal of community; relations are to be holistic, of value in themselves.
- No hierarchy of position.
- Egalitarian; reward differentials, if any, limited by the collectivity.
- Minimal division of labour. Generalization of jobs and functions. Demystification of expertise.

By contrast in the formal bureaucracy:

- Authority resides in individuals by virtue of incumbency in office and/or expertise; hierarchical organization of offices.
- Ideal of impersonality; relations are to be role-based, segmented and instrumental.
- Differential rewards by office; hierarchy justifies inequality.
- Maximal division of labour.

(Rothschild-Whitt, 1982: 37)

However, in spite of the usefulness of these ideal-typifications in clarifying some of the differences between formal and substantive rationality, it is important to be aware that Rothschild-Whitt's description of the collectivist organisation is firmly rooted in employing organisations such as cooperatives which, in the terminology which has been adopted here, are 'closed' rather than 'open'. Moreover, these organisations are engaged in some kind of economic activity with far greater frequency than the women's movement organisations. It follows that, if the limits of organisational reality are to be fully explored, then account must be taken of forms of organisation whose rationale is not primarily, or even secondarily, economic, but is essentially substantive or value based. This category could well include other types of voluntary organisations as well as those born of the women's movement. From this perspective, exploring the limits of organisational realities then involves removing the idea of a fixed boundary and a known cohort of players, and distributing organisational actions according to principles which are other than those described by formal bureaucracy.

The construction of ideal types requires the same process of abstracting 'essences' from multiple and complex instances of 'real life' as does the identification of the core values of organising in the women's movement. That is to say, while these abstractions act as reference points both for analysts and practitioners, they cannot describe the processes by which groups and individuals struggle to move closer to idealised situations. In practice we do not expect to find examples of complete, uncontaminated bureaucratic systems. Similar observations hold true for non-hierarchical approaches to organisation, but in these terms some of the attributes which define conventional organisations are absent, making 'the organisation' less easily identifiable. Although it is hard to avoid using the term 'organisation' as a convenient shorthand, this use obscures a more accurate depiction of what takes place. If we consider that Women's Centres only 'exist' when they are reliably established in a physical location then we dismiss the essential organising activity which produces the necessary conditions for 'its' existence, the context in which 'it' operates and the continuation of 'its' processes and functions after 'its' apparent demise. It follows that what we are dealing with is not a universally identifiable entity, existing independently of participants' actions, and with a momentum of its own, but rather a dynamic, variable and fragile cluster of activities and relationships, in and through which social order, organisation and leadership are emergent (Hall, 1987, Hosking and Morley, 1988). In so far as women's movement organisations fall towards the far end of Rothschild-Whitt's continuum, an understanding of their characteristic organising processes provides evidence for interrogating and modifying prevailing forms of organisational analysis.

NOTE

1   There is an exact parallel in the roles of researcher and participant discussed in chapter four.

Chapter 10

Implications for feminist organising practice

It has been the intention of this study to interrelate the theory and practice of non-hierarchical organisation. The starting point was the widespread efforts of women organising to create forms of joint action which respect and value equality between participants, and it seems appropriate to conclude by drawing on the case material to offer some observations which may be useful in understanding and enhancing the practice of organisations, such as Women's Centres, where the condition of open or fluid participation may create an additional dynamic to be managed. While it is now possible to refer to a substantial critique of bureaucratic practice from a feminist perspective (for example, Acker, 1990, Ferguson, 1984, Martin, 1990, Rothschild, 1990), relatively little work has undertaken an detailed examination of just *how* women attempting to organise non-hierarchically deal with the problems which commonly confront them.

As types of organisations Women's Centres appear to exhibit a number of characteristics which differentiate them from more conventional forms:

- Given that participation is only available to women, boundary maintenance is low and openness is striven for.
- Leaders who are other than temporally or task specific are not acceptable and participants will react to any perceived entrenchment of leadership roles.
- Similarly, hierarchical structures are unacceptable.
- The production of goods and services occupies a minor role; the primary output from the activity is a particular kind of social setting which is not widely available.
- Participation is part time and voluntary, subject to periods of greater or lesser activity.

The central problem for organisers in Women's Centres, and elsewhere within the autonomous women's movement, is that of creating and maintaining an innovative and unorthodox form of social organisation in contexts where it is rarely fully acceptable and where there are few models from which participants may learn. It must be clear by now that attempts to implement this particular form of social organisation – to establish and maintain a Women's Centre – present participants with a number of difficult and sometimes apparently intractable problems to solve. The case material described the actions and reactions of some participants to their attempts to implement the core values of participation by all, sharing of tasks and skills and the rejection of hierarchical forms, but in so doing they also illustrate how a continual process of negotiation is intrinsic to the way in which priorities are set, choices made and actions taken.

In general the following points summarise the arenas of negotiation which are involved in creating non-hierarchical organisation within the women's movement:

(i) The identification of a shared set of core values which informs organising activity within the women's movement does not presuppose that the enactment of these values is unproblematic or uncontentious.

(ii) It cannot be assumed that participants share all values and the potential for conflict on the basis of difference is maintained.

(iii) The extent to which values are shared does not affect the probability that inequalities of power and influence may persist in spite of efforts to reduce them.

(iv) All actions, strategies and tactics may be subject to assessments of legitimacy in terms of their perceived congruence with the core values.

(v) The context of these processes may vary over time, such that some aspects of the social order do not enter the arena of negotiation in a given period of time and acquire a taken-for-granted character.

The remainder of this chapter discusses these issues as a number of overlapping themes.

PARTICIPATION

It is part of the basic ideology of Women's Centres that they offer open access to all women. This is true in the sense that any woman coming to a Centre will receive attention, and is likely to be offered some kind of invitation to become involved in activities. However, two problems arise when the formulation 'participation by all' is applied to Women's Centres; first, participation is more than simple access – it depends on being able and choosing to make influential contributions to social order – and second, that different definitions of 'all' pertain at different times and in different circumstances. At Greystone in particular the requirement that participation be open to all-comers and that participating women should be broadly representative of the locality was an added factor in the construction of non-hierarchy which produced its own problematic.

For illustration we may look at the kinds of problems which often follow in the wake of attempts to handle the 'openness imperative'. One statement in the case material made about the ideal situation described it as one in which those working in the Centre were also running it, but women come to Women's Centres for a variety of reasons. With some simplification these may be typified as those who come primarily for problem-solving, seeing a Centre as one advice agency among others, and those who already value the idea of women-only space and wish to contribute to it in some way (or possibly simply to be consumers). For many of the first group the notion that they might also become part of running the Centre may be a novelty to which they need introduction. As Ann remarked: 'I spent a lot of time encouraging local mums – talking them into coming to the Centre and doing their morning stint and supporting them through that.'

For the second group the idea of a participative and collective form of organisation can be a basic assumption. The dilemma these two groups present may be compounded when one is perceived to have a greater 'right' to participate. In the first phase at Greystone the management committee consisted of a 'representative' number of voluntary workers and a number of women from outside bodies. Here the infrequency of meetings and their unfamiliar style for some members did little to further the aim of building a strong group of volunteers. (The secondary aim, of building useful relationships with these outside bodies, was also only met to a limited extent.) On the other hand the selection process left some who were active in the Centre without a means of contributing to its management. Later when an open participative version of a collective was accepted as desirable, the dilemma between women as users and women as organisers remained and was compounded by the existence of a group of women who were prepared to give their support to the ideas and policy-making aspects of the Centre by attending meetings but who were unwilling or unable to spend time working in the Centre. More generally women vary in the extent to which they are 'mobilisable' around a particular issue or inclined to participate in a particular setting. The high attendances which occurred on workshop days or at 'important' meetings could not realistically be expected to carry over into more routine aspects of Centre organisation without some overall change in an individual's pattern of commitment (cf. Gerson, 1976). Given the likely difficulty of affecting more than a few individuals in this way, and hence of bringing about the participation of all who could, or should, be involved, some other means of dealing with this shortcoming must be sought.

The representativeness of participation in relation to the demographic mix of the area can also be an issue. At Greystone, after the initial spate of enthusiasm had run its course, there was always a sense that the number of women involved with the Centre was smaller than was desirable and specifically that it did not represent the composition of women in the locality, working-class and Asian women in particular being under-represented. Neither of these characteristics was quantified, and it is their experience which mattered since this provided the basis on which action was taken. Acknowledgement of a consistent failure to involve working-class and Asian women did not necessarily change the ultimate aim – as one worker put it, 'to be all things to all women' – but it did suggest a change in tactics. This was expressed in another worker's view, that 'A Women's Centre can be OK just to provide a service for feminist women, and then hopefully the rest will follow'. Later the near total distinction between 'the collective' and 'the workers' after the second open meeting led to a reassessment of the nature of participation. Moral and ideological support was welcomed by the paid workers but it was no longer seen to be a sufficient basis for full participation. Nevertheless, in spite of variations in the basis on which the 'right' to participate was negotiated (class, interest, action or whatever) at different times, there was also a requirement for endorsement, if not participation, by as many women as possible. The importance of sheer numbers, as was evident from the frequent use of the strategy of altering the timing of meetings to enable as many women to attend as possible, meant that those who experienced their routine working situation as isolated and unacknowledged could draw on the support and energy of others. While large open meetings did not, in the longer term, greatly increase levels of participation, one of their main functions appeared to be to give a boost to the morale of the smaller groups and to endorse their activities and proposals. It appears that the confidence Centre workers have in the legitimacy of their endeavour depends, ultimately, on endorsement from a larger and sometimes quite hypothetical constituency of women.

Thus in ideal terms Women's Centres operate in such a way that participants are also organisers, and the women who are involved with a Centre are representative of the community in which it is located. In practice women participate in different ways and vary in the extent to which they are 'mobilisable' around any given issue, event or task. In all cases where there is an intention to combine some of the attributes of a cohesive group, together with an emphasis on accessibility and responsiveness to a wider constituency of women, competing pulls on the organisational style will have to be managed. In the light of this two possible organisational outcomes are observable:

(i)   defining the nature of legitimate participation so as to exclude some categories of women and/or delegitimate some forms of involvement, and
(ii) initiatives aimed at increasing participation levels, both in general and in relation to certain categories of women in order to increase representativeness.

POWER AND INFLUENCE

One feature of case study research which emphasises organising activity in these kinds of setting is that some actors attain greater visibility than others since their contributions to the production of social order are more influential than others. (I imagine that a straightforward ethnographic account of the same series of events and interactions would have looked rather different.) This is so for two reasons. First organising activity, as we have argued, requires the exercise of certain skills which may not be held by all participants and second, in circumstances of 'fluid participation' (Cohen, March and Olsen, 1983) those who are most often present or who choose to make more commitment to the setting will be more influential. These two factors have obvious applicability to the position of paid workers

who are more wholly 'within' the organisation than most other participants, particularly when a longitudinal perspective is taken. They
therefore have greater access to the knowledge base as well as contributing to the creation of that knowledge. The problem, in terms of the
desire for equality of participation, is how to manage this situation.

For both Jo and Linda part of the reason they had wanted to work
in the Centre was the non-traditional nature of the setting: 'What
appealed to me was that it was this very locally based project.' '[I was]
really pleased that it was a job within the feminist network.' It was
therefore part of their intentions that, while being paid, they wanted
to work in a way which widened the basis of power. Jo made this
statement very clearly when she insisted that the newly formed
collective was the sovereign body. Linda stated her position as: 'The
paid workers shouldn't be running the Centre; they should be there
to facilitate other women to run the Centre.'

However, they both experienced considerable difficulties in
effectively distributing power to the extent they wished. The level of
support from other women was variable – at its highest during
periods of crisis, but for many participants reduced to attendance at
meetings after the crisis had passed. Without a sufficient group of
women to share the day-to-day tasks the paid workers found
themselves assuming almost total responsibility for necessary
administrative tasks, such as bookkeeping, coupled with the feeling
that they had to provide a support for other women who came to the
Centre, as their comments vividly show. The greater degree of
'establishment' the Centre achieved increased the level of
maintenance activity required to service it. Conversely, the support
which could be activated at times of crisis did not carry over to
periods when this threat had been removed.

To a large extent their efforts to share power and influence became
no more than sharing of information. For both the management
committee and the later version of the collective the 'degenerate'
form of meeting was one in which reporting back from paid workers
to the other members became almost the sole function of meetings.
Jo had a particular distaste for this style of meeting.

I don't like the reporting back bit; the last few collective meetings
have really made me think what collective meetings are for.
Because we were all members of the collective you didn't know
what was happening so we had to bring you up to date, and having
done that, well, what do we do next?

The hoped-for solution, that 'users who come to the collective are actually involved day-to-day in the Centre', is frequently expressed but rarely enacted. The workers in Greystone Women's Centre experienced the tension between providing a 'sufficient' basis for action by maintaining the establishment of the Centre, while at the same time retaining the flexibility to attend to the solidary-affective dimensions of participation as a persistent, almost daily, issue. Simply put, the paid workers were more influential than other participants primarily because they spent more time in the Centre and had acquired more organising skills. This is not to discount the efforts of Jo and Linda to effect changes in the situation, notably in the amount of work which was put into establishing a workers' group, and finally the decision Jo made to resign when Linda's funding came to an end, which was dictated by her feeling that one paid worker in a collective was an impossible anomaly, but the examples do illustrate the considerable difficulty of achieving equality of power and influence with a mix of paid and voluntary workers. It is open to others to match the level of commitment of the paid workers, but in practice few do so for more than a limited period of time.

To summarise: inequalities of power and influence were characterised as 'a persistent problem' in the review of organising activity within the autonomous women's movement and the evidence from the case material reinforces this assessment. Paid workers are often identical with those who spend most time on the work of organising, and these women hold (or acquire) greater skills and knowledge than other participants. The means of redressing this situation makes demands on those who are already occupied on other organisational tasks, while lack of attention to this area may create a spiral of disinvolvement on the part of less committed participants. A condition of complete non-hierarchy in participatory groups, where all members make some influential contributions to social order, in situations of 'fluid participation' are arguably almost impossible to achieve because of the demands of attempting to minimise differentials on a continual basis.

SKILLS AND DIFFERENTIALS

As a consequence of fluid and variable participation, as one woman observed, 'You've got two tiers whether you like it or not, and the question is what you do with that'.

Women come to a Women's Centre for a variety of reasons and with different expectations. However, encouragement to 'become involved', if accepted, implies some form of learning process for most incomers. In the first phase at Greystone the operation of the Centre was relatively bureaucratised, including extensive information files and case records of 'clients', and the associated training courses included sessions on complex social security rights and counselling techniques. Later, when the original high levels of expertise expected had been reduced, members were still expected to be able to relate to outside agencies and generally be able to run an office. These activities were not familiar to some participants and a system of 'apprenticeship' was introduced to handle the problem of induction. Clearly there was a desire to share skills and to increase the level of expertise of all participants, but as time passed the question of whether the most appropriate types of skills were being developed was raised. By the time the personal case records were thrown out the view of women as either clients or advice workers was seriously challenged and the development of group work as a less divisive alternative was fostered. Nevertheless, in most cases the effects of differences between individuals persisted, and both Jo and Linda spoke of the way they felt about continually being asked, 'What shall I do?' Although unresolved, there was some suggestion that a solution to the problem lay as much with those who appeared to hold the appropriate skills as with those who did not. Referring to one of the 'local' women who did a lot of work in the Centre, Linda said: 'She somehow assumes that because there's this group of us who've got degrees we should be deferred to. It's really difficult to overcome. I think that's our problem to take on, not hers.'

The need for the 'more skilled' to act as enablers is recognised, but how can this be done? At Greystone the tension between providing a sufficient basis for action while at the same time attending to the affective dimensions of participation has been noted as a constant theme. A particularly clear example was the meeting where the paid workers proposed the restructuring of meetings along more conventional lines, while other members of the collective argued that the meetings were important for 'seeing people and keeping in touch'. The need to 'get what needs to be done, done', in addition to being 'this catalyst, this caring person', led one worker to question the viability of the way the Centre was run; 'I think I would be more into being very specific about people's responsibilities . . . it's very difficult working collectively'; in effect asking for the introduction of some degree of bureaucratisation in order to make her work less open-ended, more predictable. For paid workers the nature of their contractual position allows little escape from the demands of this dilemma. The only means of ameliorating the situation is to persuade other participants to become as closely involved and as knowledgeable as they are, but as volunteers. For participants whose involvement is voluntary the same restrictions do not apply. They may contribute to or consume whatever aspect of the social order appears most attractive to them and exercise choice about the extent and timing of their involvement. Given this, it is not surprising that there were few takers for the more routine administrative and clerical tasks.

A common 'career' for participants is to move through involvement with a Women's Centre to a group with a more focused identity, such as a women and health group, as an arena for support, education and campaigning. In the women's movement as a whole, as one participant remarked, 'there's enough for people to do, and more'. By moving into more specialised groups members may be spared the 'tedium' of continually accommodating newcomers and renegotiating the 'task' of the group, and are in a position to develop their own interests and to enjoy the benefits of building a shared set of assumptions. Consequently many women's active involvement in a Centre is limited in time. While they are likely to remain supportive of the idea, and can be mobilised on that basis, it is unusual for their specific commitment to be attached to a Centre in the long term, either for the reasons just noted or because of another common transfer of commitment – into paid employment. Except in rare cases, such as Karen who was able to make her work in the Centre part of her job description, it can be difficult to combine paid employment with continual involvement in a Women's Centre. It follows that in many cases those women who hold the skills of organising, whether acquired through their experiences in the Centre or elsewhere, may be mobilised to contribute these skills at times of crisis or to provide support for the idea and for those working to enact it, but the persistence of their contributions cannot be assumed as routine. The paid workers and the few longer-term participants will continually have to manage the induction of new participants while at the same time carrying out the necessary maintenance activities. Differentials are again a persistent problem in these circumstances. In chapter one some tactics for managing or minimising differentials between participants were described, but these were drawn from groups which generally are relatively 'closed'. (It is usually only groups which have a sufficiently long-term sense of identity who publish accounts of their experiences.) Similar tactics may be employed in 'open' situations, but the cumulative effect of any learning process is very likely to be reduced by the transitory nature of participation.

LOCATING IN THE ENVIRONMENT

A particular feature of women's movement groups to which attention has already been drawn is that the environment within which they locate cannot be represented as an undifferentiated entity. Broadly, sections of the environment may be seen as supportive, neutral or antagonistic, although any particular actor in the environment may behave or be perceived differently at different times. Thus, for example, at Greystone the local social services office and other advice agencies gave their support to the second attempt to acquire charitable funding when the Centre had reformed as a collective. Conversely, Simpson School was generally, if not wholeheartedly, supportive in the first phase but withdrew this support in response to initiatives from the local council. The council in turn never accepted the Centre as a body with whom they could form a contractual relationship, unlike the funding charities who were prepared to do so.

Interaction with the extra-movement environment was essentially intermittent. Here a balance was sought between assembling and maintaining a level of resources – typically, adequate premises and sometimes payment for workers – which were sufficient to fulfil the minimum requirements of a Women's Centre, building sufficiently good relations with some sections of the environment so that these may provide support if required, or at least will not constitute a threat, and, on the other hand, retain a level of autonomy and self-determination which is necessary to protect the core values.

As a consequence of these calculations, at some periods interactions with the environment were at a low level. When the minimum requirements of premises and workers could be taken for granted, attention was focused at the level of the group and its internal functioning and was only directed outwards in so far as the number or mix of participants was in some way defined as inadequate, such that modification or enlargement was sought through recruitment. For Women's Centres as examples of 'open' rather than 'closed' groups the imperative to be responsive to the needs of many women prevents a sense of complacency or completeness developing in periods where everything else is sufficient.

To summarise: as the previous discussion has shown a Women's Centre depends for the legitimation of its existence on the endorsement of as many women as possible. Therefore the section of the environment which is seen as consisting of actual or potential participants in the women's movement cannot be neglected. With respect to this group efforts are made to keep the boundary low and permeable. With other sections of the environment the situation is different; relationships are sought which are sufficient to provide support if required, but not overly collusive such that the freedom to act and develop is restricted by the need to refer to other organisations whose values may be different. Thus, entering into relationships with any section of the extra-movement environment is appraised in terms of the net gains or losses in the autonomy of the Women's Centre which may ensue.

NON-HIERARCHICAL ORGANISATION IN WOMEN'S CENTRES

The case material suggests that in these circumstances instances of fully enacted non-hierarchical organisation are rare and limited in time. While the definition of the ideal Women's Centre – the one that exists some time in the future – is used as a reference point and a source of motivation by participants, the accounts of the Women's Centres have shown that movement towards the desired end-state may be delayed or inhibited by such factors as a shortage of resources or information, or a failure to delegitimate the status quo. The (generalised) situation in Women's Centres also differs from the experience of 'closed' groups in that groups which do not include a value for open participation in their construction of non-hierarchical organisation are able to make assumptions about the nature and extent of participation, can therefore work out interpersonal and organisational relationships on a long-term basis, and have only a limited need to assimilate newcomers. Such closed groups may have the capability to go through a process of group maturation such that their internal processes approach congruence with the preferred mode of conduct. Thus particular difficulties arise in the case of Women's Centres which may not apply to the same extent to 'closed' groups:

- The requirement for open participation creates circumstances where skill differentials must be constantly managed.
- Full legitimacy of the endeavour is defined as endorsement by the whole constituency of women in the locality. This cannot be achieved and therefore failure, in this respect, is persistent.
- Participation is voluntary and intermittent. It cannot therefore be assumed that skilful participants will choose to make consistent contributions.
- A degree of *establishment* is usually desirable in terms of the requirement for autonomy. However, this is likely to involve some degree of bureaucratisation and, as Rothschild-Whitt (1982) has noted, 'wholly different values' are implied by bureaucratic and collective forms of organisation. Where participants in Women's Centres are successful in achieving a degree of establishment they must also manage the competing value imperatives.
- Similarly, interactions with the environment are likely to involve some engagement with bureaucratic values. Interactions with the extra-movement environment make demands on participants in that they are required to operate in more than one mode.

SUMMARY

It has been a central feature of the arguments presented here that the core values of the autonomous women's movement do not determine action but act as symbolic referents. Focusing on the arena of negotiation between action and its symbolic referents, it becomes apparent that the legitimacy of action is understood by participants in terms of its perceived congruence with their core values.

In relation to the organising processes involved the argument has been in terms of the role of skills – as information search, interpretation, influence and choice – in the construction and maintenance of non-hierarchical organisation. These skills are central to all organising activity; the particular relevance in this context is that the core values which inform organising activity in Women's Centres (and in the women's movement as a whole) contain the requirement that leadership be distributed. However, the facts that: (i) the relationship between values and action may be unclear, ambiguous or disputed; (ii) the process by which strategies and tactics are legitimately linked to values is 'political' and hence negotiated; (iii) constructing and maintaining non-hierarchical organisation makes demands on participants' organising skills, and minimising skill differentials makes further demands on participants; and (iv) innovation is difficult in contexts where the endeavour is rarely fully legitimated, and is without the benefit of a received body of knowledge and practice – all these considerations demonstrate that the construction of non-hierarchical forms of organisation is not, as some have claimed, a naturally occurring outcome of human social activity. While it is reasonable to argue (see, for example, Rothschild, 1990) that women's socialisation makes them better equipped than men to perform the skills[1] necessary for the creation of democratic and non-hierarchical organisation, this evidence should not be promoted to the status of an alternative determinism. Rather, women who are involved in organising as women are engaged in a creative struggle to build the future through their actions in the present – what Ehrlich (1979) has described as 'the reinvention of everyday life'.

NOTE

1 Describing work organisations Rothschild (1990) lists a 'tendency in negotiating to seek equitable agreements rather than self-advantage, a preference for involving others rather than a unilateral style, a habit of cultivating others' talents and crediting them, a sense of responsibility for others' well-being and a desire for relationships at work that are valued in themselves'.

Bibliography

Abrams, P. and McCulloch, A. (1976) *Communes, Sociology and Society*, Cambridge: Cambridge University Press.

Acker, J. (1990) 'Hierarchies, jobs, bodies: a theory of gendered organizations', *Gender and Society* 4, 2: 139–158.

Aldrich, H.E. (1979) *Organizations and Environments*, Englewood Cliffs: Prentice-Hall.

Altheide, D.L. (1988) 'Mediating cutbacks in human services: a case study in the negotiated order', *Sociological Quarterly* 29, 3: 339–355.

Argyris, C. (1957) *Personality and Organization*, London: Harper & Row.

—— (1965) *Organization and Innovation*, Holmwood, Ill.: Irwin and Dorsey Press.

—— (1979) 'Some unintended consequences of rigorous research', in R.T. Mowday and R.M. Steers (eds) *Research in Organizations: Issues and Controversies*, Santa Monica: Goodyear.

Argyris, C. and Schon, D.A. (1978) *Organizational Learning: A Theory of Action Perspective*, Reading, Mass.: Addison-Wesley.

Ashridge Management College (1988) *Management for the Future*, Ashridge Management Research Group/Foundation for Management Education.

Asplund, G. (1988) *Women Managers: Changing Organizational Cultures*, New York: John Wiley.

Bartölke, K. (1988) 'Leadership: nothing but constructing reality by negotiation?', in J. Hunt, R. Baliga, P. Dachler and C. Schriesheim (eds) *Emerging Leadership Vistas*, Lexington, Mass.: Arlington Heights.

Batstone, E., Boraston, I. and Frenkel, S. (1977) *Shop Stewards in Action*, Oxford: Basil Blackwell.

Bennis, W.G. and Shepard, H. S. (1965) 'A theory of group development', *Human Relations* 9, 415–457.

Benson, J.K. (1977) 'Innovation and crisis in organizational analysis', in J.K. Benson (ed.) *Organisational Analysis: Critique and Innovation*, London: Sage.

Berg, P.-O. (1979) *Emotional Structures in Organizations: A Study of the Process of Change in a Swedish Company*, Lund: Studentlitteratur.

Beynon, H. (1975) *Working for Ford*, Wakefield: E.P. Publishing.

Bittner, E. (1974) 'The concept of organization', in R. Turner (ed.) *Ethnomethodology*, Harmondsworth: Penguin.

Bouchier, D. (1983) *The Feminist Challenge: The Movement for Women's Liberation in Britain and the United States*, London: Macmillan.

Brown, M.H. (1986) 'Organisational aspects of Women's Centres', unpublished thesis, University of Warwick, England.

—— (1989) 'Organising activity in the women's movement: an example of distributed leadership', in P.G. Klandermans, H. Kriesi and S. Tarrow, (eds) *Organising for Change: Social Movement Organisation in Europe and the United States*, Greenwich, Mass.: JAI Press.

—— (1990a) 'Leadership and non-hierarchy: examples from the women's movement'. Paper presented to the XIIth World Congress of Sociology, Madrid, Spain. 9–13 July.

—— (1990b) 'Women's Centres: relationships between values and action', *Journal of Management Studies* 27, 6: 619–635.

Brown, M.H. and Hosking, D.M. (1986) 'Distributed leadership and skilled performance as successful organisation in social movements', *Human Relations* 1: 65–79.

Brown, R.H. (1978) 'Bureaucracy as praxis: towards a political phenomenology of formal organizations', *Administrative Science Quarterly* 23, 356–382.

Brunsson, N. (1982) 'The irrationality of action and action rationality: decisions, ideologies and organisational action', *Journal of Management Studies* 19, 1: 29–44.

Bucher, R. and Stelling, J. (1969) 'Characteristics of professional organizations', *Journal of Health and Social Behaviour* 10: 3–15.

Burgess, R.G. (1984) *In the Field: An Introduction to Field Research*, London: George Allen & Unwin.

Burowoy, M. (1979) *Manufacturing Consent*, Chicago: University of Chicago Press.

Burrell, G. and Morgan, G. (1979) *Sociological Paradigms and Organizational Analysis: Elements in the Sociology of Corporate Life*, London: Heinemann.

Cadman, E., Chester, G. and Pivot, A. (1981) *Rolling Our Own: Women as Printers, Publishers and Distributors*, London: Minority Press Group.

Carroll, S.J. (1984) 'Feminist scholarship on political leadership', in B. Kellerman (ed.) *Leadership: Multidisciplinary Perspectives*, Englewood Cliffs: Prentice-Hall.

Cassell, J. (1977) 'The relation of observer to observed in peer group research', *Human Organization* 36, 4: 412–416.

Charlton, V. (1977) 'A lesson in day care', in M. Mayo (ed.) *Women in the Community*, London: Routledge & Kegan Paul.

Chermers, M.M. (1984) 'The social, organisational and cultural context of effective leadership', in B. Kellerman (ed.) *Leadership: Multidisciplinary Perspectives*, Englewood Cliffs: Prentice-Hall.

Child, J. (1984) *Organization: A Guide to Problems and Practice*, 2nd edn, London: Harper & Row.

Cohen, M.D., March, J.G. and Olsen, J.P. (1983) 'A garbage can model of organizational choice', in J.M. Pennings (ed.) *Decision Making: An Organizational Behaviour Approach*, New York: Markus Wiener.

Col, J.M. (1981) 'Women's employment networks: strategies for development', in M. Rendel (ed.) *Women, Power and Political Systems*, London: Croom Helm.

Coote, A. and Campbell, B. (1987) *Sweet Freedom: The Struggle for Women's Liberation*, 2nd edn, London: Pan Books Ltd.

Dahlerup, D. (ed.) (1986) *The New Women's Movement: Feminism and Political Power in Europe and the USA*, London: Sage.

Davenport, H. (1982) 'Women at the wire', *Observer Magazine* 12 December, 10–13.

Day, R.A. and Day, J.V. (1977) 'A review of the current state of negotiated order theory: an appreciation and a critique', in J.K. Benson (ed.) *Organisational Analysis: Critique and Innovation*, London: Sage.

Douglas, T. (1983) *Groups: Understanding People Gathered Together*, London: Tavistock.

Ehrlich, H.J. (1979) 'Anarchism and formal organisations: some notes on the sociological study of organisations from an anarchist perspective', in H.J. Ehrlich, C. Ehrlich, D. De Leon and G. Morris (eds) *Reinventing Anarchy*, London: Routledge & Kegan Paul.

Elger, A.J. (1975) 'Industrial organizations – a processual perspective', in J.B. McKinley (ed.) *Processing People: Cases in Organizational Behaviour*, New York: Holt, Rinehart & Winston.

Emery, F.E. and Trist, E.L. (1965) 'The causal texture of organizational environments', *Human Relations* 18: 21–32.

Ferguson, K.E. (1984) *The Feminist Case against Bureaucracy*, Philadelphia: Temple University Press.

Ferree, M.M. (in press) 'Political strategies and feminist concerns in the United States and Federal Republic of Germany: class, race and gender', in M. Spenser (ed.) *Research in Social Movements: Conflict and Change*, Greenwich, Mass.: JAI Press.

Finch, J. (1982) 'A women's health group in Mansfield', in A. Curno, A. Lamming, L. Leach, J. Stiles, V. Ward, A. Wright and T. Ziff (eds) *Women in Collective Action*, The Association of Community Workers in the UK.

Freeman, J. (1975) *The Politics of Women's Liberation*, London: Longman.

—— (1984) *The Tyranny of Structurelessness*, London: Dark Star Press and Rebel Press.

French, J.P. and Raven, B.H. (1960) 'The bases of social power', in D. Cartwright and A. Zander (eds) *Group Dynamics: Research and Theory*, 2nd edn, New York: Row, Peterson.

Gerlach, L. and Hine, V. (1970) *People, Power, Change: Movements of Social Transformation*, Indianapolis: Bobbs Merrill.

Gerson, E.M. (1976) 'On "quality of life"', *American Sociological Review* 41: 793–806.

Gibb, C. (1954) 'Leadership', in G. Lindzey and E. Aronson (eds) *The Handbook of Social Psychology* (vol 2), Reading, Mass.: Addison-Wesley.

—— (1969) 'Leadership', in G. Lindzey and E. Aronson (eds) *The Handbook of Social Psychology* (2nd edn, vol 4), Reading, Mass.: Addison-Wesley.

Giddens, A. (1976) *New Rules of Sociological Method: A Positive Critique of Interpretive Sociologies*, London: Hutchinson.

—— (1984) *The Constitution of Society*, Cambridge: Polity Press.

Giorgiou, P. (1973) 'The goal paradigm and notes towards a counter paradigm', *Administrative Science Quarterly* 18: 291–310.

Gott, R. (1982) 'A man at Greenham', *Guardian* 15 December.

Gouldner, A.W. (1959) 'Organizational analysis', in R.K. Merton, L. Broom and L.S. Cottrell (eds) *Sociology Today*, New York: Basic Books.

Gray, B. (1985) 'Conditions facilitating interorganizational collaboration', *Human Relations* 38, 10: 911–936.

Grieco, M.S. and Hosking, D.M. (1987) 'Networking, exchange and skill', *International Studies in Management and Organization* XVII, 1: 75–87.

Hall, P.M. (1987) 'Interactionism and the study of social organization', *Sociological Quarterly* 28, 1: 1–22.

Handy, C. (1988) *Understanding Voluntary Organizations*, Harmondsworth: Penguin.

Hartley, J., Kelly, J. and Nicholson, N. (1983) *Steel Strike: A Case Study in Industrial Relations*, London: Batsford.

Haug, F. (1989) 'Lessons from the women's movement in Europe', *Feminist Review* 31: 107–116.

Hedberg, B.T.L., Nystrom, P.C. and Starbuck, W.H. (1977) 'Designing organizations to match tomorrow', in P.C. Nystrom and W.H. Starbuck (eds) *Prescriptive Models of Organizations*, Amsterdam: North-Holland.

Herbst, Ph. G. (1976) *Alternatives to Hierarchies*, Leiden: Martinus Nijhoff.

Herzberg, F. (1976) *Managerial Choice: To be Efficient and To be Human*, Holmwood, Ill.: Dow Jones-Irwin.

Horowitz, I.L. (ed.) (1964) *The Anarchists*, New York: Dell Publishing Co.

Hosking, D.M. (1988) 'Organizing, leadership and skilful process', *Journal of Management Studies* 25, 2: 147–166.

Hosking, D.M. and Morley, I.E. (1988) 'The skills of leadership', in J. Hunt, R. Baliga, P. Dachler and C. Schriesheim (eds) *Emerging Leadership Vistas*, Lexington, Mass.: Arlington Heights.

House, E.R. (1980) *Evaluating with Validity*, Beverly Hills: Sage.

Janis, I. and Mann, L. (1977) *Decision Making: A Psychological Analysis of Conflict, Choice and Commitment*, London: Free Press.

Jones, L. (1983) 'On common ground: the women's peace camp at Greenham Common', in L. Jones (ed.) *Keeping the Peace*, London: The Women's Press.

Kanter, H., Lefanu, S., Shah, S. and Spedding, C. (eds) (1984) *Sweeping Statements: Writings from the Women's Liberation Movement 1981–83*, London: The Women's Press.

Kanter, R.M. (1975) 'Women and the structure of organizations: explorations in theory and behaviour', in M. Millman and R.M. Kanter (eds) *Another Voice: Feminist Perspectives on Social Life and Social Science*, New York: Anchor Press/Doubleday.

Katz, A.H. (1957) 'An investigation of self-organized groups in fields of physical and mental handicap', unpublished thesis, Columbia University, New York.

—— (1981) 'Self-help and mutual aid: an emerging social movement?', *Annual Review of Sociology* 7, 129–155.

Katz, D. and Kahn, R. (1978) *The Social Psychology of Organizations*, New York: John Wiley.

Kerr, S. and Jermier, J.M. (1983) 'Substitutes for leadership: their meaning and measurement', in J.M. Pennings (ed.) *Decision Making: An Organisational Behaviour Approach*, New York: Markus Weiner.

Kotter, J. (1982) *The General Managers*, London: Free Press.

Kropotkin, P. (1904) *Mutual Aid: A Factor of Evolution*, London: Heinemann.

Levine, C. (1984) *The Tyranny of Tyranny*, London: Dark Star Press and Rebel Press.

Likert, R. (1961) *New Patterns of Management*, New York: McGraw-Hill.

—— (1984) 'The principle of supportive relationships', in D.S. Pugh (ed.) *Organization Theory*, 2nd edn, Harmondsworth: Penguin.

Likert, R. and Likert, J.G. (1976) *New Ways of Managing Conflict*, New York: McGraw-Hill.

McGregor, D. (1960) *The Human Side of Enterprise*, New York: McGraw-Hill.

—— (1984) 'Theory X and theory Y', in D.S. Pugh (ed.) *Organization Theory*, 2nd edn, Harmondsworth: Penguin.

MacIver, R.M. (1964) 'Subjective meaning in the social situation III', in L.A. Coser and B. Rosenberg (eds) *Sociological Theory*, 2nd edn, New York: Macmillan.

Maines, D.R. (1982) 'In search of mesostructure', *Urban Life* 11: 267–279.

Mangham, I. (1979) *The Politics of Organizational Change*, London: Associated Business Press.

Mansbridge, J. (1973) 'Time, emotion and inequality: three problems of participatory groups', *Journal of Applied Behavioural Science* 9, 2/3: 351–368.

Martin, P. Y. (1990) 'Rethinking feminist organizations', *Gender and Society* 4, 2, 182–206.

Martins, H. (1974) 'Time and theory in sociology', in J. Rex (ed.) *Approaches to Sociology*, London: Routledge & Kegan Paul.

Maturana, H. and Varela, F. (1980) *Autopoiesis and Cognition: The Realization of the Living*, London: Reidl.

Mayo, E. (1933) *The Human Problems of an Industrial Civilization*, New York: Macmillan.

—— (1949) *The Social Problems of an Industrial Civilization*, London: Routledge & Kegan Paul.

Mead, G.H. (1936) *The Problem of Society – How We Become Selves*, Chicago: University of Chicago Press.

Miller, E.J. (1975) 'Sociotechnical systems in weaving, 1953–70: a follow-up study', *Human Relations* 28, 349–386.

Morgan, G. (1986) *Images of Organization*, Beverley Hills: Sage.

Morley, I.E. and Hosking, D.M. (1984) 'Decision-making and negotiation: leadership and social skills', in M. Gruneberg and T. Wall (eds) *Social Psychology and Organisational Behaviour*, Chichester: Wiley.

Mueller, C. (1983) 'Women's movement success and the success of social movement theory', working paper, Wellesley College, Mass.

Neumann, J.E. (1989) 'Why people don't participate in organizational change', in *Research in Organizational Change and Development* (vol 3), Greenwich, Mass.: JAI Press.

Newman, K. (1980) 'Incipient bureaucracy: the development of hierarchies in egalitarian organisations', in G.M. Britan and R. Cohen (eds) *Hierarchy and Society*, Philadelphia: Institute for the Study of Human Issues.

Nystrom, P.C. and Starbuck, W.H. (eds) (1977) *Prescriptive Models of Organizations*, Amsterdam: North-Holland.

Parsons, T. (1960) *Structure and Process in Modern Societies*, Glencoe: The Free Press.

Perrow, C. (1978) 'Demystifying organizations', in R.C. Sarri and Y. Hasenfeld (eds) *The Management of Human Services*, Columbia, SC.: Columbia University Press.

Pettigrew, A. (1973) *The Politics of Organisational Decision-Making*, London: Tavistock.

—— (1985) *The Awakening Giant: Continuity and Change in ICI*, Oxford: Basil Blackwell.

Pugh, D.S., Hickson, D.J. and Hinings, C.R. (1983) *Writers on Organisations*, 3rd edn, Harmondsworth: Penguin.

Ranson, S., Hinings, B. and Greenwood, R. (1980) 'The structuring of organizational structures', *Administrative Science Quarterly* 25: 1–17.

Read, H. (1954) *Anarchy and Order*, London: Faber & Faber.

Reason, P. and Rowan, J. (eds) (1981) *Human Inquiry: A Sourcebook of New Paradigm Research*, Chichester: John Wiley.

Reed, M. (1985) *Redirections in Organizational Analysis*, London: Tavistock.

Reinharz, S. (1983) 'Experiential analysis: a contribution to feminist research', in G. Bowles and R. Duelli Klein (eds) *Theories of Women's Studies*, London: Routledge & Kegan Paul.

Rice, A.K. (1958) *Productivity and Social Organisation*, London: Tavistock.

Riley, M. (1982) 'A woman's employment group in Milton Keynes', in A. Curno, A. Lamming, L. Leach, J. Stiles, V. Ward, A. Wright and T. Ziff (eds) *Women in Collective Action*, The Association of Community Workers in the UK.

Rokeach, M. (1968) *Beliefs, Attitudes and Values*, San Francisco: Jossey-Bass.

—— (1973) *The Nature of Human Values*, New York: The Free Press.

Rosser, J. and Davies, C. (1987) '"What would we do without her?" – invisible women in NHS administration', in A. Spender and D. Podmore (eds) *In a Man's World: Essays on Women in Male-Dominated Professions*, London: Tavistock.

Rothschild, J. (1990) 'Feminist values and the democratic management of work organizations'. Paper presented to the XIIth World Congress of Sociology, Madrid, Spain. 9–13 July.

Rothschild-Whitt, J. (1982) 'The collectivist organization: an alternative to bureaucratic models', in F. Lindenfeld and J. Rothschild-Whitt (eds) *Workplace Democracy and Social Change*, Boston: Porter Sargent.

Salaman, G. (1978) 'Towards a sociology of organisational structure', *Sociological Review* 26, 519–554.

Sargent, L. (ed.) (1981) *Women and Revolution: The Unhappy Marriage of Marxism and Feminism*, London: Pluto Press.

Segal, L. (1979) 'A local experience', in S. Rowbotham, L. Segal and H. Wainwright, *Beyond the Fragments: Feminism and the Making of Socialism*, London: Merlin Press.

Sheffield Women's Centre (1978) *Spare Rib*, January.

Silverman, D. (1970) *The Theory of Organizations*, London: Heinemann.

Simon, H.A. (1957) *Administrative Behaviour*, New York: Macmillan.

Skinner, J. (1988) 'Who's changing whom? Women, management and work organisation', in A. Coyle and J. Skinner (eds) *Women and Work: Positive Action for Change*, Basingstoke: Macmillan Education.

Smircich, L. and Morgan, G. (1982) 'Leadership: the management of meaning', *Journal of Applied Behavioural Studies* 18, 257–273.

Smith, P.B. and Peterson, M.F. (1988) *Leadership, Organizations and Culture*, London: Sage.

Stanley, L. and Wise, S. (1983) *Breaking Out: Feminist Consciousness and Feminist Research*, London: Routledge & Kegan Paul.

Steinbruner, J. (1974) *The Cybernetic Theory of Decision*, Princeton: Princeton University Press.

Stewart, J. (1978) 'Understanding women in organisations', *Administrative Science Quarterly* 23, 2: 336–350.

Stewart, R. (1976) *Contrasts in Management*, New York: McGraw-Hill.

Strauss, A. (1978) *Negotiations: Varieties, Contexts, Processes and Social Order*, San Francisco: Jossey-Bass.

Strauss, A., Schatzman, L., Ehrlich, D., Bucher, R. and Sabshin, M. (1963) 'The hospital and its negotiated order', in E. Friedson (ed.) *The Hospital in Modern Society*, New York: Free Press.

Tajfel, H. (1981) *Human Groups and Social Categories*, Cambridge: Cambridge University Press.

Taylor, M. (1982) *Community, Anarchy and Liberty*, Cambridge: Cambridge University Press.

Thompson, K.A. (1973) 'Religious organizations: the cultural perspective', in G. Salaman and K.A. Thompson (eds) *People and Organizations*, London: Longman.

Trist, E.A. and Bamforth, K.W. (1951) 'Some social and psychological consequences of the longwall method of coal-getting', *Human Relations* 4, 1: 3–38.

Tyneside Rape Crisis Centre Collective (1982) in A. Curno, A. Lamming, L. Leach, J. Stiles, V. Ward, A. Wright and T. Ziff (eds) *Women in Collective Action*, The Association of Community Workers in the UK.

Vere, M. (1977) 'Some thoughts on organisation', *Anarchist-Feminist Newsletter* 4, 1–2.

Walton, R.E. (1969) *Interpersonal Peacemaking: Confrontations and Third Party Consultations*, Reading, Mass.: Addison-Wesley.

Ward, C. (1982) *Anarchy in Action*, London: Freedom Press.

Weick, K.E. (1978) 'The spines of leaders', in M. McCall and M. Lombardo (eds) *Leadership: Where Else Can We Go?*, Durham: Durham University Press.

—— (1979) *The Social Psychology of Organising*, Reading, Mass.: Addison-Wesley.

Welford, A. (1980) 'The concept of skill and its application to social performance', in W. Singleton, P. Spurgeon and R. Stammers (eds) *The Analysis of Social Skill*, London: Plenum Press.

Westerlund, G. and Sjöstrand, S.-E. (1979) *Organizational Myths*, London: Harper & Row.
Willis, P. (1977) *Learning to Labour*, Westmead: Saxon House.
W.I.R.E.S. (1978) *Spare Rib* 70: 18–19.
Women's Liberation Bookbus 1980.
Woodward, J. (1965) *Industrial Organization: Theory and Practice*, Oxford: Oxford University Press.
Yin, R.K. (1984) *Case Study Research: Design and Methods*, Beverly Hills: Sage.
Zald, M.N. and Ash, R. (1966) 'Social movements organizations: growth, decay and change', *Social Forces* 44: 327–340.
Znaniecki, L.H. (1980) 'Interviewing American widows', in W.B. Shaffir, R.A. Stebbings and A. Turnowetz (eds) *Field Work Experience: Qualitative Approaches to Social Research*, New York: St Marthus Press.

Name index

Abrams, P. 53, 156, 157
Acker, J. 180
Aldrich, H.E. 44
Altheide, D.L. 52, 57, 60, 61, 171, 175
Argyris, C. 38, 39, 78, 79
Ash, R. 177
Ashridge Management College 2, 3
Asplund, G. 3

Bamforth, K.W. 35, 36
Bartölke, K. 167
Bennis, W.G. 16, 172
Benson, J.K. 45, 46, 47, 49, 75
Berg, P.O. 78
Beynon, H. 47
Bittner, E. 45, 47
Bouchier, D. 8
Brown, M.H. 5, 13, 22, 32, 44, 53,
    59, 63, 67, 68, 69, 71, 76, 79, 153,
    159, 162, 164, 165, 169, 172, 175,
    176, 177
Brown, R.H. 71
Brunsson, N. 158
Bucher, R. 56
Burgess, R.G. 5
Burowoy, M. 42, 57
Burrell, G. 33, 42, 55

Cadman, E. 12, 15
Campbell, B. 5, 9, 10, 32, 165
Carroll, S.J. 21
Cassell, J. 80
Charlton, V. 17, 19, 22, 23
Chermers, M.M. 63

Child, J. 37
Cohen, M.D. 184
Col, J.M. 13, 22, 55, 70
Coote, A. 5, 9, 10, 32, 165

Dahlerup, D. 5, 32, 165
Davenport, H. 13
Davies, C. 1
Day, J.V. 48, 49, 55–6, 170
Day, R.A. 48, 49, 55–6, 170
Douglas, T. 35, 164

Ehrlich, H.J. 192
Elger, A.J. 42, 48
Emery, F.E. 54, 58, 173, 176

Ferguson, K.E. 3, 180
Ferree, M.M. 153
Finch, J. 17–18, 19
Freeman, J. 21, 32, 163, 164
French, J.P. 66

Gerlach, L. 33, 34, 53
Gerson, E.M. 50, 169, 183
Gibb, C. 38, 68
Giddens, A. 42, 46, 48, 49
Giorgiou, P. 44
Gott, R. 14
Gouldner, A.W. 43
Gray, B. 70, 172, 173
Grieco, M.S. 67

Hall, P.M. 50, 52, 58, 61–2, 68, 70,
    78, 179

Handy, C. 6, 7
Hartley, C. 6, 7
Hartley, J. 176
Haug, F. 51
Hedberg, B.T.L. 36
Herbst, Ph.G. 33, 37, 66
Herzberg, F. 41
Hine, V. 33, 34, 53
Horowitz, I.L. 6
Hosking, D.M. 30, 44, 59, 66, 67,
  68, 69, 71, 76, 79, 159, 162, 164,
  165, 169, 170, 175, 176, 179
House, E.R. 78, 79

Janis, I. 163, 176
Jermier, J.M. 38, 164
Jones, L. 14, 15

Kahn, R. 43, 64, 65–6
Kanter, H. 14
Kanter, R.M. 35
Katz, A.H. 177
Katz, D. 43, 64, 65–6
Kerr, S. 38, 164
Kotter, J. 71, 162
Kropotkin, P. 6

Levine, C. 22
Likert, J.G. 33, 39, 40, 44, 163, 165
Likert, R. 33, 38, 39, 40, 44, 66, 163,
  165, 172

McCulloch, A. 53, 156, 157
McGregor, D. 38, 39, 66
MacIver, R.M. 153–4
Maines, D.R. 52
Mangham, I. 41–2
Mann, L. 163, 176
Mansbridge, J. 20, 21, 158
March, J.G. 184
Martin, P.Y. 180
Martins, H. 53, 54
Maturana, H. 60
Mayo, E. 34, 35, 36
Mead, G.H. 168, 169
Miller, E.J. 37, 38
Morgan, G. 2, 3, 33, 42, 55, 161

Morley, I.E. 66, 67, 68, 159, 164,
  170, 179
Mueller, C. 5

Neumann, J.E. 172
Newman, K. 26, 28, 29, 174–6

Olsen, J.P. 184

Parsons, T. 43
Perrow, C. 45, 46, 47–8
Peterson, M.F. 63, 72
Pettigrew, A. 45, 48, 54, 55, 154
Pugh, D.S. 36, 48

Ranson, S. 49
Raven, B.H. 66
Read, H. 38
Reason, P. 80
Reed, M. 166–7
Reinharz, S. 80
Rice, A.K. 35
Riley, M. 23, 27
Rokeach, M. 50
Rosser, J. 1
Rothschild, J. 180, 191, 192
Rothschild-Whitt, J. 12, 13, 19–20,
  21, 26, 28, 32, 37, 56, 157, 177–9,
  191
Rowan, J. 80

Salaman, G. 45, 47, 50
Sargent, L. 46
Schon, D.A. 79
Segal, L. 10, 17, 23–4, 82
Sheffield Women's Centre 27–8
Shepard, H.S. 16, 172
Silverman, D. 45
Simon, H.A. 43
Sjöstrand, S.-E. 34, 46, 62, 165
Skinner, J. 1, 3
Smircich, L. 161
Smith, P.B. 63, 72
Stanley, L. 80
Steinbruner, J. 160, 170
Stelling, J. 56
Stewart, R. 159

Strauss, A. 45, 48, 49, 54, 55, 56, 65, 167, 168, 169, 170, 171

Tajfel, H. 176
Taylor, M. 7
Thompson, K.A. 53, 54
Trist, E.A. 35, 36
Trist, E.L. 54, 58, 173, 176
Tyneside Rape Crisis Centre Collective 11, 24–5

Varela, F. 60
Vere, M. 11

W.I.R.E.S. 13, 16, 18, 22

Walton, R.E. 70
Ward, C. 7
Weber, M. 43, 176
Weick, K.E. 55, 57–9, 77
Welford, A. 160
Westerlund, G. 34, 46, 62, 165
Willis, P. 47
Wise, S. 80
Women's Liberation Bookbus 19
Woodward, J. 44

Yin, R.K. 78

Zald, M.N. 177
Znaniecki, L.H. 78

Subject index

action: linking values and means
58–61; predictability 59;
routinisation 59; values and
53–8, 153–6
action critique 46–8
actions, essential, of organising 66,
68
actual values 53, 54
adaptiveness in non-hierarchical
organisation 12–13
Albany Women's Forum 22
alternative, creation of 147
anarchism, *see* social anarchism
Anarchist Feminist 11
Ann (community worker) 104, 105,
110–11, 132; sets up Greystone
Women's Centre 84–7, 90, 93,
95–6, 97, 99, 149; and Simpson
School 99–100, 113, 149;
withdraws 106, 107, 108, 113,
118, 124
Arlington Women's Centre 151
Asian women's groups 101–2
attendance, and communication
22–3
authority, and collectivity 21
autonomy, development 15, 74

banks, women-owned 26
boundaries: management 32, 37;
negotiable 60; permeability and
flexibility 67
British Pregnancy Advisory Society
103

bureaucracy: and collectivity 28–9,
56; ideal-typification 177–8;
negotiated order theory 56;
rules, inadequacy 56; value
systems, relating to 26–9
bureaucratisation 174–7

Cadbury Trust 114–15, 116–17,
121, 122–3, 125, 135
capacities of participants 71–2; and
demands 161–2
capitalism: and patriarchy 46; value
systems, relating to 26–9
case study: analysis 51; participants,
centrality 47; research 78
class, *see* social class
closed groups, absence from 22
coal industry, socio-technical
systems 36
collaboration: enhanced 174;
inter-organisational 173–4;
relationships 70; three-stage
process model 173
'collective dream' 6
collectivity 6; ambivalence towards
7; authority and 21; bureaucracy
and 28–9, 56; communication
and 22–3; and control over work
12; defining 138–42;
environmental costs 26; external
relationships 26–9; networks 26;
and other value systems 26–9;
paid workers 24–5; value of 4;
workers' relationships 132

commitment: appropriate 142–3; creation 75; managing 22–5; in non-hierarchical organisations 74; paid workers 24–5; and personal choice 122
communalities, identification and articulation of 156
communes 156, 157
communication, and collectivity 22–3
community, collectivity in 6
Community Enterprise Programme (CEP) 111, 118, 120
community groups, difficulties of 176
community work 112, 123; see also Ann concerted action 58; creation of 59; repetitive 59
conduct, transferable mode 79
consensus 7; decision-making 13, 14–15; legitimacy as moral authority of 56; meaning of 44; values, in society 43
contamination thesis 174
context of interactions 59; see also environment
control over work 12
cooperation, spontaneous 33, 36, 50, 73
cooperative behaviour in work groups 35
cooperative values 38, 39, 42
core values 54, 55, 153, 156; identification 181
cost-effectiveness criteria 26
counselling services 102
creativity in non-hierarchical organisation 12, 13–14
criticism, impersonal 19
cultural disjunction 26

data collection methods 78–82
decision-making 140; consensus 13, 14–15; dilemmas 71–2, 162–4; in leadership 69; networking in 69–71; and paid workers 25; processes 158; salient events 69; selection in 69; time taken 158; women's groups 40

demands, capacities and 161–2
democracy and delay 13
determinism 53
differentials 186–9; minimising 19, 20–1, 29, 40, 74, 78
dilemmas, managing 162–4
distributed leadership 68, 76, 83, 164–5, 176
double task 66
dynamic homeostasis 33

education, internal 19
'efficiency' argument 75; non-hierarchical organisation 50; of symmetrical relationships 172
elite domination, problem of 21
elitism, acceptable 21–2
enablers 18
environment: boundaries 60–1; creation 60; knowledge of 159; locating in 189–90; notional and enacted quality 60–1; turbulent–placid continuum 35
equality: constraints on 73–4; enactment of value for 17, 19, 21–2, 25, 29, 74; and individual capabilities 10; of influence 19–20; negotiation 165; and paid workers 25
equilibrium 33
essential actions of organising 66, 68
Essex Road Centre 23–4
experience, shared 80–1
expert power 65–6
external relationships, problems of 26–9

failure, criteria of 156–8
feelings, as legitimate input 79
feminism: Marxism and 46; and organisational change 3; and social anarchism 8; and social class 133–4; values 8–9
feminist organising 6, 9–12, 171
feminist publishing 15–16
flatter organisational forms 2, 174
flexibility: in non-hierarchical

organisations 12–13, 74; of social
   order 59
focused leadership 68, 83
formal rationality 177–8
funding: influence of 60; value
   systems of 26

Gina, volunteer 91, 92, 93, 97
goal-directed motivation 176
goals: of management 33, 35, 39,
   41; of workers 33, 35, 39, 41
Greenham Common peace camp
   13–14
Greystone Women's Centre 83;
   activities 101–4; autonomy and
   self-determination 151; barriers
   142; bureaucratisation 174, 175,
   176, 187, 188; clients' records 89,
   131–2, 145, 149, 152, 187;
   collective 117–22, 125, 130–1,
   132, 137–8, 138–42, 143–4, 145,
   182–3; commitment 183; as
   community project 84–106, 108,
   145, 148, 149–50; community
   team and 112–13; and
   controversy 99, 105, 106, 107;
   and council 174, 175; counselling
   102–3; decision-making 93–4,
   140, 143, 145, 155; feminism
   124, 132–4, 144–5, 150, 152; and
   flexible social order 136–7, 141;
   function 129, 130; funding 96–7,
   99, 114–15, 116–17, 119, 121,
   122–3, 125, 135–6, 144, 151,
   160; goals 151; group work
   101–2, 111, 119; interim goals
   155; January workshop 128–30,
   138, 139, 145; joint action 92–9;
   key dilemmas 133, 163; learning
   process 187; lease, signing 135,
   143, 151; and local women 90,
   91, 149; location, original 100;
   management committee 93–4,
   95, 96, 98, 106, 111, 112–13, 156,
   182; and men 87, 132–3, 152;
   modification of social order 131,
   149, 150; name, changes 131;
   networking 128, 159–60;

November workshop 142–4,
   146; organisational change
   106–7, 111, 113, 128–9, 130,
   131; and other agencies 99, 103,
   106–7, 108, 112–13, 114–15;
   paid workers 130, 131, 139, 144,
   145, 183, 185, 186, 188;
   participants, balance 154–5;
   participation, legitimate form
   142, 152–3; power, concentration
   143; problem-solving 89, 93, 149;
   professionals in 84, 90–1, 92,
   94–5, 107; Project Co-ordinator
   123–4; relocation 110–25; 127–8,
   135, 138, 140, 151; reopening
   142; representativeness 183; rota
   system 88–92, 162; and Simpson
   School 99–100, 105, 106, 107,
   115–16, 118, 159–60, 189; as
   social environment 92–3; and
   training 85–7, 88, 103;
   'volunteers' 130, 131; workers
   131, 132, 134, 135–8, 144, 145;
   workers' group 134, 138, 139,
   154, 156
group maturation, characteristics 16
group, use of term 78
group work 101–2, 111, 119
groups: difference 67; purposive
   79–80; social location 26–7
'groupthink' 163
Gulbenkian Foundation 123

'helicoptering' 170
hierarchical assumptions,
   dominance 33–4, 50
hierarchical organisations: demands
   on workers 59; negotiated order
   theory in 56; small groups in 74
hierarchy: degree of and leadership
   skills 165; elimination 2; see also
   non-hierarchical organisation
homeostasis 43
horizontal management 2
hospitals, negotiated order theory
   55–6
human relations school 32, 33,
   34–8; and leadership 66;

managerial slant 66; and referrent
power 66
human resources approach 32–3,
38–42, 74–5; moral component
38, 50

ideal types, construction 177–8
imagination 34; failure of 33
Indian textile mill, socio-technical
systems 35–6, 37
individuals, and range of settings 59
inequalities, irreducible 20; see also
equality
influence: differentials 19–21;
equality of 19–20, 65–6;
inequality of 184–6; lateral
linkages 66; negotiation 164–5;
problems 18–22
infrastructure 33
innovation in non-hierarchical
organisation 12, 13–14, 74
integration mechanisms 2
interaction processes and
psychological goods 41
interactionism 44–5; Marxism and
46–7; and systems theory 44–5
interlocking 171
internal education 19
interorganisational collaboration
173–4
Iris, volunteer 91, 123
Islington Women's Centre 82

Jill, community worker 148–9
Jo (counsellor) 90–1, 97, 105,
120–1, 128, 143; and
bureaucracy 176; and clients
102; and closure 113, 114;
demands on 124–5, 136, 137–8,
141, 145, 176, 187; feminism
133, 134, 139, 185; and funding
114, 116–17; as leader 118, 124,
163; and management
committee 95, 163; on relocation
problems 127–8; on reporting
back 140, 185; resignation 186
joint action 58, 59; structuring of
173; symmetry in 171

Karen (clinical psychologist) 104–5,
113–14, 115, 119, 121, 125, 141,
150, 188
Kington Women's Centre 150–1

leaders: and leadership 5; as more
skilful organisers 68
leadership: distributed 68, 76, 83,
164–5, 176; focused 68, 83;
important aspects of 66; leaders
and 5; location within
organisational processes 67; as
political process 69; processes 67,
72; redundant 38; as set of
organising skills 165; skills of 76,
165; spread of 40
leadership acts 68, 71, 76;
identification 67–8;
non-hierarchical organisation
154; unacceptable 164, 165
leadership behaviour 65, 68
legitimacy: as moral authority of
consensus 56; primary source 172
Linda, project coordinator 124, 125;
and clients' records 131–2; and
collective 139, 140, 141, 163;
demands on 135–8, 145;
feminism 131–2, 133–4, 144,
152, 185; and funding 144, 186;
influence of 131–2; and workers'
group 186

macro analysis 45–6
management: goals of 33, 35, 39,
41; horizontal 2; responsibility,
abdication 39; tasks 32, 37, 38,
39; vertical 2
managing commitment 22–5
Marxism: and feminism 46; and
interactionism 46–7
Marxist critique 45–6
mature group 172; characteristics 16
meaning: context of 59; source of 54
medical schools, negotiated order
theory 55–6
men: naturally cooperative 21; in
women's movement 10, 87,
132–3, 152

meso domain 52
micro analysis 45–6
mode of conduct, transferable 79
Mondragon system 26
motivation, goal-directed 176
movement organisation, as network
   33
myth of structurelessness 164

National Coordinating Committee,
   dissolution (1971) 9, 10
National Union of Public
   Employees (NUPE), strike
   120–1
negotiability, factors affecting 54
negotiated order 52
negotiated order theory 5, 48–9,
   55–6, 75–6; criticisms of 168–70;
   and culture 61; development
   168–70; and historical context
   168–9; and large-scale
   institutional arrangements
   168–9; and limits of negotiation
   59; phenomenological aspects
   49; and politics 61
negotiation: additive 171; between
   combatants 167; as central
   concept 167–8; and contextual
   contingencies 56; as core process
   68, 72, 167–8; effective 171; as
   exchange and trade 167; joint
   action, creation 170; language of
   167; limits to 150, 169–70; in
   non-hierarchical organisation 16;
   shared meaning, creation 170;
   shifting arena 83; of social order
   147–53; successful 156;
   variations in 53
networking 69–71; importance
   159–61, 173
networks 33, 55, 77
non-hierarchical organisation 73;
   arenas of negotiation 181;
   bureaucratisation 174;
   construction 4, 192; distributed
   leadership 68; efficiency
   rationale 50; external
   relationships 17, 26–9, 31;

flexibility 141; within hierarchies
   37; ideal-typification 177–8;
   internal relationships 17, 31; key
   features 31, 38; leadership acts
   154; 'managerial' tasks 38;
   mythical quality 174; negotiation
   in 4, 16; organisation theory and
   1–2, 4–5; organising, skilful 68,
   69; positive aspects 12–17, 29;
   problems of 17–29; processes 7,
   8–9, 11–12; and psychological
   goods 41; size 37; skills, role of
   191, 192; 'spontaneous' 31, 50;
   in Women's Centres 190–1
non-hierarchical relationships in
   inter-organisational domain 70
non-hierarchy 9
Norwegian navy, status differentials
   37

objectives, see goals
Onlywomen Press Collective 12
open groups: attendance 22–3; paid
   workers in 24–5
opportunities, threats and 159–61
organisation: as activity 75; as
   aggregation of role-determined
   behaviours 75; alternative forms
   1–2, 7; conditional and
   temporary nature 76; dynamic
   aspects 42–3; feminist critique 3;
   group-based 39; organising
   activity and 5; systems
   perspective 42; values, and type
   38
organisation theory: hierarchical
   assumptions 1, 33–4; language of
   1; managerial bias 33, 35;
   non-hierarchy and 1–2, 4–5, 7,
   166; small groups in 32, 34–5,
   36–7, 74
organisational analysis 47, 55
organisational change, feminism
   and 3
organisation/environment relations
   26–9
organisations: boundaries with
   environment 60–1; continually

produced 57; effective 40, 41, 50;
flatter 2, 174; flexibility 36; and
organising ability 55;
socio-technical systems 35–7;
women in 3; see also
non-hierarchical organisation
organising: ability 55; as assignment
of meaning 57–8; as complex
decision-making 77–8; core
processes 66, 68, 167; core skills
69, 70, 72; as cycle of tasks 57;
location of activities 79; mode of
55; process 74, 77–8, 159–65;
skills of 69–72, 76, 87, 159–65,
184
organising activity: characteristics of
58; and organisation 5; values in
5; in women's movement 79–80

paid workers: commitment 24–5;
and core values 74; and
hierarchy 55; power and
influence 186; problems of 24–5;
reporting back 185; role 139,
185, 188; and volunteers 25, 188
participation 181–4; dilemmas of
182; fluid 184, 186; increasing
184; legitimate, defining 184;
organisational advantages of
32–3; representative of
demographic mix 183
patriarchy, capitalism and 46
persistence, and continual
production 57
Petra, probation officer 150
political groups, and deviance 59
politics as management of meaning
55
power: available to all members
65–6; concentration of 143;
differences in 174; expert 65–6;
inequalities of 184–6; referent
65–6; sufficient distribution of
174
predictability, sufficient degree 59
principle of supportive relationships
172
problem-solving in Women's

Centres 89, 93, 182
psychological goods, interaction
processes and 41
publishing, feminist 15–16
purposive groups 79–80
pyramidal values 38–9, 40;
constraining 39

Rape Crisis Centre Collective 21
rationality: formal 177–8;
substantive 177–8
reality, organisational, limits of 178
referent power 65–6
relationships: collaborative 70;
emphasis on 59; external 17,
26–9, 31, 69–70; internal 17, 31,
34; nature of 41;
non-hierarchical, in inter-
organisational domain 70; open
and supportive forms 39, 41–2
religious symbols and organisational
forms 54
reporting back 140, 185
researcher as group member 80–1
resource base: legitimacy 171;
maintaining 161
resources: applications of 54; tasks
and 161; value systems 26
risk-taking: and autonomy 15–16; in
non-hierarchical organisation 74
rota system in Women's Centres
88–91, 155
routinisation, sufficient degree of 59

Sally, volunteer 121
scripts: creation of 161; salience 161
self-help projects, and graduate
outsiders 91, 104–5
settings, variable 59
shared experience 80–1
Simpson School and Community
College 84, 95; Annex 100,
110–12, 120; and Greystone
Women's Centre 99–100, 105,
106, 107, 115–16, 118, 159–60,
189
skill differentials 71–2, 73–4;
minimising 19, 29, 74, 78

skills 186–9; role of 191, 192; sharing 17–19, 29, 90
small groups: and social needs 32, 34–5; within hierarchies 74
social action, values and 5
social anarchism 6–7, 10; cooperative values 39; and feminist values 8; and non-hierarchical organisation 73; principles 38
social class: differences 46; feminism and 133–4
social definition, interactive process 58–9
social location 26; negotiation 27
social movement groups, difficulties of 176
social order 76; consciously experimental 60; flexible 59, 162–4; legitimate contributions to 76; negotiation 32, 147–53; and restricted negotiation 169–70; as series of temporary agreements 168; shared sense 54; and social anarchism 7; taken for granted 150–1
social organisation: cultural components of 55; negotiative processes 55; as process 77
society, concensus values 43
socio-technical systems 32, 35–8
Spain, Mondragon system 26
specialisms, temporary 19
spontaneous cooperation 33, 36, 50, 73
status differentials, de-emphasising 40
structuration 48
structure: dynamic 48; static connotations 33, 47
structurelessness: myth of 164; tyranny of 21
substantive rationality 177–8
success, criteria of 156–8
supportive relationships 39, 172
symmetrical relationships, efficiency of 172
symmetry, in joint actions 171

System 4T 39–40
System 5 organisation 40–1
systems theory 33, 42–4; action critique 46–8; interactionist critique 44–5; Marxist critique 45–6

talking through 22
task: definition 32; double 66; repertoires 36; and resources 161; rotation 17, 18–19, 29; temporary specialisms 19
temporary specialisms 19
'Theory X', see pyramidal values
'Theory Y', see cooperative values
threats, and opportunities 159–61
transferable mode of conduct 79
Tyneside Rape Crisis Centre 11, 24–5
tyranny of structurelessness 21

United States, women-owned banks 26
Urban Programme 84, 99

valuations, and values 53–4
values: and action 53–61; 153–6; actual 53, 54; cooperative 38, 39, 42; core 54, 55, 153, 156; modification 28–9; in organising activity 5; pyramidal 38–9, 40; role of 176; shared 54; and social action 5; as source of meanings 54; valuations and 53–4
vertical management 2
voluntarism, limits of 27
voluntary sector organisations, social order change 60
volunteers: commitment 22–5; ideal career 91–2; training 85–7, 88, 90; two-tier system 90, 91

Weber-Michels model 176–7
Whitefield Women's Centre: contamination 174; genesis 148; legal status 162; and local council 175; reports to management committee 174–5; rota 155, 162

women: autonomous organisations 4; in organisations 3; power hungry 21; socialisation 192
Women's Centres: additive negotiation 171; attendance at 22, 23; boundaries 67; characteristics 180; core processes 66, 67; core values 153, 156, 191; decision-making 40, 157–8; definition 82; distributed leadership 191; enduring 57; environment 175, 189–90; 'existence' 178–9; external funding 61; external relationships 27, 28, 189–90; feminism 80, 152; flexible boundaries 67; functions 161–2, 182; funding 61; ideal 184; influence, inequality of 184–6; leaders delegitimised 68; learning process 187; linkages, types 60; location 27, 61, 156, 157; middle range goals 155–6; moving around environment 175; networking 159–61; non-hierarchical organisation, interpretation 77; as open groups 22, 23, 181–4; organising activity 53, 79–80, 159–65; paid workers in 24–5; physical location 156, 157; power, inequalities of 184–6; problems of 181; problem-solving 89, 93, 182; reasons for 57; right of disagreement 175; rota system 88–91, 155; social location 27; social order 'taken for granted' 150–1; social organisation, successful 157; success, evaluation 156–8; task 161–2; value enactment 153–4; see also Arlington; Greystone; Whitefield; women's organisations
Women's Liberation Bookbus 19
women's movement 8, 9; arenas of negotiation 181; autonomy 4; distributed leadership 164; environment 189; external relationships 26–7, 28; hierarchical organisation, rejection 10–11; and Left 10; men in 10; non-hierarchical organisation 10–11, 73; and organisational transformation 177; organising activity 58, 79–80; problems of 181; social location 27; stance 73; tyranny of structurelessness 21; value system 31, 164; see also feminism
women's organisations: cooperative values 42; core processes 66, 67; decision-making 40; small group behaviour 37
work, control over 12
workers: and collectives, relationship 132; goals of 33, 35, 39, 41; paid 24–5, 55, 74, 139, 185, 186, 188; social needs 34–5